SAGE was founded in 1965 by Sara Miller McCune to support the dissemination of usable knowledge by publishing innovative and high-quality research and teaching content. Today, we publish over 900 journals, including those of more than 400 learned societies, more than 800 new books per year, and a growing range of library products including archives, data, case studies, reports, and video. SAGE remains majority-owned by our founder, and after Sara's lifetime will become owned by a charitable trust that secures our continued independence.

Los Angeles | London | New Delhi | Singapore | Washington DC | Melbourne

ADVANCE PRAISE

This book is one of the most outstanding works and a commendably successful attempt in exploring and providing deep insights into the functioning of corporate boards in the Indian context. It carries the clear imprint of the great thought leader and management guru, Dr Pritam Singh, in saying what needs to be said and in suggesting what is needed to make India reach the top. The book rightly recognizes that most of the Indian companies suboptimize their potential due to their short-sighted approach for quick gains, rather than taking a long-term view for attaining sustainable growth. It is a must-read for all corporate leaders, board members and students of commerce and business.

R. V. Shahi, *Former Power Secretary,*
Government of India

Boards have a key role to play in steering organizations towards a sustainable future by adopting sound ethical governance and financial management policies. Their role assumes more significance at this watershed moment of global disruption and potential change in the world order. The book by Dr Pritam Singh, Asha Bhandarker and Dr Subir Verma has been timely and is about organizational competitiveness and the key roles that boards can play to make Indian organizations more sustainable and competitive. It adopts a unique approach of examining boardroom functioning from the lens of organizational performance. One rarely comes across such a comprehensive account on behavioural approach to boardroom governance.

The book is a monumental exercise and the amount of empirical work involved in gathering views and experiences of board members is impressive. It is a good read and is recommended for its excellent coverage, thorough research and rich insights on the subject. I am sure that it will be of use to not only boards and top teams but also corporate India to meet the objective of building organizational resilience and sustainability.

Mallikarjuna Rao, *MD, Punjab National Bank*

This book truly has a profound meaning for shaping an Atmanirbhar Bharat when the Indian economy will grow towards becoming the third largest economy of the world, with good governance in the management as well as the boards of all the companies. With his deep experience, Dr Pritam Singh has brought many key learnings and insights for all managers and directors to inculcate these best practices in their day-to-day working. I'm sure that the book will significantly lift governance quality in India and have a positive impact on business success in the future.

Manoj Kohli, *Country Head, SoftBank India,*
SoftBank Group International

I read the book *Role of Boards: Building Sustainable Competitive Edge* with great interest. In the current context, it is very relevant and highlights the role of the board in the development and future of a corporate entity. The authors did an excellent job in bringing out the role of the board. I personally feel that this book should not only be an integral part of an MBA programme but also should be read by all board members and all those who aspire to join the board. It is full of practical examples and personal experiences. I would like to congratulate the authors for this excellent contribution.

Jyoti Gupta, *Professor Emeritus,*
ESCP Business School, Paris, France

Corporate governance and the role of boards are often the object of heated debates most of the time as a result of wrongdoings or strategic mistakes that the boards were unable to manage. This book authored by Dr Pritam Singh and team not only frames the key issues but, most importantly, offers practical and tangible ways to make the role of boards much more effective in steering the strategy of an organization to build a sustainable competitive edge. Even though most of the research is based on evidence from India, I believe that the recommendations are truly boundaryless. The book is a must-read for not only current board members but also for everyone who will be playing leadership roles in organizations as well as students of management and commerce.

Davide Sola, *Professor of Strategy and Management,*
ESCP Business School, London

The book, *Role of Boards: Building Sustainable Competitive Edge* is an outstanding work of immense importance to understanding the effectiveness of corporate governance and institutional sustainability. The issues of ethics, sustainability and governance, which are at the heart of the functioning of corporate boards, have been examined in this outstanding book in the most comprehensive and compelling manner. The authors, Dr Pritam Singh, Dr Asha Bhandarker and Dr Subir Verma, have provided a passionate tour de force on the future of corporate boards and how they can be made more ethical, effective, competitive and indeed sustainable. This work has to be made compulsory reading for all students of management but more importantly, it is a valuable work for everybody who is working and leading in all organizations and institutions. Congratulations to the authors for producing a fantastic book that will have a longer shelf life for what it has examined and enunciated in a thorough and threadbare manner.

Professor (Dr) C. Raj Kumar *Founding, Vice Chancellor,*
O.P. Jindal Global University

This unique book has amply demonstrated that effective governance is the lifeline of any organization to outcompete and increase their longevity. Dr Singh's vast and diverse experience in the arena of leadership and boardroom governance is unrivalled. He along with the co-authors provides valuable insights and analyses of boardroom functioning from the lens of organization performance. This book is a must-read for all the stakeholders involved in the governance of the organizations.

P. Dwarakanath, *Former Chairman, GSK India*

This is a unique book on corporate governance, coming up at an appropriate time in the history of corporate India. Every corporate leader, board member and scholar must read this book not only to meet the compliance requirements, but also to gain sustainable advantage in this disruptive digital world by shifting central principle of corporate governance from shareholders alone towards People-Planet-Profit.

Dr B. A. Metri, *Director, IIM Nagpur*

Role of Boards: Building Sustainable Competitive Edge by Pritam Singh, Asha Bhandarker and Subir Verma describes the blueprint of a corporation and its board. It explains where the load-bearing pillars are and the layout of the essential pipes and wires that all board members must know to manage a corporation effectively.

A leader is the one who takes the first step towards something she or he deeply cares about and in ways that others wish to follow. This blueprint is also useful for those inspired to lead a movement of change in corporate conduct, to make the world better for everyone and who want to break out of the prevalent corporate management paradigm. They must read this book, not because they want to be better board directors, but because they want to make change happen.

Arun Maira, *Author and Thought Leader,*
Former Chairman, BCG India

This book is an instant classic that will be read and consulted by all CEOs, corporate board members and regulators, and those who seek to become one, for years to come. The book has brought out, with remarkable ease and candour, compelling anecdotes and insider's insights, empirical research and conceptual analysis, the issues and challenges of boardroom functioning and performance. Good governance is going to become a competitive advantage of business in future. The book provides the foundation and road map for good governance necessary for sustained corporate success. It is a must-read for all leaders and boards of organizations as well as future leaders and students.

S. Y. Siddiqui, *Executive Advisor, Maruti Suzuki India Ltd*

The uniqueness of this outstanding book is that it looks at board effectiveness and value addition through the lens of individual behaviour and group dynamics, rather than through the usual legal or financial approach. It is an excellent blend of state-of-the-art theory and practice which demystifies board governance through evidence-based research and practical recommendations. The book also highlights the critical role of purpose, values and mindsets in determining the focus and strategic decision-making processes of the board. It is a must-read treasure house for those connected with boards, especially in the Indian context.

Rajeev Dubey, *Principal Advisor, Mahindra and Mahindra*

This is a terrific book which will undoubtedly add to the authors' reputation as talented analysts of the role of boards in steering corporations along sustainable paths. The book is cunningly well-written, sassy even, besides being very perceptive and timely. It should prove most enlightening, particularly in regions of the world where we cannot afford to waste more time or people.

Alfredo Behrens, *Professor of Cross-cultural Leadership, University of Salamanca, Spain, and FIA Business School, Brazil*

ROLE
OF
BOARDS

ROLE
OF
BOARDS

BUILDING SUSTAINABLE
COMPETITIVE EDGE

PRITAM SINGH
ASHA BHANDARKER
SUBIR VERMA

Los Angeles | London | New Delhi
Singapore | Washington DC | Melbourne

First published in 2021 by

SAGE Publications India Pvt Ltd
B1/I-1 Mohan Cooperative Industrial Area
Mathura Road, New Delhi 110 044, India
www.sagepub.in

SAGE Publications Inc
2455 Teller Road
Thousand Oaks, California 91320, USA

SAGE Publications Ltd
1 Oliver's Yard, 55 City Road
London EC1Y 1SP, United Kingdom

SAGE Publications Asia-Pacific Pte Ltd
18 Cross Street #10-10/11/12
China Square Central
Singapore 048423

Published by Vivek Mehra for SAGE Publications India Pvt Ltd. Typeset in 11/14pt Sabon by Fidus Design Pvt Ltd, Chandigarh.

Library of Congress Control Number: 2020952291

ISBN: 978-93-5388-721-6 (HB)

SAGE Team: Namarita Kathait, Syeda Aina Rahat Ali, Sudeshna Nandy and Kanika Mathur

Dedicated

to

Indian board directors.

May you have the courage to live your role and build sustainable and competitive organizations and an Atmanirbhar India.

Thank you for choosing a SAGE product!
If you have any comment, observation or feedback,
I would like to personally hear from you.

Please write to me at **contactceo@sagepub.in**

Vivek Mehra, Managing Director and CEO, SAGE India.

CONTENTS

FOREWORD

The board of directors is at the apex of decision-making in a company. Even in normal times, members of well-intentioned boards, seeking to effectively discharge their responsibilities of superintendence, direction and control are required to invest quality time and effort. In abnormal contexts such as the situation caused by the disastrous effects of COVID-19, the responsibilities of the board increase significantly. Managements that are challenged to keep the ship afloat, legitimately expect a fair measure of handholding by the board. Needless to say, the board of directors is at the centre of the efforts to ensure the sustainability of businesses, by putting in place the highest corporate governance practices and ensuring that a culture of compliance pervades the whole organization.

This is perhaps the appropriate time for a book which comprehensively, and without fear or favour, addresses the challenges in the area of governance, especially the manner in which the functioning of boardrooms is impacted. It is neither didactic nor preachy. It does not decry Boards as a bunch of non-performing entities. At the same time, it holds the mirror to boards to identify perceived shortcomings which can then be put right.

Unlike many other books which lose sight of the specificities of the Indian context, this book is rooted in ground realities and the need to address them in a constructive manner. The important aspects of strategic management and organizational behaviour feature significantly. While identifying the actionable steps for those charged with the responsibility of architecting their organizations and preparing them for the long haul, the authors manifest a rare combination of both the discipline of researchers and the perspective of philosophers.

Corporate governance in India has mostly been looked at from the perspective of either law or finance. Hence, the focus has tended to be on compliance with financial rules and regulations, and conforming to the law of the land. The missing piece, namely, the behavioural aspects that impact boardroom functioning, is in focus in this book. The board's role in helping to craft an appropriate long-term strategy, and consequently to prepare the organization for the future, is an aspect that has been strenuously argued by the authors.

The various levers of competitive advantage, that together ensure sustainable success, have been appropriately highlighted. It has been made abundantly clear that pushing any one lever of competitive advantage, and ignoring the other levers, will not work for organizations that are seeking long-term existence. The purpose of the organization is yet another matter that has been closely examined and clearly established.

The unique methodology of this book deserves comment. It effectively combines qualitative study with rigorous quantitative research. Consequently, the book rests on the solid bedrock of both empirical findings of the study and logical deductions from existing best practices.

This book gains significantly from the fact that late Dr Pritam Singh, its first author, was always known for being a builder of several academic institutions, which he then took to their commanding heights. His rich boardroom experience has also been woven into the conclusions that emerge from this book. I take this opportunity to congratulate Dr Pritam Singh, Dr Asha Bhandarker and Dr Subir Verma for this significant contribution to the literature on boardrooms and corporate governance.

Improving the effectiveness of boardrooms will always be work in progress. This book, I am sure, will serve as an aid to making significant progress on that journey.

M. Damodaran
Chairperson, Excellence Enablers Private Limited and
Former Chairman, SEBI

ACKNOWLEDGEMENTS

Many institutions, colleagues and friends have contributed to bring this book to fruition. Our deep thanks go out to AICTE (the All India Council for Technical Education), which funded this research work. Special thanks to Dr Anil Sahasrabudhe, Chairman, AICTE, and Dr M. P. Poonia, Vice-Chairman, AICTE, for their wholehearted support. Our respective institutions—International Management Institute (IMI), Delhi and FORE School of Management—deserve thanks for supporting us with the needed infrastructure and other help to ensure completion of this work. Dr Himadri Das, Director, IMI, and Dr Jitendra Das, Director, FORE School of Management, have been very encouraging throughout the process and deserve our thanks.

Anil Khandelwal (former Chairman and Managing Director [CMD], Bank of Baroda), Girish Chaturvedi (Chairman, National Stock Exchange; Chairman, ICICI Bank), Major General D. N. Khurana, L. V. Prabhakar (Managing Director [MD], Canara Bank), Mallikarjuna Rao (MD, PNB), Manoj Kohli (Country Head, SoftBank India), P. Dwarakanath (former Chairman, GSK India), R. V. Shahi (former Secretary, Ministry of Power, GOI), R. K. Dubey (former CMD, Canara Bank), Dr Santrupt B. Misra (CEO, Birla Carbon, Aditya Birla Group), S. K. Chaturvedi (former CMD, Power Grid Corporation of India Ltd), S. Viswanathan (former MD, SBI Caps), S. Y. Siddiqui (Chief Mentor, Maruti Suzuki India Ltd), S. Panse (former CMD, Allahabad Bank), S. K. Bose (ED, IOCL) and Dr A. K. Rath (former Secretary, Ministry of Human Resource Development; Professor, IMI) deserve special thanks for providing us deep insights into boardroom functioning. Shri Sunil Mehta (CEO IBA) and Shri Sunil Mehta (Chairman, Yes Bank) deserve special mention—the second author learnt a lot by observing their actions and conduct on the Board of PNB while they were MD and chairman, respectively.

The large number of board members who participated in this study and narrated their experiences deserve our gratitude for sharing their valuable thoughts and time. Many people encouraged and supported us on this journey. Professor B. A. Metri (Director, IIM Trichy) and Professor Nand Dhameja (Professor, Manav Rachna International Institute of Research and Studies) were with us when we needed them. Subrat Kumar (CEO, People Labs) was with us, providing assistance and emotional support. Dr Jyoti Gupta, Dr Davide Sola (both from ESCP, Europe) and Dr Alfredo Behrens (Universidad de Salamanca, Portugal) motivated us by taking deep interest in this work.

Special thanks go out to our respective families for tolerating our 'absence in presence' while being fully immersed in this work. Purva Choudhary who assisted us on this project was our rock, always there for us.

Dr Pritam Singh has been the architect of this book, and it was born out of his rich experience on 20 different boards across public and private sectors. The three authors spent many hours brainstorming on the issues of boardroom governance in 2018 and 2019. Once the lockdown commenced in March 2020 and when we needed hours of joint working, the only solution was daily WhatsApp calls at 5.30 PM. The three of us worked together until 26 May 2020, steadily soldiering on towards the goal of completing the book by 31 August 2020. Then the unforeseen happened and Dr Pritam Singh left us for his heavenly abode on 3 June. Most of the work on the book was completed by then, and it was more a matter of taking the write-up to its conclusion. This finally took place on 25 September—sorry Dr Singh, we missed the deadline by a few weeks, but thank you for being with us, guiding us every step of the way. When in trouble, we would ask the question: What would Dr Singh say? How would he express his thoughts? And the answer would present itself to us.

We just cannot close our acknowledgements without mentioning Vivek Mehra and his team for going out of their way on this project. A big thank you!

INTRODUCTION

*We should all be concerned about
the future because we will have to
spend the rest of our lives there.*

—*Charles F. Kettering* [1]

At the core of national development is robust economic activity which creates jobs and incomes and thereby enables people to enhance their quality of life. India, with its population of 130 crore, has gigantic challenges of creating jobs and providing basic amenities to all. More than 1.2 crore become eligible every year to join the workforce and eagerly seek ways to build their lives. The task is so enormous that multipronged approaches are needed at the national level to boost job creation. Although the economic progress made in the last 20 years has shifted millions out of poverty (27.1 crore from 2006 to 2016) [2], there is a sizeable chunk of the population (24.3% in May 2020) [3] which still remains in abject poverty (unemployment stood at 24.3% in May 2020).

No wonder then that in 2015, the Honourable PM Narendra Modi gave the slogan of manufacture in India, start-up India and stand up India, all with the intent of giving a boost to the economic activity and creating more entrepreneurs and more jobs. In fact, in his speech to the nation on 15 August 2020, the PM made it very clear that it is not only about Make in India but also about 'Make in India for the World'. The new realignment taking place in the Indo-Pacific region between Japan, Australia and India is another historic opportunity for the Indian industry. The emerging advantages can, however, become a non-starter unless the Indian industry steps up and produces world-class competitive products. Once these activities take off, India will be able to take advantage of the demographic dividend available today and reach a level of relative prosperity in a few decades.

India has to absorb more than 1.2 crore people (of working age 15–64 years [4]) every year; otherwise, the demographic dividend will turn into a gigantic disaster. Economic activity was given a boost when deregulation took place in 1992 and India could successfully shake off the 'Hindu' growth rate of 3.5 per cent and shift to the next orbit of growth. Post the year 2000, India witnessed the golden period of economic growth—the growth rate touching as much as 8 per cent [5], fuelled by the information and technology (IT) services boom and the demand for skilled IT talent which India had developed plentifully in the late 1990s and early 2000s post the Y2K revolution. This has tapered off in the last few years as the government's focus shifted to social development and many other issues plaguing India.

It is sobering to note the global ranking of India on ease of doing business, in a context where we are seeking to become a manufacturing hub for the world. The World Bank ranks India at 63 (2019) [6] on ease of doing business, based on many quantitative parameters. Thus, despite many strengths that India has to its credit, the ranking (though was improving steadily in the last few years) has not been enough to attract more international businesses into India. Investors ($51 million[i] investment in 2019 [7]) are daunted by the complexities of doing business here and view the bureaucratic red tape and political risks as a big threat. The corporate scams and scandals which regularly pop up on the business horizon in India are also contributing to the trust deficit among investors regarding Indian businesses and implementation of corporate laws.

The pandemic may have given India yet another window of opportunity to attract more investors to set up business. COVID is changing the game by creating a level playing field for all nations. New opportunities are evident in healthcare, pharma, products made with new-age materials and so on, which can protect people from the pandemic. It remains to be seen whether this opportunity fructifies or will be passed on to other nations such as Vietnam, Indonesia, Bangladesh and other Southeast Asian countries who have developed business-friendly ecosystems. It all depends on whether India can transit beyond its hindering business ecosystem and create a more facilitative one.

Examination of India's global competitiveness rating (domestic environment for doing business) shows that India has slipped 10 notches from 58th in 2018 [8] to 68th in 2019 [9]. India's GDP was at the fastest rate in the world—between 7 per cent and 8 per cent [10]—for the past few years. However, the growth rate slumped down to 4.5 per cent [10] in 2019. India has to take many strong measures if it has to get back on track and return to its record of being the fastest-growing economy in the world. The dream of pole vaulting to become a five trillion economy (by 2025), spelt out by the finance minister in the FY 2019–2020 sounds like a dream. It will need some bold decisions and serious, coordinated and sustained efforts by the industry and the government. The government has to create a business-friendly environment facilitating both international and national businesses.

On their part, if Indian organizations have to embrace the opportunity thrown up in the new emerging COVID scenario, they have to reinvent their mindsets and approaches and ways of doing business aligned to the new realities. India has the third highest number of promoter-driven companies (publicly listed family-owned businesses were 108 in 2015 [11]). These entities annually contribute 79 per cent to the GDP. Yet a bulk of them are satisfied with the opportunity available in the vast internal market. Few seek to globalize and make their presence felt outside India. Seeking to globalize is not only for the purpose of exports, but it is also a quick test of how to develop world-class products to cope with the global competition in one's own backyard.

The growth opportunities are in plenty. For example, the McKinsey Global Institute [12] estimated in 2019 that the use of digital technology could create some $ 1 trillion value in India. Cost structures can be slimmed to make companies more resilient in the present conditions. Reshaping the business by the allocation of capital and resources towards value creation and knowledge and innovation-led businesses with minimal capital requirements is the need of the hour. Digitalizing business-to-business (B2B) and business-to-consumer (B2C) can bring greater customer satisfaction and engagement and, therefore, can help to reduce the consequences of the economic slowdown. The advantages that accrue are thus too valuable to be ignored by companies and their boards. A deep mindset change is needed, and Indian organizations must get out of the stupor brought about by the lockdown. Dreaming that things will snap back into position and that we will step back into the earlier world and earlier ways is a futile dream. Kumar Birla's recent statement [13] that COVID-19 has accelerated digitization across the Aditya Birla Group businesses and that business models have changed is a reminder to companies to respond to the contextual shifts and change in business demands.

Most Indian companies suboptimize their potential either because of their short-sightedness and lack of vision or because they want to make quick gains. This general mindset prevalent among most Indian (promoter-driven) companies has resulted in short-term approaches to business and solutions. They do not professionalize adequately, wanting to retain control of their business; as a result, their growth is suboptimal. The private sector thrives on the loans sanctioned by government banks, and when businesses falter, they once again expect the government to bail them out using public money. Although the era of 'License–Quota Raj' of the pre-liberalization era has long gone, the mindset is to look to the government for a bailout when things fail. Many are the prominent business names who declared their companies bankrupt and yet personally grew wealthy at the expense of public money. Public sector companies are more bureaucratic rather than business oriented in their decision-making. They are busier placating their government and bureaucrat masters presiding over ministries, rather than devising ways to enhance organizational growth.

Another major concern regarding Indian businesses—whether in the public or private sector—has been the preference to import technology rather than innovate to find customized solutions to problems that are uniquely Indian. The most glaring example is in solar energy. It is ironical that while the Indian government wants to push usage of solar power, India is almost totally dependent on China for solar panels. Hardly any Indian company has invested in the manufacture of solar panels. Given that the bulk of our import bill consists of petroleum purchase, switching to solar by investing in R&D would have been the most strategic and sustainable national-level decision to have been made in the last two decades. Another glaring example is coal which is one of the most polluting forms of energy and contributes to 72 per cent [14] of India's energy requirements. Yet there is hardly any focus among Indian coal giants to innovate and at least reduce its polluting qualities by bringing in small innovations in the manner in which it is processed. It is not about the money; it is about the mindset. At one time, there was a chairman of Coal India Limited (CIL) who very proudly boasted (to the senior author) about the high dividend that CIL was giving to the government. The senior author replied, 'If you had invested the same money in R&D, perhaps your company and the country would have benefited manifold.'

The dependence on China is so high that India even imports Ganesh idols from there for the annual festival. In August 2020, in the aftermath of the Galwan face-off, India banned many Chinese products and realized the extent of heavy dependence which exists even on the smallest products (India's imports from China were at $48.66 billion in 2019–2020, while exports were only one-third at $16.6 billion in the FY 2019–2020 [15]). Just as South Korea bloomed under the shadow of a looming China, India should make similar efforts to leapfrog economically and strengthen its might. If India can take the China threat as a challenge, then it can certainly give thrust to develop its business and economy. For the first time in the history of independent India, the government in power has directly appealed to the corporate sector to innovate. The signals are clear from the government, and businesses need to rise up to the occasion. Both have to work in tandem.

Societal values are changing with the changing demography, and the classic example of this change is sensitivity to social causes. It is well known that the millennial generation has a high focus on doing social good. Smart companies are responding to that value priority on matters ranging from energy, environment and sustainability to diversity. The new generation of customers seeks social accountability from companies, and this is a huge factor affecting the success of companies.

The above scenario—geopolitical, economic and social factors—has been mapped out to bring the attention of the Indian industry to broader strategic matters—with a long-term view—which ought to be factored in by boards and top managements of companies, when making critical decisions for reducing business risk and ensuring a sustainable competitive advantage to the organization. Sitting at the apex of companies, boards ought to be closely tracking various contextual shifts like the above which play a key role in this process. In today's scenario of disruptions in the business, geopolitical and economic scenarios and emergence of new competitors, the most important mantra for organizations to follow is to 'innovate or perish'.

There is nothing constant but change.
            —Heraclitus, ancient Greek philosopher [16]

Yet Indian organizations continue with their old techniques of management, which are fast depleting value in the context of today's changed realities. In fact, such depletion of value has been happening over the decades, and now it has reached a tipping point where it can no more be ignored. COVID has dramatically magnified the scale of the problem as indicated by the downgrading of the economy by Moody's from Baa2 to Baa3. 'The downgrade,' Moody's says, 'has not factored in the economic impact of the pandemic.' Prior to Covid-19, S&P had cautioned (December 2019), 'If this recovery does not materialise, and it becomes clear that India's structural growth has significantly deteriorated, we could lower the rating [17].'

Companies need to prepare for a post-COVID world where they must go back to the drawing board and recreate new forms of working and seriously consider how they can create a unique value proposition for the customer. On the positive side, this means that myriad opportunities have been thrown up, new lines of businesses are opening up and new product requirements are emerging to handle the challenges thrown up by COVID. The clarion call given by the government to create an *atmanirbhar* (self-reliant) India has thrown up new opportunities for Indian entrepreneurs in multiple segments of the economy.

The capitalistic perspective encourages maximization of profits by companies, rather than promoting sustainability, and advocates quick gains. However, in today's deeply unequal world, especially in view of India's massive socio-economic problems, it is essential to view organizations through the lens of the stakeholder perspective which supports sustainability over quick gains. In this context, the statement by Nawshir Mirza drives home the basic point that organizations should be thinking about longevity rather than quick gains.

A basic failing of capitalism is to measure success by growth rather than by survival. The eight-ton Tyrannosaurus

Rex is history. The unicellular Cyano-bacteria is still around after nearly three billion years.

—Nawshir Mirza [18]

The core value question which emerges as the Indian industry gears up to get back in action is whether the industry wants to continue its old ways, grow at the expense of others, run the risk of greater devastation of environment, jeopardize its very existence, ruin its reputation and hasten its demise or be humane and fair, have concern for multiple stakeholders, contribute to social and national development and sustain itself over a longer term. Such value-level questions need to be addressed by boards of companies since the value position of the company has a key impact on all decisions and actions.

New reporting regulations are already being brought in to ensure such a changed mode of functioning. According to Securities and Exchange Board of India (SEBI) executive director Amarjeet Singh, due to increasing trends of environmental, social and governance (ESG) investing, the demand for non-financial reporting is growing, given the changing context. The Business Responsibility and Sustainability Report (BRSR) framework will set the stage for sustainable investing. The recent setting up of an expert panel by the Ministry of Corporate Affairs for business reporting is thus a timely measure. The panel has proposed a new regime for businesses to report their practices for ensuring sustainability, doing business responsibly and contributing to the society. This would also give investors an opportunity to assess the company orientation on the 3 Ps (people, planet and profit) while making investment decisions.

The government is thus signalling to the corporate sector to play its part in helping the country reach Sustainable Development Goals on poverty reduction, gender equality and adoption of clean energy. According to Rajesh Verma

(Secretary, Ministry of Corporate Affairs), SEBI will play a role in ensuring such reporting [19]. Although such reporting will have a positive effect on the reputation of Indian companies, the challenge lies in ensuring implementation. He also laid emphasis on the fact that Indian companies are aspiring to have a global foothold and, therefore, they cannot ignore the emerging global trend of corporate governance (CG), that is, responsible business. He also implored professional institutes and business associations to carry out the advocacy campaign for BRSR and to reflect better the intent and scope of reporting on non-financial parameters and capacity-building of their respective members.

Examples of leading companies in different parts of the world show that organizational effectiveness and long-term sustainability depend on innovation—in products, processes, approaches and frameworks. Somehow, Indian organizations—even those that are successful—don't invest adequately in this as reflected by the woeful research and development (R&D) spend of around 0.6 per cent [20] of GDP. Contrast this with the countries like the Republic of Korea (4.6%), Japan (3.2%), Sweden (3.3%), the USA (2.8%), Germany (3%), Austria (3.2%) and Denmark (3.1%).

According to one of India's most distinguished leaders of the energy sector,

> It is very unfortunate.... An approach has developed in the country that whether it is technology upgradation or new technology, somebody else will develop it.... Even if it is related to a country specific situation or issue or problem, there is an expectation that somebody else will do the research—this is an unrealistic expectation.

It is this myopic mindset which the corporate sector needs to reverse. Countries like the USA, Germany, Japan and now China have the opposite mindset in terms of innovation as a source of a competitive advantage.

One of the biggest enemies of innovation is the bureaucratic mindset across the sectors, with its emphasis on precedence, rules and regulations, which build rigidity rather than enabling agility and flexibility. The tendency is to convert everything into formats and then the format becomes more important than the substance; and the process becomes more important than outcomes. The effort is to maintain status quo and avoid risk. This goes against the very principles of continuous improvement, which if applied to every area of a company would bring tremendous innovation. In fact, the mindset is more like that of a trader—short-term focus on immediate gains, rather than investing in the future.

There are many promoters who believe in taking shortcuts —jugaad (somehow or anyhow without know-how and the know-why)—the quick-fix approach to win. Bypassing processes, cutting corners and using unethical means have led to a serious credibility crisis for Indian products, especially in the pharma and automobile manufacturing spaces [21]. This attitude of Indian businessmen characterized by temporary and tenuous solutions to immediate problems through clever shortcut tactics cannot pass off as an innovation. Jugaad is more reactionary, solving immediate problems without clearly drawn-up plans for creating value over the longer term. It is the last recourse for survival of those at the bottom of the pyramid and should not be the 'go-to' solution for companies. In fact, the jugaad mindset goes against the very principles of creating sustainable competitiveness for Indian organizations.

Under the Atmanirbhar banner of India, it is clear that as a nation we have to think for ourselves and work for ourselves. In fact, around the world, starting with the USA, 'country first' has now become the key slogan, although many global interdependencies continue. The only route forward is through innovation. It is high time that Indian organizations give thrust to innovation in organizations. No one 'out there' will work to solve 'our' problems—we have to help ourselves, by investing in research, to solve myriad challenges. If companies and entrepreneurs can take up this opportunity, reimagine and recreate their competitive edge, it will give a new thrust to the Indian economy and make India self-reliant, not in the Nehruvian sense, but in the 21st-century sense of *balancing being strong and capable without losing global focus.* There is no shortcut to excellence in quality manufacturing. The sane solution for the Indian economy is to Make in India for the world, which can happen only when companies go back to the basics of achieving excellence.

The business landscape is turning into a war zone as global competitors eye India for a piece of the huge market. In such a Darwinian scenario where companies compete to win, using various tactics and strategies, only the fittest will survive. The only solution is to build world-class products in terms of quality, cost and time to market. Indian companies are extremely vulnerable to the market forces, and they have to either become strong and powerful enough to withstand the winds of competition or die. As the poet Mehshar Badayuni said,

Ab hawaien hi karengi faisla,
jalaega woh diya jisme jaan ho.
(Now the winds will decide the fate of the lamp,
only the robust one will sustain.)

There is a renewed chance for India in 2020 to revive manufacturing, as countries look for new bases to move to as they leave China. In fact, the government has responded to the global scenario by trying to woo companies into India. Indian companies must also manufacture for the world, so that more jobs get created and the economy gets stronger.

At this watershed moment of disruption on a global scale and a potential change in the world order, boards of organizations have a key role to play in refocusing organizations. They need to partner with top management teams and together actively reimagine the business scenario, recast the priorities and prepare organizations for a new world. If they don't do this sitting right on the top of the organizational hierarchy, they can quickly become bottlenecks and hasten organizational decay. In fact, the well-known phrase 'a fish rots from the head down' is an apt description of how boards themselves can destroy organizations when they don't play their roles adequately. The old ways of working of boards will not serve anyone. Boards have to re-examine their contribution to the organizations they head and ask themselves whether they have a right to be there at all, unless they contribute to organizational well-being and that of the stakeholders.

Organizations are the manifest constructions of entities based on the accretion of myriad capabilities, tacit knowledge, systems and processes which are energized with human vision and will. They may also be viewed as semi-permanent communities which come together to serve a particular purpose. Unless organizations and those who create them invest in all these myriad aspects, organizational longevity cannot be ensured. Unfortunately, the trader mentality of making a quick buck on a minimum investment does not serve well in the long run simply because companies are not investing in their own future—through research, innovation, technology, training and upgradation.

This book is about organizational competitiveness and the key role that boards can play to make Indian organizations more sustainably competitive. The book starts with an examination of the ground realities of Indian organizations, of the manner in which selfishness, scams and scandals are destroying value, hurting stock markets, increasing the gap between the rich and poor and reducing trust. It then moves to conceptually study the role of various levers of competitive edge in building sustainable competitive organizations—strategic leadership, ethical culture, customer centricity, strategic planning and discussion on innovation, quality, speed and cost management.

How do these levers get mobilized? How are priorities established? Who charts the strategic direction for the organization? This can only be done by the management and the board. In fact, examination of those organizations who have done well and sustained for a longer period (e.g., TATA, Infosys, Wipro Ltd and Hindustan Unilever Ltd) brings out that managements and boards have assiduously worked together to build and shape their organizations, keeping their eye on the future and steering the organizations accordingly. There is no doubt that boards have a significant role to play in giving direction and ensuring that organizations stay focused on building a sustainable competitive edge.

If management is about running the business, governance is about seeing that it is run properly.

—R. Tricker [22]

It is not enough for boards to script the direction in tandem with the managements of organizations. They have a bigger role to play in ensuring good governance, keeping not only the interests of the organization in perspective but also that of various stakeholders—that is the only way organizations can become sustainable. Another important factor to be acknowledged by boards is the survival threats thrown by the rise of myriad business and environmental factors which threaten the very existence of organizations. In view of such factors, there is a dire need for Indian boards to recast their roles so that they can serve the companies more as partners and work together to jointly future-proof the companies they head. As Mark Twain succinctly observed,

If you want to change the future, you must change what you're doing in the present.

—Mark Twain [23]

The senior author of this work has worked on more than 20 boards, one of the other authors serves on a couple of boards and the third author is a senior professor. All three have come together to put together this unusual book, which seeks to re-examine the roles played by Indian boards, with the speculation that boards are not doing enough to develop sustainable and competitive organizations. The book is different from the typical books on this subject because it examines boardroom functioning from the lens of organizational performance. This work examines how organizations can continuously move to the next orbit as this is the way for them to outcompete and increase their longevity. It takes a behavioural rather than legal or financial approach, which is typical while studying CG. Many researchers have tried to identify demographic factors at the board level and their impact on organizational performance without stable results.

Behavioural approaches to boardroom governance research are very few. We are of the view that the behavioural approach is perhaps the one which can give more reliable answers. Boards are ultimately comprised of a group of people who come together and serve as a board. In this sense, the individual factors, as well as group-level functioning, are key success factors for boards to become value adding.

In this book, the role played by Indian boards in building organizations with a sustainable competitive edge has been empirically examined. The book is unique in that it has gathered views and experiences of board members. A study comprising interviews and questionnaire-based survey was carried out (for details, see Appendix A).

The focus of this work is on understanding board functioning in India, with a view to assess board level-focus and thrust. The position of this work is that boards can no longer function in the traditional mode. Unless boards take keen interest in organizational strategy and performance of the companies they head, companies cannot build a sustainable competitive edge.

The empirical portion of the work seeks to identify the nature of boards and factors contributing to their ineffectiveness and the dominant focus of board-level discussions, developing insights into board members' focus, attitudes and behaviour on boards, and to assess the constraints to effective board functioning.

The book is organized as follows.

Chapter 1. *Landscape of Corporate Governance: Issues and Challenges*

This chapter briefly scans the landscape of Corporate Governance (CG) in India and different parts of the world, highlighting the prominent corporate scandals and examining them from a CG perspective. The literature indicates that corporate misgovernance plays a significant role in the fall of organizations. It also highlights the various conceptual frameworks, parameters and definitions of CG which are in vogue. The existing challenges of CG in India are delineated.

Chapter 2. *Architecting Sustainable Competitive Edge: Role of Boards*

This chapter has been organized around the seven levers of competitive advantage emerging from a study of the literature —innovation, customer centricity, cost and quality, time to market, agility, organizational ambidexterity, culture and people power. This has been done with a view to identify the importance assigned to these levers by management thinkers and to draw lessons for the corporate sector.

Chapter 3. *Contours of Boardroom Functioning and Sustainable Competitive Advantage*

This chapter presents empirical evidence about the boardroom scenario in India. An attempt is made to assess whether the levers which were emphasized in Chapter 2—quality, cost, time to market, customer centricity, strategic focus, innovation, ethical governance and people power—are appropriately focused upon in boardroom discussions from the perspective of the levers of sustainable competitive edge.

The chapter also presents the findings of the study conducted by the authors on prominent themes around boardroom governance—thrust of boardroom discussions, composition of boards, board agenda, board behaviours and organizational collapse, accountability of independent directors on the board and needed board member competencies.

Chapter 4. Towards Value-adding Boards: Recommendations

This chapter dwells on how Indian boards can become value-adding by working on the key enablers for building a sustainable competitive edge, sharpening the weapons for the corporate war and giving focus to developing strategic thinking and innovation in organizations.

Chapter 5. Effective Boardroom Governance: Recommendations

This chapter focuses on ways to improve boardroom processes in order to enhance boardroom governance.

Epilogue

The epilogue identifies the direction in which companies need to move forward to build competitive advantage.

Note

i.   1 million = 10 lakh; 1 billion = 100 crore.

References

1. Kettering, C. F. (n.d.). Quotes on Future. https://todayinsci. com/K/Kettering_Charles/KetteringCharles-Future-Quotations. htm
2. *The Hindu*. (2019, 12 July). India Lifted 271 Million People out of Poverty in 10 Years: UN. https://www.thehindu.com/ news/national/india-lifted-271-million-people-out-of-poverty-in-10-years-un/article28397694.ece
3. Sharma, Y. S. (2020, 26 May). India's Unemployment Rate Continues to Hover above 24%. *The Economic Times*. https:// economictimes.indiatimes.com/news/economy/indicators/ indias-unemployment-rate-continuestohoverabove24/articles how/75998561.cms?utm_source=contentofinterest&utm_ medium=text&utm_campaign=cppst
4. Thakur, A. (2020, 22 July). India Enters 37-year Period of Demographic Dividend. *The Economic Times*. https://economic times.indiatimes.com/news/economy/indicators/india-enters-37yearperiodofdemographicdividend/articleshow/70324782. cms?utm_source=contentofinterest&utm_medium=text&utm_ campaign=cppst
5. World Economic Forum. (2018). *This Is the Story of India's GDP Growth*. https://www.weforum.org/agenda/2018/04/india-s-remarkably-robust-and-resilient-growth-story
6. *The Economic Times*. (2019, 24 October). India Jumps to 63rd Position in World Bank's Ease of Doing Business 2020 Report. https://economictimes.indiatimes.com/news/economy/ indicators/india-jumps-to-63rdpositioninworldbanksdoingbusiness 2020report/articleshow/71731589.cms?utm_source=contentof interest&utm_medium=text&utm_campaign=cppst
7. *The Economic Times*. (2020, 16 June). India 9th Largest Recipient of FDI in 2019, Will Continue to Attract Investments: UN. https://economictimes.indiatimes.com/news/economy/ indicators/india-9th-largest-recipient-offdiin2019willcontinue toattractinvestmentsun/articleshow/76400055.cms?utm_ source=contentofinterest&utm_medium=text&utm_campaign= cppst

8. World Economic Forum. (2018). *The Global Competitiveness Report 2018*. https://reports.weforum.org/global-competitiveness-report-2018/competitiveness-rankings/
9. World Economic Forum. (2019). *The Global Competitiveness Report 2019*. http://www3.weforum.org/docs/WEF_TheGlobal CompetitivenessReport2019.pdf
10. The Conversation. (2020, 14 January). India's Economy: How the World's Fastest Growing Nation Went Off the Rails. https://theconversation.com/indias-economy-howtheworldsfastest growingnationwentofftherails129714#:~:text=India's%20 GDP%20was%20growing%20at,the%20slowest%20in%20 six%20years
11. A&M. (2014, 1 May). Family Businesses in India. India Corporate Solutions Group. https://www.alvarezandmarsal. com/sites/default/files/77597_tag_india_familybusinessreport_ 05_singles.pdf
12. McKinsey Global Institute. (2019, March). Digital India Technology to Transform Connected Nation. https://www. mckinsey.com/~/media/McKinsey/Business%20Functions/ McKinsey%20Digital/Our%20Insights/Digital%20India%20 Technology%20to%20transform%20a%20connected%20 nation/MGI-Digital-India-Exec-summary-April-2019.pdf
13. *The Economic Times*. (2020, 16 August). Covid-19 Pandemic Will Curtail India's GDP Growth in FY21, First in Four Decades: Kumar Mangalam Birla https://economictimes.indiatimes.com/ news/economy/indicators/covid-19-triggersonceinacentury crisiseconomymaycontractinfy21kmbirla/articleshow/77572729. cms?utm_source=contentofinterest&utm_medium=text& utm_campaign=cppst
14. *The Economic Times*. (2019, 12 May). Coal Here to Stay Despite India's Ambitious Goals for Renewable Energy. https://economic times.indiatimes.com/industry/energy/power/india-will-not-be-abletoachieveitsrenewableenergytargetsanytimesoon/article show/69286279.cms?utm_source=contentofinterest&utm_ medium=text&utm_campaign=cppst
15. *The Economic Times*. (2020, 2 July). India's Trade Deficit with China Reduces to USD 48.66 Bn in FY20. https://

economictimes.indiatimes.com/news/economy/foreign-trade/indiastradedeficitwithchinareducestousd4866bninfy20/articleshow/76750117.cms?from=mdr

16. Kingsley, S. (2019, 28 August). Innovate or Perish: A Growth Strategy. https://www.xinova.com/innovateorperish/#:~:text=For%20as%20the%20wise%20old,are%20immature%20and%20even%20infantile

17. *Financial Express*. (2020, 2 May). Covid Crisis: India at the Cliff Edge of a Rating Downgrade. https://www.financial express.com/opinion/covid-crisis-india-at-the-cliff-edge-of-a-rating-downgrade/1945915/

18. Mirza, N. (2018). Board Failures: What Makes Boards Effective—an Independent Director's Views. BloombergQuint. https://www.bloombergquint.com/opinion/board-failures-what-makes-boards-effective-an-independent-directors-views

19. Press Information Bureau. (2020, 11 August). Ministry of Corporate Affairs Releases the Report of the Committee on Business Responsibility Reporting. https://pib.gov.in/Press ReleaseIframePage.aspx?PRID=1645169

20. UNESCO Institute of Statistics. (2019, 19 June). New UIS Data for SDG 9.5 on Research and Development. http://uis.unesco.org/en/news/new-uis-data-sdg-9-5-research-and-development

21. Bhandari, B. (2013, 1 August). Say No to Jugaad. https://www.business-standard.com/article/opinion/say-no-to-jugaad-113080101343_1.html

22. CGF Research Institute. (n.d.). Corporate Governance Quotes. https://www.corporate-governance.co.za/Home/Corporate GovernanceQuotes/tabid/148/Default.aspx

23. AZ Quotes. (n.d.). Mark Twain Quotes. https://www.azquotes.com/author/14883-Mark_Twain

1

LANDSCAPE OF CORPORATE GOVERNANCE: ISSUES AND CHALLENGES

The true measure of any society can be found in how it treats its most vulnerable members.

—*Mahatma Gandhi* [1]

Prominent management thinkers and practitioners across the world are of the view that effective boardroom governance plays a critical role in steering organizations towards greater sustainable competitive edge. Thus, good governance is the most important factor continuously driving organizations towards the next orbit. Before examining the role of the board in ensuring continued organizational growth in the contemporary world, it will be important to understand the context in which organizations operate today. This is because it is the context which has a tremendous impact on the thought process of board members and in turn is likely to significantly influence the organizational strategy. Competent and outward-looking boards are alert to the unfolding business scenario, and based on it they evolve a suitable strategy and organizational processes which are in alignment with the opportunities and challenges thrown up by the business environment. On the other hand, inward-looking boards are oblivious to contextual imperatives, make plans which are misaligned to the business environment and drag the company down, sometimes even taking it to the brink of ruination.

The contemporary business world is a confluence of uncertainties, complexities and volatility, which is characterized by dynamic disruption, posing a threat to the very survival of companies. In fact, business organizations today are operating in a war-like situation, where it is difficult for them to predict where the new competitor will emerge from and hurt their businesses. The downfall of once-glorious organizations such as Nokia, Motorola, IBM, Kodak, AT&T, Escorts, Modi, DCM, HMT and ITI shows that disruption spares none. On the other hand, new-age companies such as Amazon, Apple, Google, Facebook, Alibaba and Samsung have become global giants by responding to the unmet needs of customers and killing many established giants in the process. They operate on the fundamental principle of the strategy 'begin with the end in mind' (stakeholders). Subsequently, they do backward integration to create business strategies, processes, systems, styles, etc., relevant to the market segment they wish to serve.

Given the disruptive nature of the business environment, both coping with the competition and continuing on the growth trajectory are major challenges not only to the internal management of companies but also for creating relevant strategies at the board level. In this context, continued fresh thinking, futuristic orientation and binocular vision with microscopic focus are absolutely essential at both board and operational levels. Boards devoid of such thinking will significantly erode the value of the company and eventually bring ruination. In fact, given the myriad challenges that boards face in today's context, there is an even greater need for committed, capable and active boards which can contribute to set strategic direction for organizations and ensure sustainable organizational growth and competitive edge.

Perusal of the growth and competitiveness of many successful organizations brings out that very few have been able to sustain their performance and growth over the decades. For example, 88 per cent of the companies that featured in the Fortune 500 list of 1955 had dropped from the list decades later [2]. Several of the firms praised by Jim Collins in his books *Built to Last* and *Good to Great* have since fallen from grace [3]. Globally, many giants such as Merck, HP, Motorola, Nokia, Bank of America, Rubbermaid, Scott Paper, Zenith, American Airlines and Circuit City fell from their once-mighty positions as industry leaders in the decade of the 2000s. This occurred perhaps because their boards were not alert enough to comprehend and handle the changing environmental demands and challenges. From the above discussion, it is evident that whether it is growth or decay, competitiveness or non-competitiveness, success or failure of companies, it is the board quality which plays a central role.

Organizations fail because there is inadequate long-term strategic thinking, low concern for organizational sustainability and insensitivity to dynamic environmental shifts. Many companies are hooked on operational matters and focused on the immediate, whereas their attention needs to be more on the future, on crafting a strategy and its execution, and on continuous innovation [4]. In fact, in many large Indian companies, we have observed (as consultants and board members) that the dominant mindset is that of trading, focused on the immediate returns, devoid of long-term orientation and strategic thinking.

Corporate Governance

There are various ways in which CG has been defined depending on the type of perspective—financial, legal or strategic.[i] The most well-known and comprehensive definitions are as follows.

CG is 'a set of relationships between a company's board, its shareholders and other stakeholders. It also provides the structure through which objectives of the company are set, and the means of attaining those objectives, and monitoring performance, are determined' [5].

'Corporate governance is concerned with holding balances between economic and social goals, between individual and communal goals.... The aim is to align as nearly as possible the interests of individuals, corporations and society [6].'

In this work, we view CG of a company as the process by which conformance to governance regulations is ensured and guidance is provided to the company to develop sustainable competitive edge.

CG as a term first evolved in the mid-1980s; however, questioning governance of corporations in modern perception has its roots in the 1840s [7]. There are various theoretical approaches to CG, of which the prominent ones are agency theory, stakeholder theory, resource dependency theory, stewardship theory and trusteeship.[ii]

Researchers [8] have found that while each theory can explain some aspect of a situation, no single theory is able to explain the general pattern of results. The authors suggest that the board–performance link is likely to be highly dependent on context-specific situations such as stage of organizational life cycle, sector regulation and competitive conditions.

The above theoretical distinctions are for conceptual ease, although in practice—based on our observation as board members we can say that—board functioning is not divided into such neat and water-tight compartments. In an economy which is dominantly capitalistic in orientation, corporate boards tend to see their role as that of maximizing shareholders' interest. In the context of the debates over sustainability and increasing income inequities globally, such a narrow definition of the board's role is being increasingly questioned, indicating the need for revisiting and resetting of the role of the board.

Board Functioning and Outcomes

It would be appropriate to briefly bring out the manner in which typical corporate boards appear to have been functioning as well as dwell on how they ought to function. On the plus side, the 'agentic board' drives high achievement orientation in the organization to maximize shareholder returns. When agentic orientation gets carried to the extreme however, it leads to outright self-aggrandizement by CEOs and CFOs, many times at the expense of the organization and other stakeholders—customers, employees, society and planet. The dominant owner/CEO/CFO's focus becomes unfortunately toxic for the organization and can even go to the extent of destroying it by using organizational resources for personal gain. Destruction can be of its reputation, financial stability and long-term sustainability. It is small wonder therefore that the following questions are being vociferously asked: Which shareholders' interest is being perpetuated by boards—majority or minority? How much focus exists on protecting the interests of minority shareholders?

Sadly, excess focus on profiteering at the board level is inevitably at the expense of other key stakeholders—people, society and planet—which constitute the key pillars for sustainable organizational growth. As a result, today capitalism is in deep crisis. Even capitalists agree that the economic model is broken. The free market model has managed to generate a triple crisis for capitalism: Today, it is financially unstable, environmentally unsustainable and politically unpopular [9]. Extreme concentration of wealth in the hands of a few and high inequity at the global level are further reflections of this phenomenon. The World Economic Forum's (WEF) annual Global Risks Reports have identified severe income disparity as a serious risk since 2012 [10]. In addition, global woes continue as unemployment [11] continues to hurt human development globally.

Extreme weather threatens food production globally. Severe degradation of soil, air and water quality is hurting majority of the population across the world. The United Nations [12] predicts that by 2025, two-thirds of the world population is expected to face water stress conditions. Given the extreme wealth in the hands of a few and the downright inhuman conditions in which bulk of the global population lives, it is no wonder that issues of long-term sustainability are taking the centre stage and capitalism is being criticized and opposed worldwide. Thomas Pikkety's [13] work showed that vast inequalities in societies are an outcome of capitalism which creates levels of inequality that are unsustainable.

In 1987, the Brundtland [14] Report first mentioned the term 'sustainable development', which refers to ways in which needs of the present generation are met without hurting the ability of future generations to fulfil theirs. Sustainability has also been seen as striving to improve the social and environmental performance of the present generation without hurting the ability of future generations to meet their social and environmental needs [15]. In sum, sustainability is concerned with the effect of actions taken in the present upon the options available in the future [4]. In management literature, sustainability has been used to imply continuity [16]. Authors [17] have talked about continuous improvement and innovation as the root of sustainability. Sustainability and reputation are—in our judgement—two of the most critical organizational factors which need to be viewed by company boards from the risk perspective.

The United Nations Principles for Responsible Investment (UNPRI) [18] developed by a 20-person investor group (drawn from institutions in 12 countries) are based on the notion that ESG issues can affect the performance of investment portfolios and thus cannot be ignored while making investment decisions. Since the launch, the number of signatories has grown from 100 to over 3,000. This codification is itself a recognition that business and society operate in the same world and need to be viewed in an organic way. It was launched at the New York Stock Exchange in 2006. The rise of the UNPRI and sustainable, responsible and impact (SRI) investing networks signals a growing shift in priorities among investors where business investments are made keeping factors of sustainability and inclusivity in sight. The Business Roundtable, a powerful CEO lobbying group led by JPMorgan Chase's Jamie Dimon, adopted a definition of the purpose of the company that includes responsibilities to all stakeholders, customers, employees, suppliers and the environment as being on par with the responsibility to shareholders [19]. Caring corporate leaders have taken the lead. For example, Tim Cook said, 'When we work on making our devices accessible by the blind,' he said, 'I don't consider the bloody ROI [20].' He said that the same thing applies about environmental issues, worker safety and other areas where Apple is a leader.

Kotak Mutual Fund was the first in India to sign the UNPRI in 2018 followed by SBI, Avendus Capital and Quantum Advisors who launched ESG/ESG-based funds [21]. As per the signatory page of UNPRI, UTI Asset Management Company Ltd, 3one4 Capital Advisors LLP, ECube Investment Advisors, SBI Funds Management Pvt. Ltd, Equicap Asia Management Pvt. Ltd and INDUS Environmental Services Pvt. Ltd are the new additions.

The WEF's Davos Manifesto [22] asserts that the role of the company management is to 'serve clients, shareholders, workers, and employees, as well as societies, and to harmonize the different interests of stakeholders'. It specifically states that management must ensure the 'humanization of the workplace' and 'assume the role of a trustee of the material universe for future generations'.

Trusteeship

This brings us to another board-level orientation—trusteeship—which is a socio-economic philosophy propounded by Mahatma Gandhi more than a century ago [23]. It provides a means by which the wealthy would take responsibility of trusts that looked after the welfare of the people in general. Gandhi [24] untiringly spoke and wrote about the importance of trusteeship as a model to benefit all stakeholders and for businesses to sustain themselves in the long run. Gandhi's vision of trusteeship was based on his foresight about the failure of capitalism and communism, owing to the greater importance given by these ideologies to ends rather than means.

Viewed from the organizational perspective, key outcomes of trusteeship can be organizational sustainability and creation of a great brand attracting the best-quality talent, as well as a great work culture. This has been aptly demonstrated by the TATA Group whose chairman J. R. D. Tata was deeply influenced by the trusteeship model of Gandhi [25] and used it in the running of the Tata empire. Tata continues to be one of India's most trusted brands along with Wipro, whose chairman Azim Premji is a self-confessed Gandhi-phile, deeply influenced by his philosophy. He said at a Gujarat Vidyapith convocation address, 'The Mahatma's idea that the wealthy must be trustees of their wealth for the good of the people and the community has resonated with me....'

Ideas around trusteeship have been gaining traction in the last decade as the world is witnessing economic collapse, values erosion and challenges for sustainable growth [26]. Trusteeship is becoming increasingly attractive, especially in the current context of scams and scandals and failures of large corporations. According to some researchers [27], there is now a move to not only hold organizations responsible to maximize shareholder wealth but also to hold them responsible for social issues. Even as these discussions take place, the disparity between the rich and the poor is only widening.

The above discussion clearly indicates the dire need for a significant shift in orientation on CG. Boards need to shift their orientation from preponderantly maximizing shareholder's interests to taking care of the interests of all stakeholders. They will have to focus on the 3 Ps (people, planet and profit) for ensuring long-term sustainability.

Saga of Corporate Misgovernance

Perusal of board-level functioning in the last few decades has revealed some intriguing facts which raise serious questions about the role of CEOs and boards. The scams and scandals spawned in the corporate world show how greedy corporate honchos are destroying organizations and unfortunately hurting common citizens. CEOs in the USA defrauded public investors as well as employees of billions of dollars. Ironically, some of them such as Enron and Lehman Brothers enjoyed top-notch ratings by magazines like Fortune just prior to the debacle. The collusion between Enron (under CEO Jeffrey Skilling and his predecessor Kenneth Lay) and the accounting firm Arthur Andersen led to an accounting fraud, which affected many investors and shareholders who lost their life's savings. In 2002, WorldCom CEO Bernard Ebbers and Freddie Mac President Glanow and Chairman Leland and in 2008, Lehman brothers were all guilty of accounting frauds worth billions. Likewise, issues of CG came to the fore in the UK when Colloroll and Poly Peck collapsed in the 1980s and the Maxwell Group went bankrupt in the 1990s. Carillion, BHS, Metro Bank, Patisserie Valerie, Northern Rock, Powa Technologies, Royal Bank of Scotland of UK and Parmalat of Italy are in trouble over CG issues. Carrefour, Orange, Lafarge, Vicendi, France Telecom (during the period of Didier Lombard) and Crédit Lyonnais are some of the French companies in trouble over similar CG issues. Carlos Ghosn has become highly controversial for the manner in which he generously handed out bonuses to himself and used the properties of Nissan when he was CEO.

The Indian scenario is no different. According to media reports, there has been a spate of high-profile scandals in the last decade allegedly perpetrated by business tycoons such as Ramalinga Raju (Satyam), Vijay Mallya (Kingfisher Airlines), Anil Ambani (ADAG), Nirav Modi (Firestar Diamond, Firestar Diamond International Pvt. Ltd) and Rana Kapoor (Yes Bank). What is surprising is the manner in which 'star performer' companies of the previous decade—Jaypee, Sahara, ADAG, Bhushan Steel, Amrapali, Essar, Unitech, Alok Industries, GMR, RattanIndia Power, Electrosteel Steels Ltd, Gitanjali Diamonds, Antel Auto Ltd, etc.—have got into trouble in the last five years. Aircel, DHFL, Punjab and Maharashtra Co-operative (PMC) Bank, IL&FS, Religare and Jet Airways are some of the leading companies that are also in the limelight.

In the recent past, the media was filled with reportage regarding dubious actions by companies such as Aircel, IL&FS, PMC Bank and HDFL, the details of which are discussed further.

Former Aircel promoter Sivasankaran and companies controlled by him and his son defaulted on loans taken from IDBI to the tune of ₹600 crore. IL&FS began evading its loan repayments in 2018. IL&FS group of companies have an external debt of ₹94,216 crore, of which ₹57,000 crore are bank loans, bulk of the borrowing (70%) being from public sector banks [28]. PMC Bank—a cooperative lender—has been in the midst of a scam for underreported non-performing assets (NPAs). The bank lent nearly 70 per cent of capital to the developer, which is against RBI lending norms. This was possible because non-banking financial companies (NBFCs) were not regulated closely by the RBI. Existing account holders were badly hit, and the bank got into serious trouble over its lending of ₹6,226 crore to HDIL (approximately 73% of its loan book size). The managing director (MD) himself confessed to the bad lending practices to HDIL—fudging of NPA position of HDIL, falsification of records, creating 21,049 dummy accounts to hide HDIL NPAs—'to protect the reputation of the bank [29]'. As much as ₹2,416 crore of the loan was transferred to accounts held by the Wadhawans—the founders of HDIL. DHFL from the housing finance sector, which has a housing loan outstanding of over ₹100,000 crore, defaulted on its ₹1,000 crore payment obligation and got onto the radar of the authorities [30]. The scions of the promoters of the erstwhile company Ranbaxy—Malvinder Singh and Shivinder Singh—were supposed to be the key actors in the ₹3,000 crore Religare group fraud. It has been alleged that the brothers indulged in practices to divert money from Religare Finvest Ltd (RFL), thereby endangering the very survival of RFL [31].

The list of defaulters on bank loans is quite long. In fact, the finance minister recently stated in the Parliament that the total number of wilful defaulters stood at 8,582 at the end of FY 2018–2019. This signifies a 60 per cent surge in the last five years. As much as ₹71,542.93 crore worth of frauds were existing in the Indian banking system in 2018–2019. Unfortunately, more than 90 per cent of these losses were to government-owned banks, which ironically are supposed to be the trustees of the public money. Overall, 3,766 fraud cases were detected in 2019, a 15 per cent hike from FY 2017–2018. Losses increased by 70 per cent in FY 2017–2019 compared to FY 2017–2018.

The biggest share of losses has been owing to frauds related to advances, most of them from public sector banks [32]. It is interesting to note that the top 30 defaulters account for one-third of the gross NPA in the banking sector, amounting to ₹2.86 lakh crore. Clearly, it is the big fishes who are taking advantage of the system, thus exposing the inept functioning of boards. It is shocking to note that according to the RBI report, the bulk of these frauds were because of cheating and forgery.

According to the RBI, lack of early detection is one of the major factors allowing the borrowers adequate time to flee, as banks on average take two years to detect frauds, while large frauds (₹100 crore plus loans) take four and a half years to detect. Unfortunately, this long time period gives the default-ers adequate leeway to find ways and means to evade the law. On their part, bank boards also contribute to perpetuating frauds, since they delay declaration of frauds in order to save the company's reputation and postpone facing investigative agencies. A combination of these factors has resulted in rising fraudulent activities with the perpetrators of frauds getting away without any retribution.

It is possible to conclude the following from the above discussion:

- The quality of board-level functioning in the corporate sector as well as in the banking sector is flawed and needs to be urgently addressed as indicated by the various frauds taking place under the very noses of the boards of directors of leading companies.
- Boards of most Indian organizations appear to be short-sighted and either ignorant or unethical and appear to be generally bereft of strategic thinking. Companies adopt unhealthy business practices which give them short-term gains at the cost of long-term sustained competitive advantage. In fact, such unethical board-level practices have been the biggest cause of ruination of many companies.
- If Indian organizations are committing frauds and getting away scot-free, boards are contributing to the same either directly or indirectly.

Speaking about boards, M. Damodaran (former Chairman SEBI) stated that 2018 will be remembered in India as the year when independent directors and indeed whole boards emerged as top non-performers closely followed by auditors [33].

Frauds in the Corporate Sector: Modus Operandi

At this stage, readers may be curious to know about the manner in which the frauds were carried out.

The Satyam fraud was reportedly conducted through falsification of accounts including overstatement of revenues as well as diversion of funds to related parties. While Fortis appears to have adopted the Satyam model, Kingfisher and United Spirits appeared in the news for illegal funding to related parties and falsification of accounts [34].

Religare appears to have been cheated by the promoters and their trusted aides. Representatives of key shell companies (which were part of the scam) gave replies to the Economic Offences Wing (EOW), which makes it apparent that they were part of the criminal conspiracy to whisk away hundreds of crores from RFL [35]. ₹47,000 crore loans were given over a 10-year period, and total losses on paper were ₹2,399 crore according to EOW. The RBI had been making observations to the board regarding unsecured loans being given to other entities by RFL and also raised issues of CG [36].

There have been reports that the PMC episode occurred because powerful shareholders/borrowers took advantage of the weak systems and procedures of the cooperative banks (as the borrowers do not come under the direct radar/surveillance of the RBI) to raise huge sums of money to fund their business interests [29]. Big sharks use the deposit route for conversion of unaccounted cash. Thankfully, after this loophole got badly exposed in the PMC scam, NBFCs have now been brought under RBI scrutiny. One wonders how a transaction involving ₹6,226 crore to a single party by PMC could go undetected by the inspection teams of the RBI.

The media went into a frenzy over the ICICI case over the alleged nexus between the CEO and the borrower [37]. According to the reported story, the ICICI Bank authorized a loan of ₹3,250 crore to Videocon in 2012 and the CEO Chanda Kochhar was on the committee that sanctioned the loan. Companies controlled by Venugopal Dhoot of Videocon Group invested in the company of Chanda Kochhar's husband Deepak Kochhar, NuPower Renewables Ltd (NPRL), indicating the conflict of interest. According to the CBI, the day after the ₹300-crore loan was disbursed to Videocon International Ltd (VIL), Dhoot of Videocon had transferred ₹64 crore from VIL to NPRL, the company owned by her husband [38]. This makes us wonder how come the board could not identify such transgressions. Is it that such matters never reach the board? Or are there other behavioural dynamics at play? If the board of India's leading professionally managed and highly reputed bank has come into such a situation on CG, what would be the ground realities in the case of the rest?

Yet another approach is through collusion among four key actors—CEO, board, rating agencies and auditors. In many cases, auditors and credit rating agencies do not alert the banks well in time about the impending frauds [39]. In fact, there is suspicion that these agencies may be hand in glove with the borrower. Questions have been raised about IL&FS continuing to get top ratings over the years and suddenly going bust. Is it possible that rating firms colluded with IL&FS executives?[iii] Was it a case of incompetence of the concerned executives?

According to a report published in the RBI's latest bulletin [40], nearly one-fourth of borrowers who defaulted to banks carried an investment grade credit rating up to a quarter before they defaulted. That is, ratings plunged from at least BBB to D within just three months, showing that ratings do not seem to reflect the asset quality of borrowers in a timely manner.

The phenomenon of frauds, diversion of funds, etc., cut across sectors and are probably the key reasons for the ₹2,100 crore NPAs in the public sector being borne by banks such as SBI and PNB. SBI and PNB have put their 15 NPAs worth ₹1,063 crore for sale. All the 21 public sector banks had gross loans of over ₹733,000 crore as on 31 December 2017. Out Of these loans, SBI had the highest share of ₹201,000 crore, followed by PNB (₹55,200 crore), IDBI Bank (₹44,500 crore) and Union Bank of India (₹38,000 crore), among others [41].

The Indian regulator SEBI has responded by further modifying and tightening norms of CG in India. The moot point is whether regulations by themselves are enough to set the house in order or other measures are needed to ensure compliance.

The above exposition brings to the fore serious questions about the quality of boardroom governance in Indian organizations: How could boards be oblivious of many of the above actions? Were the board members ignorant or were they in collusion? Are there some structural issues involved which weaken the functioning of boards?

Tsunami of Frauds: Indian Realities

The above examples clearly indicate that frauds are taking place because of the ineffective functioning of the board or owing to incompetent CEOs or collusion between boards and CEOs with the support of board members having vested interests and weak moral fibre. These frauds have had a tremendous impact on the Indian economy. The collapse of IL&FS (highly reputed among the NBFCs) proved to be the tipping point, leading to a liquidity crisis in the Indian banking sector, brutally bringing the NBFC sector down on its knees. Of the ₹91,000 crore borrowed from banks, ₹57,000 crore (70%) are from public sector banks [28]. In the aftermath of the Nirav Modi and Gitanjali Gems episodes, the gems and jewellery sector has been crippled by lack of access to bank finance. The impact of loan defaults has been acute on the key lenders—the Indian banks—themselves. They have had to perforce do higher provisioning for bad loans coupled with lower profitability and an inability to lend in a big way. It is appalling that a few sharks with overweening ambition have caused so much damage to individuals, organizations and entire industry sectors.

The Honourable Prime Minister of India Narendra Modi has shown his increasing concern on the matter of frauds, scams and scandals in India. The periodic discovery of newer cases at a great frequency makes one wonder what is happening—just how many older frauds can there be? It perhaps reveals the presence of a terribly rotten system which has been in operation for a long time.

Different views have been expressed by bankers on this matter. According to a former MD of SBI, Arundhati Bhattacharya (currently Chairman SWIFT), 'Most of the frauds getting reported are credit related.... [42]' The bulk of credit-related payment defaults barring the top wilful defaults mentioned earlier from the RBI report indicate the poor quality of project appraisal by bankers and inadequate understanding of the credit worthiness of the borrower.

Further examination indicates that of the reported frauds, 73 per cent have been worth ₹100 crore and above. Ninety-two per cent of these loans originated in the public sector. Above all, majority of the frauds (92%) were committed 5 years ago and some even more than 10 years ago [43]. Some of the so-called frauds are taking place because of defaults by a promoter lacking equity due to stalled or zombie projects. Although public sector banks are badly affected, apparently they don't readily declare frauds. Their reluctance emanates from factors such as reputational risks to the organization and fear of subsequent interference by various agencies impairing business as usual. The seriousness of underreporting is evident from the fact that by August 2019, the RBI fined banks a record 76 times for non-reporting of fraud [44]. Interestingly, only 10 per cent of frauds were cyber frauds, putting to rest the bogey—which has been getting large amount of attention—as an important cause of frauds. Most importantly and a matter of great concern, frauds are continuing because the guilty get away with their actions. In fact, all the above cases bring out that the defaulter is rewarded (for committing frauds) rather than being punished.

The above raises strong questions about the role of the CEO and the boards. *Just as the fish rots from the head down,* so does organizational decay begin from the top, namely board and CEO levels—and then creeps down the organization. In the above examples, both boards and CEOs seem to have failed as custodians and trustees of the organization to protect the interests of various stakeholders. In some cases, boards themselves seem to have been complicit in the perpetration of frauds.

The above exposition clearly brings out details regarding the weak and indifferent functioning of boards characterized by (a) inadequate understanding of board-level nuances, (b) managerial incompetence in strategic thinking, (c) lack of commitment to attend board meetings and, above all (d) weak moral fibre.

CG in India: Key Challenges

One of the major grievances of both domestic and foreign investors has been the poor CG standards in India. These standards have adversely affected price recovery (post the global financial crisis in 2009) and have played a key role in the exodus of retail investors from stock markets, limiting the depth and liquidity of these markets. While India's financial markets have been set up to protect ordinary investors in actual fact, they do the opposite by protecting insiders who get access to company-related information well before the general public. This loads the dice in favour of insiders at the expense of the retail investor [45]. No wonder there is suspicion about the stock markets in the public domain.

According to U. K. Sinha, former Chairman, SEBI [46], nearly one-fifth of listed companies in India do not comply with basic shareholding reporting norms set by the regulator. Although the top 1,000 listed companies have complied with SEBI norms, they still have a long journey ahead in becoming more inclusive, progressive and futuristic in their approach. Even blue-chip companies have been found to have governance issues. A little over half the companies in the NIFTY 50 index received a cumulative 4,552 whistle-blower complaints in FY 2018–2019—30 per cent higher than the previous year.

There is no doubt that weak CG can be perilous for organizations. Franklin Templeton Investments India said that the recent expose of the unsavoury governance practices is a big concern for investors. In the light of this revelation, the company has withdrawn six of its debt funds from the Indian market, owing to some exposure to lower-rated bonds, where liquidity is an issue. The crises at Essel Group, Jet Airways, Yes Bank, DHFL, IL&FS and many others have raised serious investor concerns. The international rating agency Fitch Ratings expressed concern regarding the allegations that ICICI Bank extended a loan with a probable conflict of interest [47]. According to them, it raised questions over the lender's governance practices and created reputational risks. Ten per cent companies on the NIFTY 50 index are facing CG issues and have experienced erosion of their value in the stock markets [48].

In recent years, the lack of adequate authority to meaningfully contribute to the firm, while facing the risks of being summoned, investigated and arrested by adjudicating authorities, has triggered independent directors to resign from their posts. A fallout of the spate of CG scandals in 2019 has been a record number of resignations of auditors and independent directors midway through their term on company boards. As per data from nseinfobase.com, the number of exits of independent directors from boards of Indian companies increased 54 per cent year on year in calendar year 2019. Fifty-eight auditors stepped down mid-term in 2019, higher than the number in 2018 [49]. One thousand and three hundred and forty-four independent directors quit the boards of companies listed on the NSE in the FY 2019–2020, 45 per cent more than the same period in 2019. 'Personal reasons' was the most common explanation for resignations. According to Ravi Venkatesh, it is hazardous to one's reputation, and there are just a handful of companies that show true leadership and governance standards [49]. This is probably an outcome of the increased responsibilities placed on independent directors by SEBI and the serious repercussions in the event of frauds.

Examination of ownership of Indian organizations shows that family-managed organizations dominate the private sector in Indian business. For example, of the 100 private sector companies in India with a market cap of over ₹1,000 crore, 75 are family managed [51]. Private sector companies seem to invariably make decisions which hugely benefit the dominant shareholder, their family, friends and corporate entities, rather than in the interest of the minority shareholders, and are far from taking into consideration the interest of all stakeholders. Moody's and ICRA [52] surveyed CG practices of 32 Indian companies in 16 prominent family groups across a broad cross-section of Indian industries. They found that the issue of governance afflicts most of the organizations surveyed. Despite regulations regarding independent board directors, families retained significant control over listed companies and sometimes appeared to be acting primarily for the benefit of their group or family.

In addition to CG issues arising from the pattern of dominant family holding in Indian business companies, an additional complexity arises on account of 'promoter control' in Indian companies [53]. This is a reality today despite these companies being listed on stock exchanges, having public shareholders and not holding controlling shares. The key problems in the Indian corporate sector (public, private or multinational corporations [MNCs]) are (a) disciplining the dominant shareholder—the principal block holder—and (b) protecting minority shareholders. In view of concentration of shareholdings in the hands of the owner, the author goes on to say, 'How can one even envisage a Board that can discipline the dominant shareholders from whom the board derives all the powers ... unfortunately the board is powerless to prevent many abuses by the dominant shareholders' [54].

Examination of the norms and rules put in place by SEBI from time to time reflects that sincere efforts have been made to adopt international best practices. India's 2013 Company Act incorporated many provisions and reforms suggested by various committees (e.g., recommendations of the Birla Committee [55] [1999], Murthy Committee [56] [2003], Chandra Committee [57] [2003] and Irani Committee [58] [2005]). Responsibility and accountability have been clearly placed on independent directors and auditors. In 2014, among the many changes introduced, the reforms by SEBI focused on strengthening board independence, regulating related party transactions with greater stringency, mandating a whistle-blower policy and enhancing disclosure require-ments. These measures were put in place with the intention to bring in greater levels of transparency as well as the desired level of regulation of such transactions.

In 2018, on the recommendation of the Kotak Committee, SEBI mandated that boards should have at least 6 directors, 1 independent woman director, special resolution for inde-pendent directors beyond the age of 75 years, role separation of chairman and MD/COO, norms on minimum requirement for attendance, limit on the maximum number of director-ships, prescribed number of committee meetings, etc. In 2019, SEBI [59] announced a new set of regulations to bring in greater independence, diversity and transparency, shareholder information rights and steps towards greater promoter gover-nance, enhanced roles of the committees to perform their respective duties, disclosure of all the credit ratings, manda-tory disclosures of quantification of audit qualifications, etc. Whether the regulations are being complied with in both letter and spirit is the question. Every time there is a fraud committed or a scam unearthed, SEBI brings in new regulations. In fact, India probably has the best regulations in the world, on paper. As Adi Godrej rightly stated, there is no need for new legislations to ensure good CG. Rather, there is a need for effective enforcement of existing laws [60].

Board Focus on Strategy, Board Processes and Firm Performance: Research Findings

Scholars and practitioners are alike in their view that boards can play a key role in ensuring good CG and contribute in building a sustainable competitive edge of the organization. According to researchers [60–63], the emerging evidence is that high-performing boards across all sectors concentrate on shaping strategy, resource identification and talent management.

Studies have shown [64–69] that CG and organizational performance are strongly correlated. Studies on Indian firms have found that effective CG helps to increase market valuation [70] and has a positive impact on share prices [71]. Another study [72] on 40 companies revealed that superior governance practices and better company evaluations were positively correlated.

Research has examined the impact of board-level factors such as board capital, focus on strategy and implementation, board-level processes (organizational culture and board dynamics), board behaviour (high trust and high challenge), group dynamics and firm performance. It has been found that a relatively hands-on approach to strategy formulation and implementation is associated with high-performing organizations [62]. The board's attention to strategy is strongly linked to good financial performance [73]. Strategy planning has been found to be related to organization effectiveness [74]. Board focus on strategy is associated with positive organizational performance in the longer term [75].

Factors like board-level processes have been found to make a greater contribution to organization performance than structural factors like board composition [76]. The authors have concluded that board behaviour—high trust, high challenge and high engagement—is a key factor contributing to board effectiveness. Board effectiveness depends on the quality of the individuals who become directors and their ability as a group to get the work done [77], and, therefore, attention has to be given to understand how to develop group and team dynamics.

Challenges of CG: A Snapshot

Prominent management thinkers and practitioners across the world are of the opinion that it is good-quality boardroom governance which contributes significantly to propel organizations to the next orbit as well as ensures their growth and sustainability. However, there is also near unanimity in the view that boards in general are not adequately playing the role for which they have been constituted. The large number of scandals and frauds that regularly erupt in the corporate sector all over the world are ample testimony to this strong view held by many people. There is no doubt that current boardroom governance practices leave a lot to be desired. The famous adage 'the fish rots from the head down' necessitates closer examination of current boardroom practices in India in terms of current realities, what boards ought to do and the role they ought to be playing, in order to protect organizations and make them sustainable and competitive.

In the current disruptive business environment characterized by ambiguity, volatility and uncertainties, boardroom governance assumes even greater significance in making or breaking the organization in the long term. The rise of huge scandals and the subsequent fall of mighty organizations raise serious questions about the role played by the board. One wonders whether such frauds in the corporate world reflect collusion in operation among the various stakeholders or it can be attributed to lack of long-term strategic thinking. Is it because of the inability of boards to scan the unfolding environment and respond accordingly? Could it also be owing to the difference in focus of the board across various stakeholders—for example, some stakeholders (e.g., shareholders) get greater benefit at the cost of the others, while others wield greater power compared to the others.

The traditional perspective regarding the role of boards, namely maximization of shareholder wealth [78], continues to hold sway in most boardrooms even today. However, there is a strong emergent view criticizing the undue focus on larger shareholders at the cost of minority shareholders. The growing inequities in societies across the world, exploitation of the have-nots and their continuous fall into deeper poverty, rapacious destruction of the environment for profiteering alone are leading to a demand for change of focus at the board level, from shareholder interest to stakeholder interest. There is rising demand for conscious capitalism as well as stewardship and trusteeship as better approaches to governance in an era characterized by concerns about inclusion and sustainability. Global organizations such as United Nations Development Programme (UNDP), World Bank and Organisation for Economic Co-operation and Development (OECD) are emphasizing the need for equitable focus of boards on the 3 Ps. Many of the problems faced by the world (environmental degradation, climate change, poverty, etc.) throw up tremendous challenges for societies and organizations, and these need to be addressed by boards, so that organizational growth can become sustainable and organizations perform competitively. It has been suggested that the board must become a strategic partner of management [79]. There have been studies that emphasize that boards and managements must formulate strategy in partnership with each other [80].

We propose to examine contours of boardroom governance in India in the above perspective. The thrust will be on examining the focus of boardroom deliberations, board composition, board processes and the role played by boards. The basic assumption is that boards have a key role to play in guiding and shaping the destiny of the organization and in making it sustainably competitive.

Notes

i. Some of the definitions are as follows:

According to Solomon (2007), 'Corporate governance refers to rules, regulations and best practices for securing shareholder claims, enhancing competitive power and reaching capital within the global environment.'

CG refers to the set of processes that provide an assurance to outside investors of the firm of a fair return on their investments (Roy, 2016).

Sieben (2002) defines 'corporate governance as both the knowledge and the art of weighting divided interests of all the stakeholders. In other words, it is the effort of balancing the relationships of power. The importance of corporate governance has been realized all over the world with the integration and liberalization of financial markets'.

Another view by Tricker (1984) states, 'The governance role is ... concerned with giving overall direction to the enterprise, with overseeing and controlling the executive actions of management and with satisfying legitimate expectations of accountability and regulation by interests beyond the corporate boundaries.'

According to La Porta et al. (1999), CG refers to 'a set of mechanisms through which outside investors protect themselves against expropriation by the Insiders'.

Shleifer and Vishny (1997) state, 'Corporate governance deals with the ways in which suppliers of finance to corporations assure themselves of getting a return on their investment.' According to Parkinson (1994), 'Corporate governance is the process of supervision and control intended to ensure that company's management acts in accordance with the interests of shareholders.'

Some of the most comprehensive definitions of CG are as follows.

'Corporate governance is a framework of rules and practices by which a board of directors ensures accountability, fairness and transparency in a company's relationship with all stakeholders' (Sarbanes–Oxley Act of 2002).

'Corporate Governance refers to the structures, systems and processes which ensure the overall direction, control and account-ability of an organization' (Cornforth and Chambers, 2010).

ii. Theoretical paradigms:

- *Agency theory.* This theory is a principle that is used to explain and resolve issues in the relationship between business principals and their agents. Most commonly, that relationship is the one between shareholders, as principals, and company executives, as agents (Kopp, 2019). According to the agency theory, when the board monitors management, problems of the latter performing poorly or working for their own interests will go down. The agency theory assumes that human beings are self-interested rational maximizers and hence they need to be monitored to ensure that they do not stray. The board of directors (Berle and Means in 1932) is thus an important means to monitor and thereby minimize the problems brought about by the principal–agent relationship.

- *Stakeholder theory.* According to this theory, a corporate entity tries to balance the interests of various stakeholders in order to ensure that each constituency is satisfied (Abrams, 1951). It emphasizes morals and values in managing an orga-nization. This approach highlights the role of the board as a value creator striving to ensure the long-term survival of the organization. According to Donaldson and Preston (1995), board members represent the interests of individuals and groups who have a 'stake' in the organization—managers, employees, customers, suppliers (contractual stakeholders) and the community.

- *Resource dependency theory.* This theory assumes resources to be critical for an organization and that board directors help the organization by connecting it with relevant external entities and resources needed to survive (Pfeffer and Salanick, 1978). According to the resource-based theory, the organization consists of both tangible and intangible assets and capabilities (Barney, 1991). The resource dependency theory (Pfeffer and Salanick, 1978) suggests that managing external relationships and leveraging influence and resources are key board roles. Board directors can contribute to organizations through advice, access to information, preferential access to resources and legitimacy (Pfeffer and Salanick, 1978).
- *Stewardship theory.* This theory takes the view that there is an alignment between the goals of board directors and of their managers. Besides this, it is assumed that managers act in the best interests of the organization and are self-motivated. The underlying assumption about human nature is that there is, in general, a desire to do good and to act unselfishly, as long as a number of organizational and cultural preconditions are satisfied (Davis et al., 1997). Managers and owners work together for the organization, and the focus of the board is primarily on developing a strategy rather than on monitoring day-to-day performance.
- *Trusteeship.* According to this model (Balakrishnan et al., 2015), business managers and stakeholders integrate various rights and responsibilities into economic value creation to create a just and prosperous society. In fact, the article by Jerry Rao and S. K. Jha (2018) elucidates that the idea of trusteeship is hundreds of years old in India. In this model, the board acts as the trustee on behalf of various stakeholders, especially the general public.

iii. A forensic audit conducted by Grant Thornton reveals that agencies ranging from ICRA, Crisil, Care, Fitch, India Rating, Moody's and Brickworks were pliable in the hands of the IL&FS executives—the draft update by Grant Thornton is based on several e-mail exchanges between IL&FS executives and key functionaries of the agencies (Rajput and Sinha, 2019).

References

1. AZ Quotes. (n.d.). Mahatma Gandhi Quotes. https://www.azquotes.com/quote/877037
2. Perry, M. J. (2014). Fortune 500 Firms in 1955 vs. 2014; 88% Are Gone, and We're All Better Off Because of That Dynamic 'Creative Destruction'. https://www.aei.org/carpe-diem/fortune-500-firms-in-1955-vs-2014-89-are-gone-and-were-all-better-off-because-of-that-dynamic-creative-destruction/
3. Collins, J. (2009, 7 July). Good to Great to Gone. *The Economist*. https://www.economist.com/business/2009/07/07/good-to-great-to-gone
4. Aras, G., and Crowther, D. (2002). Governance and Sustainability: An Investigation into the Relationship between Corporate Governance and Corporate Sustainability. *Management Decision*, Vol. 43, No. 6, pp. 443–448.
5. OECD. (2004). OECD Principles of Corporate Governance. OECD Publications Service. http://www.oecd.org/corporate/ca/corporategovernanceprinciples/31557724.pdf
6. Cadbury, A. (1992). *The Financial Aspects of Corporate Governance* (Cadbury Report). London, UK: The Committee on the Financial Aspect of Corporate Governance (The Cadbury Committee) and Gee and Co. Ltd. https://www.uksa.org.uk/sites/default/files/press_releases/19920727_uksa_on_cadbury.pdf
7. Steger, U., and Amann, W. (2008). *Corporate Governance: How to Add Value*. Hoboken, NJ: John Wiley & Sons.
8. Nicholson, G., and Kiel, G. (2007). Can Directors Impact Performance? A Case-based Test of Three Theories of Corporate Governance. *Corporate Governance*, Vol. 15, No. 4, pp. 585–608. https://doi.org/10.1111/j.1467-8683.2007.00590.x
9. Jacobs, M. (2019, 8 November). Capitalism Is in Crisis. And We Cannot Get out of It by Carrying on as before. *The Guardian*. https://www.theguardian.com/commentisfree/2019/nov/08/economy-crisis-capitalists-1945-1979
10. World Economic Forum. (2014). *Global Risks*. 9th ed. http://www3.weforum.org/docs/WEF_GlobalRisks_Report_2014.pdf

11. International Labour Organization. (2015, 20 January). *World Employment and Social Outlook: Trends 2015.* https://www.ilo.org/wcmsp5/groups/public/---dgreports/-dcomm/---publ/documents/publication/wcms_337069.pdf

12. United Nations Department of Economic and Social Affairs. (2014). International Decade for Action 'WATER FOR LIFE' 2005–2015. https://www.un.org/waterforlifedecade/scarcity.shtml

13. Pikkety, T. (2014). *Capital in the Twenty-first Century.* Brighton, MA: Harvard Business School Press.

14. Brundtland, G. (1987). *Our Common Future: The World Commission on Environment and Development.* Oxford: Oxford University Press.

15. Hart, S., and Milstein, M. (2003). Creating Sustainable Value. *Academy of Management Perspectives*, Vol. 17, No. 2. https://doi.org/10.5465/ame.2003.10025194

16. Reed, R., and DeFillippi, R. J. (1990). Causal Ambiguity, Barriers to Imitation, and Sustainable Competitive Advantage. *Academy of Management Review*, Vol. 15, No. 1, pp. 88–102.

17. Zwetsloot, G. I. J. M. (2003). From Management Systems to Corporate Social Responsibility. *Journal of Business Ethics*, Vol. 44, Nos 2/3, pp. 201–207.

18. UN Principles of Responsible Investing. (2006). Integrate the Principles for Responsible Investment. https://www.unglobalcompact.org/take-action/action/responsible-investment

19. MacLellan, M. (2019). Responsible Capitalism Is Not a Form of Millennial Pandering. Quartz at Work. https://qz.com/work/1691365/business-roundtable-statement-on-purpose-of-companies-goes-back-to-the-future/

20. Russell, K. (2014, 1 March). Tim Cook Erupts after Shareholder Asks Him to Focus Only on Profit. Business Insider. https://www.businessinsider.com/timcookversusaconservativethinktank20142?IT

21. Somvanshi, K. K. (2019, 11 February). Why India Is Turning into ESG Funding Hotspot. *The Economic Times.* https://economictimes.indiatimes.com/markets/stocks/news/whyindiaisturningintoesgfundinghotspot/articleshow/67938722.cms?

utm_source=contentofinterest&utm_medium=text&utm_campaign=cppst

22. World Economic Forum. (2019). *Davos Manifesto 1973: A Code of Ethics for Business Leaders*. https://www.weforum.org/agenda/2019/12/davos-manifesto-1973-a-code-of-ethics-for-business-leaders/

23. Gandhi, M. K. (1960, April). *Trusteeship*. Compiled by Ravindra Kelekar. Ahmedabad: Navajivan Mudranalaya.

24. Gandhi, M. K. (1939). Trusteeship. *Harijan*, p. 145. https://www.mkgandhi.org/trusteeship/chap02.htm

25. Sarukkai, S. (2012). JRD Tata and the Idea of Trusteeship. In *Zoroastrianism: From Antiquity to the Modern Period*, edited by Murzban Jal, pp. 307–324. New Delhi: Centre for Studies in Civilizations.

26. Rana, N., and Majumdar, U. (2014, 8 January). Can a Trusteeship Model Redefine Business in the 21st Century? *The Economic Times*. https://economictimes.indiatimes.com/blogs/ResponsibleFuture/can-a-trusteeship-model-redefine-business-in-the-21st-century/

27. Margolis, J. D., and Walsh, J. P. (2003). Miseries Loves Companies: Rethinking Social Initiatives by Business. *Administrative Science Quarterly*, Vol. 48, No. 2, pp. 268–305.

28. Mudgill, A. (2018, 12 September). IL&FS Cash Crunch: Which Banks Have Biggest Exposures to Group? *The Economic Times*. https://economictimes.indiatimes.com/markets/stocks/news/ilfs-cash-crunch-which-banks-havebiggestexposuresto group/articleshow/65779707.cms?from=mdr

29. Narendra, S. (2019, 6 October). Collapse of Banking System, the Fall of the PMC Bank Is yet Another Example of the Crisis Facing the Banking Industry. *Deccan Herald*. https://www.deccanherald.com/specials/sunday-spotlight/collapse-of-banking-system-766558.html

30. Das, S. (2019, 5 June). DHFL Fails to Pay ₹1,000 Cr Interest on Bonds, Talks on. The Economic Times Bureau. https://economictimes.indiatimes.com/markets/stocks/news/dhfl-fails-to-pay-rs-1000crinterestonbondstalkson/articleshow/69658664.cms?utm_source=contentofinterest&utm_medium=text&utm_campaign=cppst

31. BS Reporter. (2019, 11 October). Religare Fraud: What Led to Singh Brothers' Arrest in the ₹2,400-Cr Case. *Business Standard*. https://www.business-standard.com/article/companies/why-were-former-ranbaxy-promoters-malvinder-and-shivinder-singh-arrested-119101100430_1.html

32. RBI. (2019). *RBI Annual Report 2018–19*. https://www.rbi.org.in/Scripts/AnnualReportPublications.aspx?year=2019

33. ET Now. (2018, 18 April). You Can't Have a Silent Board; It Must Lead from the Front: M Damodaran. *The Economic Times*. https://economictimes.indiatimes.com/markets/expert-view/you-cant-have-a-silentboarditmustleadfromthefront mdamodaran/articleshow/63815762.cms?utm_source=content ofinterest&utm_medium=text&utm_campaign=cppst

34. Roy, P. B. (2018, 18 June). The Great Corporate Governance Challenge. Business World. http://www.businessworld.in/article/TheGreatCorporateGovernanceChallenge/18-06-2018-152244/

35. IANS. (2019, 20 October). Here's How the Singh Brothers Stripped Religare Bare of ₹3,000 Crore. LiveMint. https://www.livemint.com/companies/people/here-s-how-the-singh-brothers-stripped-religare-bare-of-rs-3-000-crore-11571421 377614.html

36. Pandey, M. C. (2019, 11 October). Inside Story: How Ex-promoters of Ranbaxy Defrauded Religare of ₹2,397 Crore. *India Today*. https://www.indiatoday.in/india/story/inside-story-how-ex-promoters-of-ranbaxy-defrauded-religare-of-rs-2-397-crore-1608453-2019-10-11

37. Dubey, R. (2019, 24 January). Former ICICI Boss Chanda Kochhar Booked in Videocon Loan Case. *India Today*. https://www.indiatoday.in/india/story/former-icici-boss-chanda-kochhar-booked-in-videocon-loan-case-1438263-2019-01-24

38. *The Times of India*. (2019, 24 January). Videocon Loan Case: What CBI Said on Chanda Kochhar's Role Its FIR. https://timesofindia.indiatimes.com/business/india-business/videocon-loan-case-what-cbi-said-on-chanda-kochhars-role/articleshow/67674937.cms

39. TNN. (2019, 20 July). Rating Firms Colluded with IL&FS Executives: Audit. *The Times of India*. http://timesofindia.india

times.com/articleshow/70300713.cms?utm_source=content ofinterest&utm_medium=text&utm_campaign=cppst

40. RBI Bulletin. (2020, 11 January). Efficacy of Credit Ratings in Assessing Asset Quality: An Analysis of Large Borrowers. https://m.rbi.org.in/Scripts/BS_ViewBulletin.aspx?Id=18704

41. Press Trust of India. (2018, 9 April). State Bank of India, Punjab National Bank to Sell 15 NPAs Worth ₹10.63 Bn. *Business Standard.* https://www.businessstandard.com/article/finance/ statebankofindiapunjabnational-bank-to-sell-15-npas-worth-rs-1-063-cr-118040800228_1.html

42. Manikandan, A. (2019, 9 October). Why Indian Bankers Are Hesitant to Report Frauds. *The Economic Times.* https:// economictimes.indiatimes.com/industry/banking/finance/ banking/why-bankers-are-hesitant-to-report-frauds/article show/71496811.cms?from=mdr

43. Dave, S., and Shukla, S. (2020, 21 January). Lenders Put Cash Flows of about 500 Stressed Companies under Lens. *The Economic Times.* https://economictimes.indiatimes.com/ industry/banking/finance/banking/lendersputcashflowsof about500stressedcompaniesunderlens/articleshow/73480185. cms?from=mdr

44. ASSOCHAM. (2019). *Banking E-Bulletin.* Vol. 51. https:// www.assocham.org/userfiles/Banking%20Bulletin_October% 202019%20OK.PDF

45. Sharma, M. (2017, 21 November). Insiders Do More than Trade in India's Bull Market. LiveMint. https://www.livemint. com/Opinion/6K88JK3BOY7J24eXgQuQFP/Insiders-do-more-than-trade-in-Indias-bull-market.html

46. Banik, A., Gupta, A. D., and Bhaumik, P. K. (2015). *Corporate Governance, Responsibility and Sustainability: Initiatives in Emerging Economies.* 1st ed. London: Palgrave Macmillan.

47. The Economic Times Market. (2018, 9 April). ICICI Bank's Corporate Governance in Doubt: Fitch Ratings. https:// economictimes.indiatimes.com/markets/stocks/news/icicibanks corporate-governance-in-doubt-fitchratings/articleshow/ 63681548.cms?from=mdr

48. Somvanshi, K. K. (2019, 5 November). Governance Issues Most Important for Investors in India. *The Economic Times.*

https://economictimes.indiatimes.com/markets/stocks/news/governance-issues-most-important-for-investors-in-india/articles how/71921591.cms

49. Somvanshi, K. K. (2019, 30 December). Five Trends That Defined India Inc's Corporate Governance Standards. *The Economics Times*. https://economictimes.indiatimes.com/markets/stocks/news/five-trends-that-definedindiaincscorporate governancestandardsin2019/articleshow/73027056.cms? from=mdr

50. Vijayraghavan, K., Vyas, M., and Philip, L. (2020, 7 September). Why Independent Directors Resigning in Droves. *The Economic Times*. https://economictimes.indiatimes.com/markets/stocks/news/exodusofinddirectorsgainspaceonreputationalandlegal concerns/articleshow/77966601.cms?from=mdr

51. Bajaj, R. (2004). Competing with the Best in the World. BMA Golden Jubilee Lecture, Mumbai.

52. PTI. (2007, 22 October). Family-owned Firms Face Corporate Governance Challenges: Moody's. *The Economic Times*. https://economictimes.indiatimes.com/news/company/corporate-trends/family-ownedfirmsfacecorporategovernancechallenges moodys/articleshow/2480928.cms?utm_source=contentof interest&utm_medium=text&utm_campaign=cppst

53. Varottil, U. (2009). A Cautionary Tale of the Transplant Effect on Indian Corporate Governance. *National Law School of India Review*, Vol. 21, No. 1, pp. 1–49. https://ssrn.com/abstract= 1331581

54. Varma, J. R. (1997). Corporate Governance in India: Disciplining the Dominant Shareholder. *IIMB Management Review*, Vol. 9, No. 4, pp. 5–18. https://faculty.iima.ac.in/~jrvarma/papers/iimbr 9-4.pdf

55. NFCG. (1999). *Report of Kumar Mangalam Birla Committee on Corporate Governance*. http://www.nfcg.in/UserFiles/ kumarmbirla1999.pdf

56. SEBI. (2003). *Report of Shri N R Narayana Murthy Committee on Corporate Governance*. https://www.sebi.gov.in/reports/reports/mar-2003/the-report-of-shri-n-r-narayana-murthy-committee-on-corporate-governance-for-public-comments-_ 12986.html

57. MCA. (2003). *Report of the Committee on Regulation of Private Companies and Partnerships*. http://reports.mca.gov.in/ Reports/3Naresh%20Chandra%20committee%20report%20 on%20regulation%20of%20private%20companies%20 and%20partnerships,%202003.pdf

58. Irani, J. J. (2005). *Report of the Expert Committee on Corporate Law*. http://reports.mca.gov.in/Reports/23Irani%20committee %20report%20of%20the%20expert%20committee%20 on%20Company%20law,2005.pdf

59. Parthasarathi, V., and Tiwari, R. (2019, April). Dawn of a New Era in Indian Corporate Governance? India Corporate Law, Cyril Amarchand Mangaldas Blog. https://corporate.cyrila marchandblogs.com/2019/03/april-2019-dawn-of-a-new-era-in-indian-corporate-governance/

60. PTI. (2018, 18 February). No New Laws Needed for Good Corporate Governance: Adi Godrej. *The Economic Times*. https://economictimes.indiatimes.com/news/company/corporate-trends/no-new-lawsneededforgoodcorporategovernancea digodrej/articleshow/63015528.cms?utm_source=contentof interest&utm_medium=text&utm_campaign=cppst

61. Garratt, B. (1997). *The Fish Rots from the Head: The Crisis in Our Boardrooms: Developing the Crucial Skills of the Competent Director*. New York, NY: HarperCollins.

62. Useem, M. (2006). How Well-run Boards Make Decisions. *Harvard Business Review*, Vol. 84, No. 11, pp. 130–138. https:// pubmed.ncbi.nlm.nih.gov/17131569/

63. Ostrower, F., and Stone, M. (2005). *Boards of Nonprofit Organizations: Research Trends, Findings, and Prospects for the Future. The Nonprofit Sector: A Research Handbook*. New Haven, CT: Yale University Press.

64. Gregg, S. (2001). *The Art of Corporate Governance: A Return to First Principles*. St Leonards: Centre for Independent Studies

65. Hilmer, F. G. (1998). Strictly Boardroom: Improving Governance to Enhance Company Performance. 2nd ed. Melbourne: Information Australia.

66. Kiel, G., and Nicholson, Gavin. (2002). Real World Governance: Driving Business Success through Effective Corporate Governance. *Mt. Eliza Business Review*, Vol. 5, No. 1, pp. 17–28.

67. Maher, M., and Andersson, T. (1999). Corporate Governance: Effects on Firm Performance and Economic Growth. OECD. https://www.oecd.org/sti/ind/2090569.pdf

68. Gompers, P., Ishii, J., and Metrick, A. (2003). Corporate Governance and Equity Prices. *The Quarterly Journal of Economics*, Vol. 118, No. 1, pp. 107–155.

69. Bebchuk, L., Cohen, A., and Ferrell, A. (2009). What Matters in Corporate Governance? *The Review of Financial Studies*, Vol. 22, No. 2, pp. 783–827.

70. Ferris S. P., Kim K, Kitsabunnarat P. (2003). The Costs (and Benefits) of Diversified Business Groups: The Case of Korean Chaebols. *Journal of Banking and Finance*. Vol. 27, No. 2, pp. 275–297.

71. Khanna, V., and Black, B. (2007). Can CG Reforms Increase Firm's Market Value? *Journal of Empirical Legal Studies*, Vol. 4, No. 4, pp. 749–796.

72. Mani, G. V., and Sreedharan, R. (2004). Better Corporate Governance Pays. *Insight in Risk*, Vol. 2, No. 9.

73. Emslie, S. (2007). *Exploring the Association between Board and Organizational Performance in NHS Foundation Trusts*. London: Department of Management, Birkbeck College, University of London.

74. Ostrower, F., and Stone, M. M. (2006). Governance: Research Trends, Gaps, and Future Prospects. In *The Nonprofit Sector: A Research Handbook*, edited by W. W. Powell and R. Steinberg, pp. 612–628. New Haven, CT: Yale University Press.

75. Lorsch, J. W., and Clark, R. C. (2008). Leading from the Boardroom. *Harvard Business Review*, pp. 105–111.

76. Cornforth, C., and Chambers, N. (2010). The Role of Corporate Governance and Boards in Organisational Performance. https://doi.org/10.1017/CBO9780511762000.007

77. Finkelstein S, and Mooney, A. C. (2003). Not the Usual Suspects: How to Use Board Process to Make Boards Better. *Academy Management Perspectives*, Vol. 17, No. 2, pp. 101–113. https://doi.org/10.5465/ame.2003.10025204

78. Friedman, M. (1970). The Social Responsibility of Business Is to Increase Its Profits. *The New York Times Magazine*. http://umich.edu/~thecore/doc/Friedman.pdf

79. Anderson, D. W., Melanson, S. J., and Maly, J. (2007). The Evolution of Corporate Governance: Power Redistribution Brings Boards to Life. *Corporate Governance: An International Review*. Vol. 15, No. 5, pp. 780–797. https://doi.org/10.1111/j.1467-8683.2007.00608.x

80. Hendry, K., and Kiel, G. (2004). The Role of the Board in Firm Strategy: Integrating Agency and Organisational Control Perspectives. *Corporate Governance: An International Review*, Vol. 12, No. 4, pp. 500–520. https://doi.org/10.1111/j.1467-8683.2004.00390.x

Further Readings

Abrams, F. W. (1951). Management's Responsibilities in a Complex World. *Harvard Business Review*, Vol. 29, pp. 54–64.

Balakrishnan, J., Malhotra, A., and Falkenberg, L. (2015). Multi-level Corporate Responsibility: A Comparison of Gandhi's Trusteeship with Stakeholder and Stewardship Frameworks. *Journal of Business Ethics*, Vol. 141, pp. 133–150. https://doi.org/10.1007/s10551-015-2687-0

Barney, J. (1991). Firm Resources and Sustained Competitive Advantage. *Journal of Management*, Vol. 17, No. 1, pp. 99–120. https://doi.org/10.1177%2F014920639101700108

Berle, A., and Means, G. (1932). The Modern Corporation and Private Property. New York, NY: Macmillan.

Davis, J. H., Schoorman, F. D., and Donaldson, L. (1997). Toward a Stewardship Theory of Management. *Academy Management Review*, Vol. 22, pp. 20–47. https://doi.org/10.5465/amr.1997.9707180258

Donaldson, T., and Preston, L. E. (1995). The Stakeholder Theory of the Corporation: Concepts, Evidence and Implications. *Academy of Management Review*, Vol. 20, pp. 65–91.

Kopp, C. M. (2019). Agency Theory. https://www.investopedia.com/terms/a/agencytheory.asp

La Porta, R., Lopez-de-Silanes, F., Shleifer A., and Vishny, R. (1999). Corporate Ownership around the World. *The Journal of Finance*, Vol. 54, No. 2, pp. 471–517.

Parkinson, J. (1994). The Legal Context of Corporate Social Responsibility. *Business Ethics*, Vol. 3, No. 1, pp. 16–22.

Pfeffer, J., and Salancik, G. R. (1978). *The External Control of Organizations: A Resource Dependence Perspective.* New York, NY: Harper & Row.

Rajput, R., and Sinha, S. (2019, 22 July). IL&FS' Rating Agencies Made Professional Compromises, Says Grant Thornton. *The Economic Times.* https://economictimes.indiatimes.com/industry/banking/finance/gt-report-lists-out-issues-of-professional-compromises-by-the-cras-who-rated-ilfs/articleshow/70296758.cms?utm_source=contentofinterest&utm_medium=text&utm_campaign=cppst

Rao, J., and Jha, S. K. (2018). A Less Acknowledged Source of Gandhi's Ideas of Trusteeship. *Economic & Political Weekly*, Vol. 53, No. 37.

Roy, A. (2016). Corporate Governance and Firm Performance: A Study of Indian Listed Firms. *Metamorphosis*, Vol. 15, No. 1, pp. 31–46.

Sarbanes Oxley Act. (2002). www.soxlaw.com

Sieben, H. (2002). Concepts and Working Instruments for Corporate Governance. *Journal of Business Ethics*, Vol. 39, Nos 1/2, pp. 109–116.

Shleifer, A., and Vishny, R. W. (1997). A Survey of Corporate Governance. *Journal of Finance*, Vol. 52, No. 2, pp. 737–783. https://onlinelibrary.wiley.com/doi/abs/10.1111/j.1540-6261.1997.tb04820.x

Solomon, J. (2007). *Corporate Governance and Accountability.* London: John Wiley & Sons.

Tricker, R. I. (1984). *Corporate Governance: Practices, Producers and Powers in British Companies and Their Boards of Directors.* Aldershot: Gower Press.

2

ARCHITECTING SUSTAINABLE COMPETITIVE EDGE: ROLE OF BOARDS

The ability to learn faster than your competitors may be the only sustainable competitive advantage.

—Arie de Geus [1]

In the world of cataclysmic change and uncertainty, developing organizations with sustained high performance and competitive edge requires committed and capable boards. This is more so amid all the environmental disruptions that pose the most potent challenge to the survival of businesses. The previous chapter made it clear that boards have an important role to play in providing strategic guidance to the companies they head.

This chapter focuses on three core stages of cognition involved in acquiring and processing information to be traversed by the boards and top management of companies before they take steps to architect sustainable competitive edge (Appendix B) in the organizations they head:

- Understanding the business context and the threats and challenges inherent in the disruptions to their specific business
- Identifying the enablers of sustainable competitive edge for their company
- Detailing the levers of sustainable competitive edge

The chapter concludes by identifying some of the key strategic issues which every forward-thinking board must focus upon to architect sustainable competitive edge.

This chapter is divided into three parts:

Part 1. The Business Context
Part 2. Enablers of Sustainable Competitive Edge
Part 3. Levers of Sustainable Competitive Edge

Part 1. The Business Context

This part delineates the various issues and challenges of the business context faced by Indian companies.

The Challenge for India

Speaking from the ramparts of the Red Fort on 15 August 2019, Prime Minister Narendra Modi announced the road map for India: to become a five-trillion-dollar economy and feature among the top three developed nations in the world by 2025. This is a steep challenge that India has to cope with. In order to realize this, the Indian economy will need to grow at more than 10 per cent per annum for the next five years [2]. This is an apparently impossible challenge for a nation which in the year 2019–2020 grew at around 5 per cent. Nations such as Germany, Japan, Australia, Four Asian Tigers and China, despite their many problems and challenges, leapfrogged into growth and prosperity by riding on the power of technology and innovation. This provides a glimmer of hope that it just might be possible for India to similarly bounce back and achieve its economic aspirations. If not by 2025, the target can be achieved a couple of years down the line.[i]

At this stage, it may be worthwhile to understand the present state of the Indian economy vis-à-vis India's aspirations. According to the *Global Competitiveness Report* [3], India stood 68th in the list of 141 economies. It is only on the pillars of the market size (3rd rank), innovation capability (35th rank), financial systems (34th rank) and macroeconomic stability (43rd rank) that India scored quite well. The report also underscored the criticality of technology and innovation for economic growth. The Global Innovation Index (GII) 2019 has also shown that there is a strong and positive correlation between an economy's level of development (measured by GDP per capita) and innovation performance.[ii]

The GII, 2019 places India as the most innovative country in the region of Central and Southern Asia. Nevertheless, it is sobering to note that India has a long way to go—the score of 35.59 on innovation is just above the halfway mark of

Switzerland, which is ranked Number 1 on the innovation parameter. Clearly, India is yet to break into the elite club of top global innovation powerhouses. One of the reasons for India lagging behind is the paucity of intermediate outputs such as publications, patents and research outputs for achieving commercial success. This is not surprising given the fact that the investments of Indian manufacturing in R&D have been extremely paltry. In fact, the expenditure on R&D as a percentage of GDP [4] in India has been consistently in the range of 0.6–0.9 per cent, spending the least, among the newly industrializing countries such as South Korea, Taiwan, Singapore, China and Brazil. Even then, most of the R&D is done in publicly funded and autonomous R&D institutes with the share of industry in the national expenditure on R&D at just 35 per cent.

Indian Firms Are Globally Uncompetitive

India's contribution to world exports (currently at a meagre 2%), grew at a measly 0.87 per cent in 2018–2019 as against the world average of 3.5 per cent [5]. In the same year, the trade deficit has been huge—as much as $296 million—equivalent to 3.9 per cent of India's GDP. More revealing is its meagre growth of 5.3 per cent in merchandise exports and 8.6 per cent growth in commercial services—both are quite low when compared with other developing countries. India's script of success in software solutions and data-based technology is also slowing down. Although India is 2nd in the overall list of information and communications technology (ICT) services exporters ($58 billion) globally and growing at a steady pace of 7 per cent (2008–2018), others are quickly catching up. In comparison, China's growth in ICT is at a staggering 69 per cent, followed by Israel at 18 per cent and Canada at 10 per cent. The decline in imports, along with exports in recent times, tells another story. It is not surprising at all that just seven Indian companies featured in the Fortune 500 companies list. Even more depressing is the fact that even the highest-ranked Indian firm, namely Reliance Industries is ranked at 96th position and that three other companies, namely Indian Oil Corporation Limited (IOCL), Bharat Petroleum Corporation Limited (BPCL) and Oil and Natural Gas Corporation (ONGC) are from the government-controlled monopoly oil sector. Their membership in the exclusive group is more because of their market capitalization rather than any efforts towards growth propelled by R&D and innovation. *The Comptroller and Auditor General (CAG) Report* [6] on the expenditure of 21 select Central Public Sector Enterprise during the period (2013–2014 to 2017–2018) revealed that companies such as ONGC, IOCL and BPCL which spend between 2.5 per cent and 1.5 per cent of their respective profit after tax (PAT) on R&D do so without any well-formulated R&D plan. Much worse, these companies have normally failed to exhaust the budgeted amount on R&D and commercialization of new technologies. Indeed, it is a testimony to the sorry state of affairs that R&D and innovation which are key strategic weapons for enabling competitiveness are not emphasized even by those companies which are in the Fortune 500 list.

There is no doubt that Indian organizations have to redouble their efforts to enable innovation and business growth and thereby to enhance labour and capital productivity. Boards have a key role to play in bringing such sharp focus in their businesses and make key decisions to accelerate the global competitiveness of Indian firms.

Firms Are Masters of Their Destiny

Countries facing favourable conditions for business and the firm's conducive environment are expected to perform better than those in unfavourable business environments. The World

Bank's annual survey of 'Doing Business' is premised on this underlying assumption. It was argued, at one time, that (a) size of the home country market, (b) availability of minimum efficiency of scale, (c) abundance and costs of factor endowments, (d) co-location in regions that had agglomeration advantages and (e) the propensity of the market to accept new and innovative products gave a comparative advantage to domestic firms over rival companies [7–9].

Things have changed dramatically in today's free (liberal and deregulated), global and digitized market economy. Today, firms are masters of their destiny, unhampered by the above criteria as they have the opportunity to compete and organize their value chains for production and sales on a global level. They can make direct investments, acquisitions, mergers, make local firms a part of their globalized value chain and in this way, develop a competitive advantage in other markets. It is the firm that chooses its products and industry, along with taking on the commensurate challenges. Studies [10] have shown that firm effects explain performance variation more than industry and country factors.[iii]

Changing Business Landscape: New Opportunities

Firms excel or fail, stagnate or die, depending—among other things—on the business context and the response of boards to the challenges and opportunities therein. As long as the business landscape of firms was simple and stable, the competitive edge was based on choosing the most attractive industry and strategic position in keeping with the capabilities of the firm. A firm's performance was more a matter of fit between the organization and its external environment, the various components of the internal organizational configuration of strategy, structure, systems, style, skills and shared values. A disruptive and dynamic environment changes the game. In order to survive and succeed in such a context, organizations need to co-evolve with their environment and develop contextually aligned responses. This requires both a strong strategic focus and a focus on continued innovation.

Before delving into the details, however, at this stage, it would be relevant to understand the emerging business context. Business context refers to the trends, impact and relationship which the business has with the wider world. It consists of the entire universe minus the focal firm which has a direct or indirect effect on the functioning and outcomes of the firm. The direct effect is of the forces consisting of government rules and regulations, suppliers, buyers, technology and competitors. The broader context, consisting of factors such as political, legal, economic, social, cultural and ethical affect the firms indirectly through its effects on the direct factors.

Given below is a presentation regarding the contemporary business landscape in the light of which companies and boards have to develop a suitable strategic focus for their organizations as well as develop strategies to promote continued innovation.

The contemporary business environment is marked by globalization, complexity, hyper-turbulence, hyper-competition and ambiguity. It is not for the first time that globalization has happened in human history. People across nations came together in earlier eras as well for purposes such as trade and commerce, war and conquests, religion and ideologies. The features of contemporary globalization, its drivers and the impact on business are, however, unlike anything seen in earlier eras. The sea change has taken place because there is now a world-wide integration of goods, services, capital, labour, production process, economic activities, market and consumption patterns. In addition, the sheer expanse and velocity with which there is a flow of capital, labour, services, images and ideas across geographies, has led to 'compression of time and space' and the occurrence of opportunities to work beyond borders.

This globalization is driven by the ICT revolution. Today, business processes have become mind-bogglingly faster, effective and more cost-efficient. Innovation in the supply chain has led to the horizontal integration of manufacturers, suppliers, retailers and customers across the globe as they collaborate to plan, create, deliver and use goods and services of global standards. Firms are better able to break down their value chains into modularized activities that can be outsourced and even offshored to cost-efficient locations riding on the power of communication technologies. Intellectual property rights (IPRs) are getting shared, ideas and funding are getting crowd-sourced and open innovation has liberated R&D as an activity internal to the firm. In fact, firms have given way to networks which deliver value to customers and markets, enabled by the circuit of financial and ICT systems.

In this globally integrated world, no environment provides safety or longevity of organizations. All firms across the world are facing severe challenges because of innovations by competitive companies on the four key dimensions of business: 'offerings' (unique products) which the company creates, the 'customers' it serves, the 'configurations' or processes it employs and the 'experience' it provides to its consumers. In today's context, these four new sources of competitive advantage when used by competitors can bring down any firm no matter how big, established or mature. This has been amply illustrated by the fall of global industry leaders such as Nokia, Xerox and Pan Am among others.

Over the last two decades, most Indian firms went bust because they could not compete with the cost, quality and brand advantages of global firms that entered India. A slew of Indian companies gradually slipped into years of stagnation or simply went bankrupt because of their complacency and lack of adequate efforts at continuous improvement—HMT Limited, ITI, HEC, Hindustan Motors, Escorts, DCM, Modi,

Bombay Dyeing, Essar to name a few.[iv] Thus, it is clear that being large and successful at one point in time is no guarantee of the continued survival of organizations. In the current business context, the most common outcome for large 20th-century firms—characterized by giant managerial hierarchies and large markets with first-mover advantages—is indeed decline. They are like the dinosaurs of another era, too big, too rigid and too slow to change [11].

Despite the high rates of failure of business organizations, some companies have not only survived but also excelled over long periods of time [12–14] beating all expectations. At this stage, readers may be interested to know more about the features of companies that survived, performed and excelled. A recent study[v] by McKinsey Global Institute [15] has shown that notable companies—across industry sectors—such as Altria, Coca-Cola, Intel, Johnson & Johnson, Merck, Microsoft, Nestle, Novartis, Samsung, Toyota and Walmart have consistently featured among the top 1 per cent of the firms for the last 30 years. In recent times, they have been joined by technology firms such as Alphabet, Apple, Facebook, Oracle, Tencent, Alibaba and some Chinese banks.

These giants have mind-boggling strengths to their credit. Together, they generate more than 1.5 times sales from outside their home region, account for a majority of global trade and outperform their peers on the scale and operating performance. They show 50 per cent more productivity than firms which rank at the median and account for more than 70 per cent of R&D in the sample as well as make a disproportionate investment in intangible assets (IPRs, software and brand value and in foreign direct investment and sales).

These firms are the so-called 'superstars' because they are '…Larger, more Profitable, more Innovative, more Globalized and more Productive than their peers' [15].

It is obvious that in the current business environment, the strategic focus of firms needs to shift if they have to survive, perform and succeed on a sustainable basis. Firms should move beyond mere efficiency to become more responsive, adaptive, speedy and above all innovative. A study of the impact of innovation on firm survival revealed that there is a marked difference between innovators and non-innovators even when controlling for the effects of firm size, growth and nature of technology.[vi] In fact, innovate or perish is the mantra for the organizations, and boards need to take serious note of this.

The enablers of sustainable competitive edge have been divided into two parts: the first part unravels the role which is played by innovation in architecting sustainable competitive edge, and the second part identifies the factors that have enabled the firm's capability for continuous innovation.

Enabler 1

Innovation: The Key to Sustainable Competitive Edge

Innovation is the key to organizational longevity. It is only organizations that seek to stay ahead of the pack and anticipate and respond to the environmental changes have the best chance to live longer. Innovation has been found to have a direct relationship with organizational performance.[vii] Organizations which had a strong alignment between their business and innovation strategies outperformed their peers, with a 40 per cent higher operating income growth and a 100 per cent higher shareholder return over a three-year period [16]. Highly innovating firms had better top-line growth, customer satisfaction, bottom-line growth and profitability [17].

In contrast, organizations possessing low innovation orientation had significant negative correlations with return on investment, firm performance and overall enterprise value. Today, firm profitability is constantly under threat because of changing customer preferences and competition. Thus, it is imperative that organizations continuously align and realign with these changing preferences [18,19]. Firms that do not innovate enough to improve productivity, respond to market demands and operate in tune with the competitors have been found to display poorer performance [20]. It is not an exaggeration to say that companies which do not innovate have no future since they are made irrelevant by the competition in due course. Thus, today, every organization must have an alert antenna and radar-like collective mindset for continued innovation since the sustainability of a firm depends on finding new sources of value creation and new configurations of value propositions.

Innovation is the introduction of ideas or behaviours pertaining to products, services, production processes, organizational structures or administrative systems that are 'new to the adopting organization' [21–23]. Innovation can be either in the form of new products or services to fulfil customer needs or the adaptation of existing products or services to new markets. This is driven mainly by the organization's desire to penetrate new markets or to compete more effectively in existing markets. They enable product differentiation resulting in increased profitability and lower competitive pressure and, above all, foster market creation or renewal. Innovation can also take place either in the form of new organizational processes or the modification of existing ones, to increase efficiency or effectiveness in the production and delivery of goods and services [24].

Regardless of the form it takes, innovation is critical for the sustainable competitive advantage of the firm. The key point is whether such innovation is 'sustaining' or 'disruptive' [18,25,26]. Sustaining innovation enables companies to go up on the established improvement trajectory, that is, they bring improvements in existing products or services (e.g., faster computers, long-lasting mobile phone batteries or cameras with better quality images). Disruptive innovation, on the other hand, introduces a new value proposition. It either creates a new market or reshapes an existing market. For example, Walmart's discount retail store and Dell's direct-to-customer business are examples of how existing products or services which were 'too good' could be transformed to provide a novel value proposition to the customer. This is quite different from products like Apple's personal computer, which provided an alternative to existing cumbersome products. Innovations such as digital cameras relative to analogue cameras, cellular phones relative to wired phones, iPod relative to Walkman and electronic calculators relative to slide rules radically disrupted the market because they were better performing and provided a unique value proposition [27,28].

What Matters Is Business Innovation

As firms within an industry start pursuing the same customer with similar offerings, they will also tend to innovate on similar lines, thus nullifying the initial competitive advantage. In technology-based industry, most firms focus on product development; while in chemical, oil or power industries, all firms concentrate on process innovations. In the consumer package goods industry, manufacturers concentrate on procurement, supply chaining, branding and distribution. Adopting similar approaches as others in the industry hardly provides a competitive advantage to companies; it simply helps the laggard to catch up with the leader of the pack and bring the entire industry to the same level.

If firms really intend to create and sustain their competitive edge, their innovations must impact their business model, that is, the way they run their business to make money. The moot question to ask is whether or not the innovation will generate substantially new value for customers and firms.

Starbucks became a winner not because it serves better-tasting coffee but because it provided 'the third place'—a common meeting place between workplace and home where people can unwind, chat and connect with each other. Similarly, the competitive edge of Dell does not rest on being just a PC maker, but a PC that can be brought quickly to the market due to innovation in processes such as supply chain management, manufacturing and direct selling. Indeed, in today's world, it makes no difference as to how innovative the company is. What matters is whether that innovation is activating the customers' willingness to pay for goods or services that meet their needs and wants.

Continuous Innovation Must Be the Centrepiece of Strategy

It is not just innovation but continuous innovation which should be the central focus of firm's strategy for building sustainable competitive edge. Needless to say, in the world of hyper-competition, innovations can provide competitive edge only for a short time before other competitors catch up. Empirical studies have also shown that it was the inability to craft a winning strategy, aligned to the changing context, that led to the downfall of firms which were once industry leaders and disrupters—Nokia, Dell, GM, Qantas, Kodak, Radio Corporation of America (RCA), Pan Am, Sears, etc [29–31].

Researchers [25,32–34] have found that despite operating in an environment characterized by rapid shifts in markets and technologies, these companies failed to continuously protect the market share. They remained trapped in the headiness of success based on existing strengths such as successful products, designs, technologies and competencies in the existing product, market and customers. As a result, when new entrants started disrupting the industry, the incumbents displayed a striking inability to unlearn old deeply embedded routines and look beyond their current customers.[viii]

Given that success itself lulls companies into a false sense of security, it is vital for the board to have a forward-looking, even paranoid perspective about growth. This is more so when evaluating whether to invest in new and immature disruptive innovations that could become mainstream tomorrow; whether it makes sense to cannibalize the existing product market and competencies providing revenue and profits today. The company faces the humungous dilemma to either destroy its existing competencies and create new ones or break out of the bounded rationality of thinking and initiate pathbreaking innovations. The only way a firm can escape its nemesis is by adopting a strategy of continuous innovation which would resolve the paradoxical challenges of 'dualism', that is, functioning effectively today while parallelly providing resources to innovate for tomorrow.

Part 2. Enablers of Sustainable Competitive Edge

It is not enough for a firm to decide that it wants to be innovative. The success of the strategy of continuous innovation requires that other organizational factors such as processes, management practices and design elements are also suitably aligned to facilitate innovation. In the contemporary world, so much of innovation and change has happened that these very elements have become the basis for sustainable competitive advantage. Given below are seven key factors that provide sustainable competitive edge to firms.

Customer Centricity

The five elements of customer centricity are as follows:

1. Understanding that the purpose of business is to create value for the customers
2. Knowing what customers value
3. Innovating to take care of the unmet needs of the customers

4. Considering non-customers as potential customers
5. Using data science and digital technologies to engage with the customers

The purpose of a firm is to create value for its customers. The capacity of a firm to charge a premium on its products depends on its ability to create and communicate an attractive value proposition that the customer is inclined to trust based on its earlier experiences with the firm. The board needs to recognize the shift of economic power from the seller to the consumer, and the need for moving from a product-centric approach to a customer-centric approach. Above all, there is a need to focus on understanding the customer's needs, the product uses and the money, time and effort involved. They also ought to develop strategies to garner higher returns by seeking to acquire, retain and develop the highest value customers.

In an earlier era, the customer value proposition was based either on cost or differentiation by pursuing a low-cost strategy to reap large cost savings. Firms that chose to provide superior products at low costs were able to derive dual competitive advantage. For instance, Toyota's pursuit of quality not only reduced errors, rejects, returns and thus the overall costs, but also ensured superior products to its customers. Today, it is the same strategy that has also catapulted companies such as Apple, Singapore Airlines and similar others into impregnable fortresses of competitive advantage.

Today, the customer value proposition is about what customers value.[ix] In the 1980s, Kodak was so focused on developing the film-based camera case that it forgot to market its own invention: the digital camera. Their version of the digital camera may have been low in quality, but it was more convenient, less costly and more popular among the customers. In the 1990s and early 2000, Sony, Nikon and Canon went through the rat race of adding pixels. It was engineering that drove the business. And then, people stopped noticing the difference after 5 or 7 megapixels. This was when customers shifted to mobile cameras which afforded cost, convenience and connectedness. Today, it is Google, Apple, Samsung, etc., that have become the best sellers. Some firms have enjoyed continued success only because of the loyalty of the customers to the taste associated with their favourite product [35]. For instance, Colgate in toothpaste, Amul in milk and dairy, Nescafe with coffee, Budweiser with beer or Maggi with noodles have continued to succeed only because of the early seduction of customers taste buds to the company products. On the other hand, another set of firms have created high loyalty among the customers based on the power of the brand. Such customers go to the extent of believing that cost saving is less important as compared to the time, trouble and money spent on researching and comparing the product and its competitors. Drug companies like Bayer, TATAs in products ranging from salt to diamonds, IBM, Sony, Bose, etc., have all enjoyed competitive advantages for this reason alone. Studies have also shown [36–38] that reward and loyalty programmes help retaining customers as the high switching costs (from one service provider to another) prevents the customers from migrating.

As stated earlier, customer centricity is also about creating and providing new products or services to serve the unmet needs or under-served customer segments. P&G's 'spin brush', 3Ms Scotch-Brite and other masking tapes and medical devices, Apple's iPod and iTunes are examples of new or novel goods highly valued by the customers and which translated into huge profits for firms. Some firms have created value for the customers through the sheer breadth of their offerings, whether products or services. UPS logistics services and supply chain solutions, DuPont's building innovations for construction have all endeared them to the customers and the market only because they have provided a one-stop solution to cater to all the customer needs.

Developments in customer centricity have also exploded the myth of the hallowed marketing principle of segmentation, targeting and positioning. Firms have innovated offerings by introducing a new mantra for success: treat non-consumers as a segmentation problem, which is all about firms finding out and knowing why some people in its market category are not its customers and what products it should innovate to convert them. Virgin Mobile, for instance, customized offerings to customers below the age of 30. The global swimwear company Arena created freestyle breather to help non-swimmers, children and novices to have a better pool experience. They also created a line of swimwear (burkini) in keeping with the socio-religious sentiments of Muslim women. Firms such as Uber, Tesla and a whole host of clean and green energy and storage companies cater to the known 'unknown' needs of people. There is another group of companies that have impacted customer experience through a redesign of customer interactions across touch points and all 'moments of truth'. A whole host of firms in retail banking, travel, home services, etc., are making the customer experience more personalized, automated, contextual and digitized so that customers not only get attracted but also remain permanently loyal.

Yet another variety of firms use big data and analytics to understand customers and their changing needs by continuously engaging with them, understanding the jobs they want to accomplish (with a particular product or service) and accordingly tailoring their offerings. Mall of America extensively uses weather bulletins, mall events, foot traffic patterns, dwell times at particular locations to predict mall traffic. This is subsequently used by retail stores to predict footfalls, sales and staff requirement to enhance experience not only for customers but also retail stores as tenants. More and more companies are using multiple sources to collect data. Today, insights into customer behaviour and choices are being collected from the vendors, competitors, customers and the public. In this context, one of the most fascinating sources of new data is the mobile ecosystem. Every click, every swipe, every text on the smartphone generates data, enabling firms with the capabilities in artificial intelligence (AI), machine learning (ML) and data science in configuring specific, personalized and curated solutions.[x]

There are an increasing number of firms piloting automated real-time conversations through 'chatbots' to acquire information about customer needs, product preferences and help retailers respond quickly to the insights gathered through such automated interaction. Swiss Re, an insurance firm, uses algorithm and scenarios to generate future risks and pricing, thus transforming the actuarial work that is based upon looking at the historical data of losses, its frequency and its severity. Amazon's expertise with data analytics has facilitated its entry into pharmacy business. Google has also got into the clinical space due to its ability to generate, aggregate and analyse big data and thus engage with their customers. Amazon and Netflix have used data analytics, AI and IoT to profile customers, their behaviour and their choices so as to provide better and more targeted recommendations for purchase and viewership. Real-time analysis provided by IoT sensor data along with AI analysis by US agriculture solutions provider WinField United guide farmers through 40 make or break decisions.

In the efforts to engage at each and every touch point of customer interaction and life cycle, firms have moved beyond digital marketing and multi-channel to omnichannel strategies. Omnichannel marketing strategy anticipates customer's prospect as he/she moves from one channel to another such as from say social media to website ramped up through search engine optimization and eventually through email to the phone before turning into sales qualified lead. It then orchestrates the customer experience across all channels so that it is seamless, integrated and consistent. Research by Invesp, the conversion rate optimization experts, shows that companies with omnichannel customer engagement strategies retain an average of 89 per cent of their customers.[xi] With the use of native advertising, Toshiba got a 0.78 per cent engagement rate on its ads compared to 0.14 per cent that it got through traditional mobile ads.

Finally, due to easier access to information, consumers have started playing a significant role in information selection and screening. Today, brand differentiation and competitive advantage are getting driven by 'the superiority of customer journeys firms undertake' [39]. And this journey depends upon the firm's mastery of four capabilities: automation, proactive personalization, contextual interaction, and innovation. Indeed, in an environment defined by a new generation of users, who have sensitive and fickle consumption habits, the idea of seeking growth from a company's existing traffic, driving marketing through technology and gaining results through greater efficiency are the new skills that firms will need in order to excel.

Time to Market: Either Digitize or Die

Time to market involves responding fast, flexibly and effectively to hit the market as an early mover. In order to facilitate such speed, firms need to:

1. Digitally engage with the customer at every touch point of their journey
2. Digitally enable and transform the supply chain
3. Apply real-time data and sensing capability
4. Use collaborative models for speedy innovation

Businesses that move fast have been found to attract more customers and profits. Knowing one's customer, segmenting them, tailoring individuated personalized offerings, engaging them at each step of their customer journey is today becoming digital. AI is being used for product recommendations, campaign optimization, customer service, personalized headlines and advertising copy. Search engines are driving a huge amount of traffic, especially on Google with Accelerated Mobile Pages (AMP) technology.[xii]

Digital technologies are also transforming the business models of companies and customer-facing activities by transforming company's supply chains.[xiii] As digital advances continue to reduce communication and coordination costs, companies are finding it easier, less risky and more efficient to secure external solutions rather than invent solutions in-house.[xiv] Zara, the Spanish apparel retailer, has been able to create fast and flexible supply chains by making counter-intuitive choices in sourcing, designing, manufacturing and logistics.[xv] Amidst this, firms such as Stitch Fix and Warby Parker actually encourage customers to order multiple sizes and colours of the same item, choose the one they like best and return the rest. Their competitive edge rests in their capability to be fast, flexible, personalized and responsive.

Just a few years ago, supply chain performance was all about planning, batch quantities, timetables and lead times. Effective supply chain was about improvements in speed, efficiency and reliability. However, in the world of demand volatility, customer expectations for personalization and an increasingly unpredictable operating environment, it is not enough for supply chains to be speedy, economical and reliable. Agility demands that the supply chain should also be flexible, adaptive and reconfigurable. In fact, by embracing technology that provides real-time data and sensing capability to supply chain managers, some firms have turned volatility and unpredictability into sources of competitive advantage for their company.[xvi]

Time to market is also about the speed of innovation. As a result, there is increasing use of collaborative models to speedily design solutions to meet the current and future needs of the customers. In an earlier world where every innovation got imitated, it was IPRs—patents, copyrights, trademarks and trade secrets—which enabled a firm to enjoy competitive advantage. Today, this logic has been turned on its head; sharing proprietary rights and innovations is yielding considerably stronger competitive advantage to firms. Monsanto has benefitted by sharing its genetically modified and herbicide-resistant seeds with even the rival firms such as BASF, DuPont and Syngenta. Microsoft and Sony have shared technology with developers such as Xbox and PlayStation. Google freely licenses Android software to make sure it is ahead in the number of applications available for the Android operating systems. The evolution of business has shown that it makes sense to collaborate with companies with complementing skills operating at different levels of the value chain, that is, the complementors.

One outcome of company-level partnerships for co-creating solutions, greater connectedness and platform engagement driven by digital convergence is open innovation. This distributed innovation process is the new imperative. It is based on purposively managed knowledge flows across organizational boundaries. There are varying levels of openness as firms decide which parts of the knowledge can be made open and which part can remain proprietary. Apple develops its iPhone software with closed innovation but uses open innovation for the initial hardware design. The same approach is used for its iPhone app store. Qualcomm embraced open innovation by building an open ecosystem by licensing its proprietary technology to its 'complementors', who in turn designed and built final products for consumers.[xvii] With its product-based revenue model, Tesla has created its open innovation ecosystem around open patent systems fully realizing that it could not produce enough electric cars to solve the carbon crisis itself. Similarly, IBM has initiated Eco-Patent Commons through an open patent strategy to accelerate implementation to protect the environment. Cisco, on other hand, has used open innovation through multiple routes such as acquisition, partnering with or investing in promising start-ups. Interestingly, Cisco is at the centre of the world's finest industrial R&D organization without conducting much R&D on its own.

It is thus clear that heightened sensing capability can enable companies to identify and evaluate valuable external knowledge resources and establish cross-boundary collaboration beyond the organizations. In such companies, innovativeness is about leveraging and enhancing internal capabilities, either to enhance one's own business model (outside-in open innovation) or to explore a new business model (inside-out open innovation).

Cost Leadership: The Integrated Architecture of Distributed Value Chain

Apart from the cost efficiencies derived from process optimization and operational innovations, cost leadership is all about:

1. Geographically distributed but digitally integrated value chain for ensuring cost efficiencies and speedy response to customers
2. Decoupling, modularizing, outsourcing and offshoring processes and activities
3. Globally distributed network of partners for co-creation

It is said that a firm can have competitive advantage only when it betters its rivals in performing the primary activities (inbound logistics, operations, outbound logistics, marketing and sales and post-sales service) and support activities (procurement of inputs, development of technology and human resources and general firm infrastructure) for generating and delivering goods or services of a desired value or attributes at the least cost possible. This would require firms to do competitive cost and quality analysis of activities in the value chain catalogued for generating goods or services. As shown in the previous section, firms—by applying information and digital technologies—have been able to reconfigure and redesign their internal activities. They have thus derived competitive edge rooted in efficiency, quality, reliability, speedier cycle time and faster response to the customer.

Today, firms have geographically distributed architecture of the value chain. As companies chase low factor costs, unimpeded access to resources and markets to generate economies of scale and profitability, such a value architecture could very well be geographically and, at times, even globally distributed. However, the revolutions in ICTs have also ensured that this architecture remains well integrated. The advantages accruing from such architecture have led to the decoupling of backend and front-end, outsourcing and off-shoring of the processes that are now broken down into the constituent elements and worked upon by cross-functional teams across several companies and coordinated through well-defined protocols. Fragmentation in the production and delivery process, global value chains and partner ecosystem is the new normal.

All these developments have turned modern-day firms into a network of companies collaborating for co-creation. IT majors such as Infosys, Wipro, TCS have perfected this model of service delivery. Apple has reaped benefits in manufacturing its marquee product, the iPhone. Automobile majors such as BMW, Ford, Honda, Hyundai, Suzuki, Volkswagen and

Fiat have distributed the entire procurement, assembly, manu-facturing, sales, after-sales and customer services across the globe. This has enabled them to reap cost advantages arising out of factor endowments, learning curve and economies of scale. Factors such as flexibility, speed to market and sourc-ing of competitive talent from a global pool have provided a more complex, sophisticated and unmatched layer of com-petitive edge.

Agility: Dynamic Capabilities for Continuous Innovation

In the VUCA (volatility, uncertainty, complexity and ambiguity) world, rapid changes in competition, demand, technology and regulation have made it imperative for organizations to respond and adapt quickly. In order to ensure adaptation to the changing business realities, firms should possess:

1. Ordinary capabilities for optimization and improvement-oriented efforts and innovations
2. Dynamic capabilities for exploration of opportunities and market-creating innovations
3. Dynamic capabilities to sense and seize opportunities and to reconfigure internally for better execution and externally for better alignment with the environment

It was Jack Welch, the legendary CEO of General Electric, who stressed the importance of 'speed, agility and simplicity' [40]. Agility gained prominence in the software engineering com-munity as a more responsive and collaborative approach in the 1990s, replacing the traditional waterfall methodology. Today, agility has become a vast global movement that is trans-forming nearly every other function in the world of work. Agility has been defined as the ability to anticipate, adapt and react decisively to events in the environment that have brought about a paradigm shift in the way that organizations balance stability and dynamism. It is identified as the persistent, systematic variations in an organization's outputs, structures or processes, to plan and execute a deliberate strategy to gain competitive advantage [41]. It has given organizations the capacity to flexibly respond to rapid changes in the environment by quickly, efficiently and effectively adjusting product and service offering.

Firms compete on the basis of two kinds of organizational level capabilities—ordinary capabilities as well as dynamic capabilities. Ordinary capabilities [42] enable organizations to exploit the potential of the current product in the current market.[xviii] The objective of ordinary capabilities is resource optimization and cost minimization and is behind efforts such as benchmarking, planning, enterprise-wide optimization, routinization and standardization. However, ordinary capabilities are ubiquitous and vulnerable to be imitated by competition, and above all, they can be sourced at a competitive price. Simply put, ordinary capabilities are useful for process innovation.

It is not surprising, therefore, that ordinary capabilities will rarely suffice to support long-term competitive advantage. This is particularly true in the VUCA [43] world where efforts towards process innovation can actually detract from preparing for the future. For example, Henry Ford perfected the manufacturing efficiency of Model T but eventually lost competitive advantage because he rendered a 'wrong' car in the context of changed customer preferences. Similarly, at one time, Nokia excelled at making feature phones that employed a rudimentary operating system. The introduction of Apple iPhone post-2007 demonstrated the latent demand for a converged phone–computer experience which was seized by both Apple and Samsung to topple Nokia from its pre-eminent position as a market leader. Indeed, Nobel Laureate Herbert Kroemer remind us that 'transistors, lasers and fibre optics did not come out of six sigma or ISO 9000 certification quality control programmes', indicating the importance of dynamic capabilities over ordinary capabilities.

Dynamic capabilities thus are of great strategic value to organizations. They immensely help organizations to simultaneously exploit today's competitive advantage while at the same time, exploring innovations that will be the foundation for tomorrow's competitive advantage. For example, under Indra Nooyi, Pepsi chose to focus and strengthen its dynamic capabilities. As she illustrated in an interview, 'I had a choice... I could have gone pedal to the metal, stripped out costs, delivered strong profits for a few years and then said adios. But that wouldn't have yielded long term success. So I articulated a strategy to the board focusing on the portfolio we needed to build, the muscles we needed to strengthen, the capabilities to develop...we started to implement our strategy...and we have achieved great shareholder value while strengthening the company for the long term' [44]. Jeff Bezos at Amazon also demonstrated his understanding of the difference between ordinary capabilities and dynamic capabilities when he noted that 'there are decisions that can be made by analysis...unfortunately there are a whole lot of other decisions that you can't ultimately boil down to math problem' [42].

Dynamic capabilities are the firm's ability to integrate, build and reconfigure internal and external competences to address rapidly changing environment such as the one characterized by hyper-competition, volatility and deep uncertainty [42]. Such a firm does not focus on resources as the source of competitive advantage. On the one hand, it emphasizes those processes that allow it to complement its first-order capability to ensure technical fitness (efficiency and effectiveness). On the other hand, it also keeps the focus on the second-order capability (creating, integrating and reconfiguring its resources and capabilities) to ensure evolutionary [45] and entrepreneurial fitness [31]. Dynamic capabilities enable an organization to be agile, timely and flexible to adapt.

Organizations with mature dynamic capabilities can proactively shape their environment through innovation and collaboration. Dynamic capabilities—related to the identification of new products and services and opening of a new market—ensure that the organization does not get stifled by its fixation with ordinary capabilities, benchmarking, best practices and incrementalism. These are thus directed towards ensuring that the company does not lose its competitive edge in the wake of changing technologies and market. In sum, dynamic capabilities define the firm's capacity to innovate, adapt to change and create change that is favourable to customers and unfavourable to competitors. Viewed in this way, dynamic capabilities are the enablers of sustainable competitive advantage.

There are three primary kinds of dynamic capabilities:

1. Identification, development, co-development and assessment of opportunities and threats
2. The mobilization of resources to address needs and opportunities and capture value
3. Execution of new strategy through organizational transformation

The capability to identify and evaluate opportunities and threats is critical in the context of sudden shifts in (i) the behaviour of the customers, competitors and suppliers; (ii) government rules and regulations and (iii) advances in scientific and technological development. It enables a company to sense the unknown future by using strong peripheral vision, building and testing hypothesis and learning from the same. This requires a radar-like mindset, continuous scanning of the business horizon, sense-making and reframing conventional thinking and guarding against the normalization of risk, denial or sheer myopia. This perspective is best illuminated by the famous words of Albert Einstein, 'the intellect has little to do on the road of discovery. There comes a leap in consciousness, call it intuition or what you will...' Scenario planning and real option analysis further aid such generative sensing and are strong internal tools to manage uncertainty and take business initiatives in response to sudden changes.

The second type of dynamic capability is the mobilization of resources to address needs and opportunities and capture value from doing so. This is about 'seizing' the opportunity and implementation of new systems and putting structures in place to get things done. This capability has been witnessed in the flexible sourcing arrangements by Apple, which involved the outsourcing of manufacturing to Taiwanese company Foxconn while preserving contractual flexibility. The stumbles of General Electric, Westinghouse and Sperry Rand reflect the loss of initial dynamic capabilities.

The process of seizing can also extend over many years as in the case of DuPont's entry into biofuels which took decades of research followed by years of development. On the other hand, Kodak's precipitous decline, even after successfully recognizing the opportunities and threats, exemplifies how important it is to seize the opportunities in a timely manner. As the story goes, senior leaders as well as R&D scientists inside Kodak knew for some time that digital photography was an emerging threat. But the digital future unfolded more quickly than they forecasted. The first digital camera came in 1999, a decade earlier than Kodak's forecast. In fact, by 2009, 95 per cent of the cameras became digital as against Kodak's forecast of 5 per cent, thereby marginalizing Kodak's competitive advantage in chemical emulsion platform for analogue processing. Between 1988 and 2008, Kodak reduced its employee numbers by more than 80 per cent. In 2012, it filed for bankruptcy. In order to enable innovation, therefore, organizations need to change their perspective (cognitive reframing), bring in new leaders with a fresh eye and develop separate organization structures to enable innovation.

Execution of a new strategy is the third type of dynamic capability. Business opportunities created by sensing and seizing capabilities can be fully exploited only when the firm is able to implement its new strategies. Such execution indeed depends upon the capability of the firm to transform itself. Transformation is about maintaining competitiveness through enhancing, combining, protecting and reconfiguring the organizational resources. This capability is in terms of organization redesigning internally and aligning with the external business environment. It was dynamic capabilities of General Motors (GM) under the leadership of Alfred Sloan, which saw its restructuring from a functional design to multi-divisional form. This step taken for product diversification strategy of GM provided autonomy to the divisions and proved to be a winner. It was a similar kind of separation from the parent organization that was also required in Kodak. The needed organizational structure and cohesive strategy were not put in place at Kodak (to enable such a separation from the parent), thus leading to weak accountability and therefore, poor implementation. Many organizations have hived off units into separate organizations when new endeavours are different from that of the parent organization. Such hiving off has been able to generate internal flexibility and experimentation and entrepreneurial dynamism. Such a structural arrangement led to the success of General Motors' Saturn Division, IBM's PC unit and Roche's Genentech investment and 3M.

Transformation capabilities of an organization also include ability to 'pivot', that is, bring idea to the market through new and rapid product development.[xix]

Transforming is also about re-negotiating the environment and the company's ecosystem. At one end of the continuum is joint lobbying and creation of new industry standards. At the other end, it is about reshaping the business ecology by creating networks: customers through social sites, suppliers with supply chaining, open innovation and co-creation. VUCA is a world not only of deep uncertainties but also of bottomless risk. Sharing economy firms such as Uber and Airbnb save on capital and share risk with their contractor partners. Pharmaceutical firms such as Pfizer and Sanofi experiencing a scarcity of new drugs are experimenting with a new risk-sharing business model. They have allowed Nova Quest (a private start-up specializing in life sciences) to fund late-stage clinical trials of some of their drugs in exchange for a share in the potential profits. Strong relational capabilities and loosely coupled networks have enriched and enhanced process and product innovation, operational capabilities and business models. These have facilitated value capturing and thus have strengthened and sustained the competitive edge of several leading firms. Boards which are serious about building a sustainable competitive edge cannot afford to lose focus on dynamic capabilities, the necessary condition to help prepare the organizations for the future.

Ambidexterity: Organizational Design for Innovativeness

Organizations need to be designed for continuous innovation through the following:

1. Ambidexterity of the organization so that it can both exploit the current product market and explore new opportunities and thus enable both sustaining innovation and disruptive innovation
2. Complementarity of organic structure to provide dynamism and facilitate ideation and innovation and mechanistic structure to give stability and ensure implementation

3. Separation of organizational DNA for core business unit and new venture business unit to ensure strategic innovation
4. Embedding execution excellence in organizational DNA

Firms such as 3M, Intel, WL Gore, Ciba Vision, IBM, Amazon, etc., are great not because they innovated and became behemoths [46]. They are great because they continue to be innovative. This is the characteristic which is built upon their capability for continuous innovation. They are designed for innovation, and the central pivot of this design is ambidexterity.

Organizational ambidexterity is the ability of the firm to simultaneously pursue (a) exploitation of existing competencies (through better, efficient, optimized alignment of technologies, activities and administrative arrangement relating to current operations, product and market) and (b) exploration of new opportunities, experimenting, taking risk and innovating new products, new technologies and new markets [47–50].[xx]

Organizations that pursue exploration to the exclusion of exploitation are likely to suffer costs of experimentation without gaining much benefit; while organizations that pursue exploitation to the exclusion of exploration have a stable equilibrium and efficient operations but nowhere to go. In order to prosper, firms need to maintain a balance and 'simultaneously pursue both incremental and discontinuous innovation and change' [51].

Ambidexterity can be undertaken in two different forms: structural ambidexterity and contextual ambidexterity. Contextual ambidexterity is achieved through individual employees who divide their time between exploitation and exploration-oriented activities in their daily work. This would require organizations to create conditions such as stipulating that employees set aside a certain percentage of time for ideating or pursuing the pet projects. Structural ambidexterity involves creating separate structures for different types of activities. For example, the core business units are given responsibility for creating alignment with the existing products and markets and running the operations, and the R&D department and business development group are given the job of prospecting for new markets, developing new technologies and keeping track of emerging industry trends. Despite being complementary, both exploration and exploitation require substantially different structures, processes, strategies, capabilities and cultures to pursue and may have different impacts on firm adaptation and performance. In general, exploration is associated with organic structure involving typically cross-functional teams, information and communication density, resolution of differences through mutual adjustment and empowered decision-making based on discussion, dialogue and consensus. Exploitation is associated with mechanistic structure involving hierarchy, standardization, standard operating procedures, rigid routines and bureaucratic control.

Scholarly studies have also shown that agility in VUCA times involves balancing both to ensure stability and dynamism. McKinsey consulting [52] for one found that companies without a stable backbone (start-ups) may be too chaotic and unpredictable, while companies with a strong backbone (e.g., large hierarchical organization with standardized processes) may be too bureaucratic and risk averse. Winning companies were those which had a stable backbone comprising fixed structure as well as more dynamic elements that leveraged the stable backbone to respond and adapt to emerging opportunities and challenges [52]. The solution seems to be to design the organization in such a way that it can both focus on the present and prepare for the future.[xxi]

Designing organizations for innovations also involves separating the units organized for a new venture (the future business) and the other for the core business (existing business). It is also important that the two units have separate DNA so that new business is able to overcome the challenges that may debilitate its efforts for strategic innovation. These challenges [53] are essentially threefold: (a) the need for the organization to forget some of the key assumptions that made the current business and the business model successful, (b) the need for borrowing assets such as manufacturing capacity, supply network, distribution channels, etc., from the established business to fuel the new one and gain heft to overcome the challenge from the start-ups and (c) the need for organizational learning to test critical assumptions about the future to assess what will work and will not work. Rewiring the organizational DNA would require interventions across four main areas: staffing, structure, systems and culture.

Ideas are not enough to make a business plan culminate into profitability. In the journey from idea to execution, execution is where most of the organizations stumble. Former IBM CEO Louis V. Gerstner Jr. writes in his memoir *Who Says Elephants Can't Dance? Inside IBM's Historic Turnaround* [54] that the revival of the computer giant wasn't due to vision. 'Fixing IBM,' he wrote, 'was all about execution.' Execution excellence is embedded in the corporate DNA. The DNA of the organization is composed of (a) structure in terms of layers in the hierarchy and number of direct reports for each layer, (b) decision rights in terms of who decides what, who is involved and what is the extent of the jurisdiction of decision-makers of organizations, (c) motivators in terms of how people are incentivized and rewarded both financially and non-financially and (d) information in terms of how information and knowledge are shared, how activities are coordinated and how performances are measured and metrics used. It is how all these fit together that will determine the success or failure of the strategy of continuous innovation.

Organization Culture and People Power

It is human mind that creates, innovates and provides solutions. Such an efflorescence of human spirit in the corporate world is determined by the organizational culture. People power gets unleashed when

1. Leaders play a key role in shaping organizational culture
2. Culture is aligned to strategic change
3. Culture of entrepreneurship and organizational innovativeness is promoted.

Schein [55] defines organizational culture as a pattern of basic assumptions that the group learned as it solved its problems, and that has worked well enough to be considered valid. It is passed on to new members as the correct way to perceive, think and feel in relation to those problems.

Culture has a two-way relationship with leadership. Bass [56] demonstrated that leadership style has a significant impact on culture. Research suggests that leaders have a central role in shaping and monitoring organizational culture both by being closely intertwined and by playing a major role in nurturing appropriate culture. In other words, for any strategic change, cultural change becomes a crucial variable and an agenda for leadership.

The only thing of real importance that leaders do is to create and manage culture.' 'If you do not manage culture, it manages you, and you may not even be aware of the extent to which this is happening.
—Edgar Schein [55]

Research[xxii] has shown that companies with cultures that emphasize all the key managerial aspects (customers, stockholders and employees) outperform, by a huge margin, those firms that do not do so.

Culture has a two-way relationship with the organization design. It is clear that culture gets supported by rational tools and processes defined by the strategic architecture of the organization and through employee behaviour. Culture leads to the building of competitive advantage of an organization through its impact on work-related attitudes and behaviour. A culture supporting innovation would encourage behaviours which value creativity, risk-taking, freedom, teamwork, tolerance for mistakes, empowered enactment, equity and fairness in value and contribution. It would simultaneously reject practices and behaviours such as rigidity, control, predictability and stability, all of which militate against the innovation propensity of the company.

Organizational ambidexterity is supported by a culture which promotes behaviours that nurture innovation such as backing idea creation, empowerment and tolerance for risks, instead of rigid and inflexible responses. The combination of both an ambidextrous structure and a culture-promoting innovation helps companies to achieve a variety of positive outcomes, including robust growth and international expansion. Hence, if a culture does not have to eat strategy for breakfast, it must be aligned with the leadership, strategy, structure and system of the firm.[xxiii]

Above all, culture provides signals on how people are to be encouraged and rewarded to display those behaviours which contribute to organizational innovation and entrepreneurship. If employees resonate with organizational goals and experience an ambient work culture, they will willingly become more innovative and/or promote innovation at their levels as well as cooperate with management plans. If they are not made a part of the process, then the strategic planning will remain on paper.

Ethical Governance

Ethical governance is the key to organizational sustainability and consists of the following elements:

1. Good CG is not only about rules and compliance but also about ethics and values.
2. The philosophy of *vasudhaiva kutumbakam* (meaning, the world is one family) as the guiding principle for ethical positioning of CG.
3. Importance of ethical governance

In the early 1980s, the competitive strategy was seen as a zero-sum game, where companies were engaged in a battle to capture the maximum economic value possible [57]. As information, knowledge, capabilities and innovation came to provide a competitive advantage, the game shifted from value appropriation to value creation. The focus on value creation led to different approaches to value appropriation involving sharing among stakeholders and not benefitting shareholders alone. Organizational values are the foundation on which organizational ethics are developed—the norms, guidelines or expectations for appropriate behaviours in different situations.

Good CG goes beyond rules and regulations and involves the ethics and values which drive companies in the conduct of their business. An effective ethical practice entails synergy among vision statements, mission statements, core values, general business principles and code of conduct [58].

The phrase *vasudhaiva kutumbakam* from Maha Upanishad, rightly explains the needed position to be taken by today's organizations in the global competitive market. Embracing the world as one's family entails not only making in India for the world but conducting business through a set of ethical practices. It ensures competition in a healthy sense while maintaining ethics and integrity in the entire range of the decision-making process. In other words, *vasudhaiva kutumbakam* stresses upon thriving in a tough competitive market and incorporates an ethical dimension into company values through responsiveness, transparency and accountability. Therefore, the principle of 'ethical compliance' in every facet of decision-making translates into success in erratic global markets and earns more returns to shareholders [59].

The World Bank *Report on the Observance of Standards and Codes* [60] says that India lags in giving adequate safeguards to investors. Perhaps, the only way to advance CG in India is to give sufficient safeguards to protect the interests of minority shareholders by framing suitable laws. This can also attract greater foreign capital and investment to boost economic growth [61]. The ethical standards of a company play a key role in scripting the above.

Ethical governance does not directly lead to the sustainable competitive edge, but the lack of it leads to a steep fall in a company's reputation, goodwill and ability to thrive in adversity. When the company is marred by fraud and misdemeanours, it leads to even bankruptcy and death of the organization. Companies with a clear commitment to ethical conduct consistently outperform other companies by retaining the best talent, sustaining and building trustworthiness and loyalty and customer satisfaction.

Part 3. Levers of Sustainable Competitive Edge: Role of Boards

In an increasingly competitive environment, board members have to be more involved in setting strategy and promoting innovation. However, to do this successfully, a reasonable understanding of the business, the drivers of business and modes of achieving sustainable competitive edge is essential. They need to have a good grasp of key aspects of the above-cited pillars so that they can build, strengthen and leverage each pillar to architect sustainable competitive edge for the organization they lead. Given below is a set of such key factors to which boards need to pay attention and, in turn, provide guidance to management as well as monitor the same in the board meetings. Such an approach will immensely help boards and management to develop a laser-like focus on key issues of relevance to managing the present, as well as prepare the organization for the future.

Pillars of Sustainable Competitive Edge: A Snapshot

Strategic Focus

- Vision and goals for continued growth, high performance and excellence in the interests of the various stakeholders, common good and shared prosperity
- Wealth creation as the purpose of business
- Continuous innovation as the centrepiece of the organization's strategy

Customer Centricity

- Customer as the basis of value creation
- Understanding changing needs and wants of customers
- Involving customers in co-creation
- Innovation to provide and deliver value better than the rivals

Competitive Leadership through Cost and Quality

- Geographically dispersed and digitally integrated supply chain
- The globalized architecture of value chain
- The global market for driving scale economies and revenue generation
- The global mindset in terms of vision, goals, resources, capabilities, market and competition
- The transition from operational excellence to operational innovation

Time to Market

- Quick pivot from idea to product to market
- Big data, data analytics and digital technology for sensing needs and opportunities
- Digital Integration of the distributed value chain and dispersed enterprise
- Digital and automated supply chain to ensure fast, flexible and reliable delivery
- Models for collaborative innovation

Agility

- Ordinary capabilities for improvement-oriented innovation
- Dynamic capabilities for disruptive innovation
- Capabilities to sense and seize opportunities
- Capabilities to reconfigure and transform for execution

Organizational DNA

- Ambidexterity for simultaneous exploitation and exploration
- Complementarity of organic structure and mechanistic structure
- Separation of organizational DNA for core business unit and future business unit
- Encouragement of entrepreneurial mindset, learning orientation and knowledge management
- Relational network to ensure collaboration, co-creation and co-opetition

Culture and People Power

- Shared vision for mobilizing organizational energies
- Shared mindset for continuous innovation

- Building orientation for entrepreneurship and innovativeness
- Acquiring and retaining the 'right' talent

Ethical Governance

- Develop the inner conscience of business
- Uphold the ethical mode of functioning
- Build and display social responsiveness for organizational reputation and goodwill
- Enable business to prosper through ethical practices and trust

In Conclusion: Architecting a Sustainable Competitive Edge

This chapter maps the three core stages of cognition to be traversed by the boards and top management of companies before they take steps to architect sustainable competitive edge in the organizations they head: understanding the business context and the threats and challenges inherent in the disruptions, identifying the enablers of sustainable competitive edge and detailing the levers of sustainable competitive edge. The chapter has been divided into three parts—Part 1 presents the business context, Part 2 delineates the enablers of sustainable competitive edge and Part 3 discusses levers of sustainable competitive edge. The chapter identifies some of the key strategic issues that must be discussed by every forward-thinking board.

In today's erratic and competitive business world, innovation and technology are the keys for building sustainable competitive edge of organizations. The firm's innovative capability and strategic decision-making play a vital role in this. To move into this orbit, organizations need to develop an entrepreneurial mindset and strategic leadership at the top. Above all, strategic leadership exercised both by the top management of the company and its board can architect and create a road map for a firm's competitive advantage as well as for its sustainability and growth. This is also vital for the shared prosperity, social good, development and competitiveness of the country as a whole.

Notes

i. In the June 2020 forecast, Moody's sliced 2020 economic growth forecast for India to (–)3.1 per cent, from its earlier projection of (+)0.2 per cent in the April update (Noronha, 2020). Moody's has estimated Indian economy to grow 6.9 per cent in 2021, stating that the Indian economic recovery is underway but closely intertwined with the pandemic. The growth of Indian economy was slowed in 11 years at 4.2 per cent in 2019–2020.

ii. GII 2020 report stated that India's level of development in the last 10 years has made it surpass the consistent innovative performance. India stands at 48th position on GII 2020, among 131 economies, breaking into top 50 for the first time and 3rd among the lower-income group.

iii. Hawawini, Subramanian and Verdin (2016) in their study of the sample comprising 500 British companies, 200 German companies and 150 companies from BENELUX have shown that firm effects as compared to industry and country factors explain performance variation to the tune of 44.17 per cent of total market value per dollar of capital employed (TMV/CE), 35.5 per cent of economic profit per dollar of capital employed (EP/CE) and 35.2 per cent of return on assets (ROA).

iv. The Ministry of Company Affairs reported that more than 6.83 lakh companies in India just withered away by the end of 2019 due to the above-cited reasons. Foster and Kaplan (2001) investigated the life expectancy of firms in the Standard and Poor (S&P) 500 and showed that while in 1935, the average expectancy was 90 years; by 1975, it dropped to 30 years, and in 2005 life expectancy of firms was estimated to be only 15 years.

v. A recent study by McKinsey Global Institute (2018) of 5,750 (out of a preliminary dataset of around 600,000 corporations further pruned into 33,000 global parent companies) has shown that a few notable companies such as Altria, Coca-Cola, Intel, Johnson & Johnson, Merck, Microsoft, Nestlé, Novartis, Samsung, Toyota and Walmart have consistently featured among the top 1 per cent of the firms for the last 30 years.

vi. Cefis and Marsili (2004) investigated the impact of innovation on firm survival and found that in a firm having an 'innovation premium', there is 11 per cent and 25 per cent higher likelihood of survival because of product-market innovation and process innovation respectively.

vii. Innovation has a direct relationship with organizational performance as illustrated by the Arthur de Little study (2013) of over 650 organizations. The study found that the top quartile innovation performers obtained a 13 per cent higher profit than the average performers. Additionally, the top performers had a 30 per cent shorter 'time to break even' for new services and products

viii. Christensen (1997) calls this phenomenon the 'innovator's dilemma', that is, following a sustaining innovation path can make sense in the short run but can condemn the firm to failure in the long run. On the other hand, dedicating valuable resources to a niche and unproven opportunity might also lead to the failure of the firm. Christensen et al. (2002: 1) explained this dilemma thus: 'Most managers understand that significant, new, sustainable growth comes from creating new markets and ways of competing. But few of them make such investments. Why? Because when times are good and core businesses are growing robustly, starting new generations of growth ventures seems unnecessary; when times are bad and mature businesses are under attack, investments to create new growth businesses can't send enough profit to the bottom line quickly enough to satisfy investor pressure for a fast turnaround.'

ix. Clayton Christensen, author of the book *Competing Against Luck* (p. 171), quoting Ted Levitt wrote, 'People don't want to buy a quarter inch drill; they want a quarter drill hole.' A company may sell the best drill money can buy, but how good is it to a customer if a cheaper drill can do the job or perhaps a safer drill or perhaps a drill which does not look like a drill.

x. Companies like Lenovo exchange sensor and Internet of Things (IoT) based usage data with their customers to develop insights for inventory management. Google deploys technology to track the extent to which people who click an ad actually go offline to that particular store to complete the transaction.

xi. With the use of omnichannel marketing, Net-a-Porter company achieved a 16.9 per cent year-over-year growth to create revenues in excess of $3 billion in 2017. Firms are now building brands by combining automated and personalized emails, content marketing, native advertising, short videos, user-generated content, augmented reality and virtual reality. This has made the medium and messages cheaper, authentic, engaging and persuasive due to its fear-of-missing-out effect. The augmented reality app of IKEA drew 8.5 million downloads and many potential buyers. Similar was the benefits which Volvo derived by using Google Cardboard.

xii. AMP technology has enabled faster loading time of websites, lower bounce rate, better website experience and progressive web apps. It has eliminated app development costs by the companies and the need for app download by the users. Users can now create shortcuts on the smartphone and helped by push notification technology easily and speedily access the website. This has helped companies like Flipkart to get more access and purchase from areas with poor internet service

xiii. The whole world of the supply chain with its programme on 'plan, make, source, deliver' has evolved significantly. Firms are using AI, ML and IoT to quickly sense, source and integrate the whole mass of information flowing from the suppliers to the customers. Use of robotics and automation has led to an increase in efficiency and reduction in warehousing costs. Blockchains (digital records of transactions stored across a decentralized network of computers) are also being used for cost-savings (paperless transactions), data verification, asset tracking, 'smart contracts', accountability and compliance.

xiv. Digital advances have enabled a more robustly networked supply chain and a collaboration model based on transparent and frictionless proprietary data sharing and co-creation. Data 'clean rooms' and the digital marketplace are the orders of the day today.

xv. Zara has reduced design-to-retail cycle to just 15 days, ensuring brisk sale and at full price.

xvi. Intel, the multinational manufacturer, uses cognitive computing and Saffron, their proprietary AI tool, to manage its sourcing, supplier selection and monitoring. Pfizer is using highly innovative End-to-End In-Transit Visibility project app called Track-It, which users can launch on a smartphone, permitting them to view whatever data they require at any given time, wherever they are. BuySeasons, an online seller of costumes and party supplies, implemented a multimodal order fulfilment solution from FastFetch to integrate voice technology, barcode scanning and light-directed picking to triple the speed with which orders are filled and sent on their way.

xvii. Qualcomm, Nokia, Ericsson, Motorola, IBM and others built together a number of technology platforms under European Telecommunications Standards Institute/Third Generation Partnership Project that enhanced and combined core proprietary technologies and brought thousands of engineers across thousands of firms in the mobile phone industry to create and deliver solutions that were compatible across firms.

xviii. Ordinary capabilities relate to a firms' human resources, tangible and intangible assets, operations, processes and administrative system for efficient and effective production and sale. It is expressed in efficient manufacturing, effective marketing, partnership management and capable operational leadership.

xix. More and more organizations are incubating the build-measure-learn methodology. This has involved building a minimum viable product (MVP) launching it, learning quickly, adjusting accordingly and improving. Entrepreneurs are adapting their plans incrementally rather than wait for the final and perfect product. The lean start-up methodology also favours experimentation, failing fast, regrouping, learning and developing products iteratively and incrementally rather than planning elaborately, wasting time and resources.

xx. There is adequate support for the success of an ambidextrous organizational structure to deliver breakthrough innovations. In a study by O'Reilly, Tushman, Smith, Wood and Westermen (2004), out of 35 breakthrough innovations undertaken by 15 business units in 9 industries, the authors found that 7 were taken by companies with functional structure design, 9 by the cross-functional team but outside the managerial hierarchy, 4 by unsupported teams which were independent units outside the management and organizational hierarchy and 15 were pursued within ambidextrous structures. Ninety per cent of the breakthrough innovations succeeded in ambidextrous structure. Two out of seven succeeded in functional design structure, and none in cross-functional and unsupported teams succeeded. In fact, when the firm shifted from the earlier functional, cross-functional design, etc., to ambidextrous design, the performance improved substantially in seven out of eight cases.

xxi. The reason why ambidextrous structure leads to innovation and high performance is that it enables cross-fertilization among units while preventing cross-contamination. Despite being complementary, both exploration and exploitation require substantially different structures, processes, strategies, capabilities and cultures to pursue and may have different impacts on firm adaptation and performance. In general, exploration is associated with the organic structure and therefore with cross-functional project teams, loosely coupled systems and autonomy. Exploitation is associated with alignment and adaptation-related activities through a mechanistic structure involving hierarchy, tightly coupled systems, standardization control and bureaucracy. The 'exploit' business focuses on cost and profit, values quality, efficiency and existing customers and spurs efficiency improvement and incremental innovation.

The 'explore' business function focuses on growth through innovation, values risk-taking, speed and experimentation, tolerates failures and promotes entrepreneurship and thus spurs new product and breakthrough innovation. Sustainable competitive edge has been found to be possible only when a firm is a network of empowered teams within a people-centred culture that operates in rapid learning and fast decision cycles enabled by technology and guided by a powerful common purpose to co-create value for all stakeholders.

xxii. Kotter and Heskett (1992) studied the relationship between culture and economic success among 207 organizations from 1977–1988 and found that culture does have a bottom-line impact. Over the 11-year period, organizations that vigorously monitored and managed their cultures achieved remarkable success (revenue increased by 682%, workforce expansion by 282%, elevated stock prices by 901% and net income by 756%).

xxiii. Culture in organizations is defined as the deeply held and, at times, subconscious values and beliefs shared by employees at all levels, and it is manifested in the traits and behaviour of the organization. Culture has four attributes: (a) it is shared as it resides in shared behaviours, values and assumptions and is most commonly experienced through norms and expectations of the group, (b) it is pervasive as it is manifested in group behaviour, physical arrangement, rituals, stories and legends as well as in mindset, motivation, mental models and action logic, (c) it is enduring as it develops through critical events and learning in the collective life and becomes self-reinforcing social system due to its ability to attract and retain people who fit in and by shunning all external influence and resisting change and (d) it is implicit and works like a silent language shaping human capacity and determining how the collectivity would sense and respond to the environment.

References

1. Senge, Peter M. (1990). *The Fifth Discipline*. New York, NY: Doubleday/Currency.

2. LiveMint. (2019, 15 August). PM Modi's Independence Day Speech Highlights: India Can Be a $5 Trillion Economy in 5 Years. https://www.livemint.com/news/india/73rd-independence-day-2019-live-updates-pm-narendra-modi-delivers-speech-from-red-fort-1565763102454.html

3. World Economic Forum. (2019). *The Global Competitiveness Report.* http://www3.weforum.org/docs/WEF_TheGlobal CompetitivenessReport2019.pdf

4. Sharma, S. (2019, 25 July). India's R&D Spend Far Less than China, Korea, as Private Companies, States Abstain. *Financial Express.* https://www.financialexpress.com/economy/indias-rd-spend-far-less-than-china-korea-as-private-companies-states-abstain/1656309/

5. World Integrated Trade Solution. (2018). India Trade. https://wits.worldbank.org/countrysnapshot/en/IND

6. CAG Report. (2019). Expenditure on Research and Development by CPSEs. https://cag.gov.in/sites/default/files/audit_report_files/Chapter_7_Expenditure_on_Research_and_Development_by_CPSE_of_Report_No_18_of_2019_General_Purpose_Financial_Reports_of_Central_Public_Sector_Enterpri.pdf

7. Porter, M. E. (1990). *The Competitive Advantage of Nations.* London: MacMillan.

8. Krugman, P. R., and Obstfeld, M. (1997). *International Economics: Theory and Policy*, 4th ed. Boston, MA: Addison-Wesley.

9. Smit, A. J. (2010). The Competitive Advantage of Nations: Is Porter's Diamond Framework a New Theory That Explains the International Competitiveness of Countries? *Southern Africa Business Review*, Vol. 14, No. 1, pp. 105–130.

10. Hawawini, G., Subramanian, V., and Verdin, P. (2003). Is Performance Driven by Industry-or Firm-Specific Factors? A New Look at the Evidence. *Strategic Management Journal*, Vol. 24, No. 1, pp. 1–16.

11. Conceição, P., Hamill, D., and Pinheiro, P. (2002). Innovative Science and Technology Commercialization Strategies at 3M: A Case Study. *Journal of Engineering and Technology Management*, Vol. 19, No. 1, pp. 25–38.

12. Hill, C., and Rothaermel, F. (2003). The Performance of Incumbent Firms in the Face of Radical Technological Innovation. *Academy of Management Review*, Vol. 28, No. 2, pp. 257–274. https://doi.org/10.5465/amr.2003.9416161

13. O'Reilly, C., and Tushman, M. (2008). Ambidexterity as a Dynamic Capability: Resolving the Innovator's Dilemma. *Research in Organizational Behavior*, Vol. 28, pp. 185–206. https://doi.org/10.1016/j.riob.2008.06.002

14. Yu, D., and Hang, C. C. (2008). A Reflective Review of Disruptive Innovation Theory. *International Journal of Management Reviews*, Vol. 12, No. 4, pp. 402–414. https://doi.org/10.1111/j.1468-2370.2009.00272.x

15. McKinsey Global Institute. (2018). Superstars the Dynamics of Firms, Sectors, and Cities Leading the Global Economy. https://www.mckinsey.com/~/media/mckinsey/featured%20insights/innovation/superstars%20the%20dynamics%20of%20firms%20sectors%20and%20cities%20leading%20the%20global%20economy/mgi_superstars_discussion%20paper_oct%202018-v2.pdf

16. Jaruzelski, B., Staack, V., and Goehle, B. (2014). The Global Innovation 1000: Proven Paths to Innovation Success. *Tech & Innovation*, Winter, No. 77.

17. Dobni, C. B. (2011). The Relationship between Innovation Orientation and Organizational Performance. *International Journal of Innovation and Learning*, Vol. 10, No. 3, pp. 226–240.

18. Christensen, C. M. (1997). *The Innovator's Dilemma: When New Technologies Cause Great Firms to Fail.* Boston, MA: Harvard Business School Press.

19. Porter, M. E. (1981). The Contributions of Industrial Organization to Strategic Management. *The Academy of Management Review*, Vol. 6, No. 4, pp. 609–620.

20. Dobni, C. B. (2008). Measuring Innovation Culture in Organizations: The Development and Validation of a Generalized Innovation Culture Construct Using Exploratory Factor Analysis. *European Journal of Innovation Management*, Vol. 11, No. 4, 539–559.

21. Daft, R. (1978). A Dual-core Model of Organizational Innovation. *The Academy of Management Journal*, Vol. 21, No. 2, pp. 193–210.

22. Damanpour, F., and Evan, W. M. (1984). Organizational Innovation and Performance: The Problem of 'Organizational Lag'. *Administrative Science Quarterly*, Vol. 29, No. 3, pp. 392–409.

23. Wischnevsky, J. D., Damanpour, F., and Méndez, F. A. (2011). Influence of Environmental Factors and Prior Changes on the Organizational Adoption of Changes in Products and in Technological and Administrative Processes. *British Journal of Management*, Vol. 22, No. 1, pp. 132–149.

24. Schilling, M. A. (2005). *Strategic Management of Technological Innovation*. Boston, MA: McGraw Hill.

25. Christensen, C. M., and Raynor, M. (2003). *The Innovator's Solution: Creating and Sustaining Successful Growth*. Boston, MA: Harvard Business School Press.

26. Christensen, C. M., Anthony, S. D., and Roth, E. A. (2004). Seeing What's Next: Using the Theories of Innovation to Predict Industry Change. Boston, MA: Harvard Business Press.

27. Utterback, J., and Acee, H. J. (2005). Disruptive Technologies: An Expanded View. *International Journal of Innovation Management*, Vol. 9, pp. 1–17.

28. Govindarajan, V., and Kopalle, P. K. (2006). The Usefulness of Measuring Disruptiveness of Innovations Ex Post in Making Ex Ante Predictions. *Journal of Product Innovation Management*, Vol. 23, pp. 12–18.

29. Peters, T. J., and Waterman, R. H., Jr. (2006). *In Search of Excellence: Lessons from America's Best-Run Companies*. Reprint. New York, NY: Harper Business.

30. O'Reilly, C. A., and Tushman, M. (2004). The Ambidextrous Organization. *Harvard Business Review*, April, pp.74–83.

31. Teece, D. J. (2007). Explicating Dynamic Capabilities: The Nature and Micro Foundations of (Sustainable) Enterprise Performance. *Strategic Management Journal*, Vol. 28, No. 13, pp. 1319–1350. https://doi.org/10.1002/smj.640

32. Ahuja, G., and Lampert, C. M. (2001). Entrepreneurship in the Large Corporation: A Longitudinal Study of How Established Firms Create Breakthrough Discoveries. *Administrative Science Quarterly*, Vol. 38, pp. 51–73.

33. Assink, M. (2006). Inhibitors of Disruptive Innovation Capability: A Conceptual Model. *European Journal of Innovation Management*, Vol. 9, No. 2, pp. 215–233.

34. Slater, S. F., and Mohr, J. J. (2006). Successful Development and Commercialization of Technological Innovation: Insights Based on Strategy Type. *Journal of Product Innovation Management*, Vol. 23, No. 1, pp. 26–33.

35. Felix Oberholzer-Gee. (2016). *Sustaining Competitive Advantage*. Boston, MA: Harvard Business School Publishing.

36. Brush, T., Dangol, R., and O'brien, J. (2012). Customer Capabilities, Switching Costs, and Bank Performance. *Strategic Management Journal*, Vol. 33, No. 13, pp. 1499–1515. https://doi.org/10.1002/smj.1990

37. Shi, M., Chiang, J., and Rhee, B. (2006). Price Competition with Reduced Consumer Switching Costs: The Case of 'Wireless Number Portability' in the Cellular Phone Industry. *Management Science*, Vol. 52, No. 1, pp. 27–38. http://www.jstor.org/stable/20110481

38. Stango, V. (2002). Pricing with Consumer Switching Costs: Evidence from the Credit Card Market. *The Journal of Industrial Economics*, Vol. 50, No. 4, pp. 475–492. http://www.jstor.org/stable/3569784

39. Edelmen, D. C., and Singer, M. (2015). Competing on Customer Journeys. *Harvard Business Review*. https://hbr.org/2015/11/competing-on-customer-journeys

40. Tichy, N., and Charan, R. (1989). Speed, Simplicity, Self-confidence: An Interview with Jack Welch. *Harvard Business Review*. https://hbr.org/1989/09/speed-simplicity-self-confidence-an-interview-with-jack-welch

41. Singh, J., Sharma, G., Hill, J., and Schnackenberg, A. (2013). Organizational Agility: What It Is, What It Is Not, and Why It Matters. *Academy of Management Proceedings*, No. 1, pp. 11813–11813. https://doi.org/10.5465/ambpp.2013.11813 abstract

42. Teece, D., Peteraf, M., and Leih, S. (2016). Dynamic Capabilities and Organizational Agility: Risk, Uncertainty, and Strategy in the Innovation Economy. *California Management Review*, Vol. 58, No. 4, pp. 13–35. http://dx.doi.org/10.1525/cmr.2016.58.4.13

43. Schoemaker, P. J. H., Heaton, S., and Teece, D. (2018). Innovation, Dynamic Capabilities, and Leadership. UC Berkeley Previously Published Works. *California Management Review*, Vol. 61, No. 1. https://doi.org/10.1177/0008125618790246

44. Nooyi, I., and Ignatius, A. (2015, September 01). How Indra Nooyi Turned Design Thinking into Strategy: An Interview with PepsiCo's CEO. *Harvard Business Review*. https://store.hbr.org/product/how-indra-nooyi-turned-design-thinking-into-strategy-an-interview-with-pepsico-s-ceo/R1509F

45. Helfat, C., and Peteraf, M. (2009). Understanding Dynamic Capabilities: Progress along a Developmental Path. *Strategic Organization*, Vol. 7, No. 1, pp. 91–102. https://doi.org/10.1177/1476127008100133

46. Jaruzelski, B., and Dehoff, K. (2007). The Customer Connection: The Global Innovation 1000. *Tech & Innovation*, Winter, No. 49. https://www.strategy-business.com/article/07407?gko=3ad6f

47. March, J. G. (1991). Exploration and Exploitation in Organizational Learning. *Organization Science*, Vol. 2, No. 1, pp. 71–87. http://wwwmanagement.wharton.upenn.edu/pennings/documents/March_1991_exploration_exploitation.pdf

48. Benner, M. J., and Tushman, M. L. (2003). Exploitation, Exploration and Process Management: The Productivity Dilemma Revisited. *Academy of Management Review*, Vol. 28, pp. 238–256.

49. Birkinshaw, J., and Gibson, C. (2004). Building Ambidexterity into an Organization. *MIT Sloan Management Review*, Vol. 45, No. 4, pp. 94.

50. Raisch, S., and Birkinshaw, J. (2008). Organizational Ambidexterity: Antecedents, Outcomes, and Moderators. *Journal of Management*, Vol. 34, No. 3, pp. 375–409.

51. O'Reilly III, C., and Tushman, M. (1996). Ambidextrous Organizations: Managing Evolutionary and Revolutionary

Change. *California Management Review*, Vol. 38, No. 4, pp. 8–29. https://doi.org/10.2307%2F41165852

52. Aghina, W., de Smet, A., and Weerda, K. (2015). Agility: It Rhymes with Stability. *McKinsey Quarterly*. https://meincoach. at/pdfs/agility_rhymes_with_stability_201512_McK.pdf

53. Govindarajan, V., and Trimble, C. (2011). The CEO's Role in Business Model Reinvention. *Harvard Business Review*, Vol. 89, pp. 108–114, 180.

54. Gerstner, L. V., Jr. (2002). *Who Says Elephants Can't Dance? Inside IBM's Historic Turnaround*. New York, NY: Harper Business.

55. Schein, E. H. (1982). *Organizational Culture and Leadership*. San Francisco, CA: Jossey-Bass.

56. Bass, B. M. (1985). *Leadership and Performance beyond Expectations*. New York, NY: Free Press.

57. Bartlett, C., and Ghoshal, S. (2002). Building Competitive Advantage through People. *MIT Sloan Management Review*, Vol. 43, No. 2, pp. 34–41.

58. Nainawat, R., and Meena, R. (2013). Corporate Governance and Business Ethics. *Global Journal of Management and Business Studies*, Vol. 3, No. 10, pp. 1085–1090.

59. Vallabh, G., and Dadhich, G. (2016). Corporate Governance and Ethical Compliance—Deriving Values from Indian Mythology. *Theoretical Economics Letters*, Vol. 6, pp. 1128–1144. http://dx.doi.org/10.4236/tel.2016.65108

60. World Bank. (2004). *Report on the Observance of Standards and Codes (ROSC), Corporate Governance Country Assessment*. Washington, DC: World Bank.

61. Srivastav, N., and Singh, J. P. (2012). Corporate Governance in India: Case for Safeguarding Minority Shareholders Rights. *International Journal of Management and Business Studies*, Vol. 2, pp. 7–11.

Further Readings

Amed, I., Balchandani, A., Beltrami, M., Berg, A., Shedrich, S., and Rölkens, F. (2019, February 19). Fashion and Demand. McKinsey & Company. https://www.mckinsey.com/industries/retail/our-insights/fashion-on-demand

Blank, S. (2013, 5 May). Why the Lean Start Up Changes Everything. *Harvard Business Review*, Vol. 91, pp. 63–92.

Bogers, M., Chesbrough, H., Heaton, S., and Teece, D. (2019). Strategic Management of Open Innovation: A Dynamic Capabilities Perspective. *California Management Review*, Vol. 62, pp. 77–94. https://doi.org/10.1177%2F000812561 9885150

Cefis, E., and Marsili, O. (2004). A Matter of Life and Death: Innovation and Firm Survival. *Industrial and Corporate Change*, Vol. 14, No. 6, pp. 1167–1192.

Christensen, C. M., Hall, T., Dillon, K., and Duncan, D. S. (2016). *Competing against Luck: The Story of Innovation and Customer Choice*. New York, NY: HarperCollins

Christensen, C. M., et al. (2002). Foundations for Growth How to Identify and Build Disruptive New Businesses. *MIT Sloan Management Review*, Vol. 43, No. 3, p. 22.

Foster, R., and Kaplan, S. (2001). *Creative Destruction: Why Companies That Are Built to Last Underperform the Market— And How to Successfully Transform Them*. New York, NY: Currency.

Google. (n.d.). New Progressive Web Helps Flipkart Boost Conversion 70%. https://developers.google.com/web/showcase/2016/pdfs/flipkart.pdf

Kotter, J. P., and Heskett, J. L. (1992). *Corporate Culture and Performance*. New York, NY: Macmillan.

Muhammad, F. (2020, 9 April). What Is AMP? The Complete Guide to Accelerated Mobile Pages. https://instapage.com/blog/amp

Noronha, G. (2020, 22 June). India's GDP to Contract 3.1% in 2020: Moody's. *The Economic Times*. https://economictimes.indiatimes.com/news/economy/indicators/indias-gdp-to-contract-3-1-in2020moodys/articleshow/76515744.cms?utm_source=contentofinterest&utm_medium=text&utm_campaign=cppst

Paap, J., and Katz, R. (2004). Anticipating Disruptive Innovation. *Research-Technology Management*, Vol. 47, No. 5, pp. 13–22.

Press Trust of India. (2020, 25 August). India to Post Strong GDP Growth Pick Up in Second Half of 2020: Moody's. *Business*

Standard. https://www.business-standard.com/article/economy-policy/india-to-post-strong-gdp-growth-pick-up-in-second-half-of-2020-moody-s-120082501828_1.html

Ransbotham, S., and Kiron, D. (2018, 30 January). Using Analytics to Improve Customer Engagement. *MIT Solan Management Review*. https://sloanreview.mit.edu/projects/using-analytics-to-improve-customer-engagement/

Schoemaker, P., Heaton, S., and Teece, D. (2018). Innovation, Dynamic Capabilities, and Leadership. *California Management Review*, Vol. 61, No. 1, pp. 15–42. https://doi.org/10.1177/0008125618790246

Teece, D. J. (2016). The Foundations of Enterprise Performance: Dynamic and Ordinary Capabilities in an (Economic) Theory of Firms. *The Academy of Management Perspectives*, Vol. 28, No. 4, pp. 328–352. http://dx.doi.org/10.5465/amp.2013.0116

Thuriaux-Alemán, B., Eager, R., and Johansson, A. (2013). Getting a Better Return on Your Innovation Investment, Results of the 8th Arthur D. Little Global Innovation Excellence Study. Technology and Innovation Management. Arthur D Little. https://www.adlittle.com/innovex/assets/file/TIM_2013_Innovex_Report.pdf

Tushman, M., Smith, W., Wood, R., Westerman, G. and O'Reilly, C. (2002). Innovation Streams and Ambidextrous Organizational Designs: On Building Dynamic Capabilities. Harvard Business School Working Paper, No. 03–106.

WIPO World. (2020). Global Innovation Index 2020. https://www.wipo.int/edocs/pubdocs/en/wipo_pub_gii_2020.pdf

3

CONTOURS OF BOARDROOM FUNCTIONING AND SUSTAINABLE COMPETITIVE ADVANTAGE

Governance and leadership are the yin and the yang of successful organizations. If you have leadership without governance you risk tyranny, fraud and personal fiefdoms. If you have governance without leadership you risk atrophy, bureaucracy and indifference.

—Mark Goyder [1]

As mentioned in Chapter 1, the Fortune 500 list powerfully illustrates [2] that high mortality rates of companies are a painful corporate reality. This is a bitter lesson for managements that they cannot take their existence for granted. In such a scenario, both the leadership of companies and the boards have a critical role to play in developing and ensuring sustainable competitive edge for organizations.

We examined issues of board role, board governance and board functioning in the context of the frauds and scandals taking place in the corporate sector in India and in different parts of the world. In fact, it is the occurrence of these frauds and scandals which spurred us to examine the ground realities of board-level functioning in India, in order to find out what boards contribute to enhance the sustainable competitive advantage of organizations. As discussed earlier, in the last two decades, SEBI has been periodically introducing world-class practices to regulate Indian boards. However, despite the introduction of new regulations by SEBI, financial scandals have continued to pop up on the corporate horizon suggesting that perhaps regulations are not enough to achieve the desired goals.

Board Role: Business Leadership and Governance

According to Ram Charan [3], a board's most valuable role is as a thinking partner to CEO and that together, the board and CEO should address strategic issues facing an organization. It is generally accepted that boards have to play the twin roles of both governance and performance [4]. While governance refers to compliances and oversight of management; performance includes guiding the organization through policy formulation and strategic thinking. The emerging evidence indicates that high-performing boards across all sectors concentrate on shaping strategy, resource identification and talent management [4,5,6].

Building sustainable competitive edge in the corporate sector depends a lot on the strategic mindset, perspectives and decisions of both the managements and the boards of organizations. A conceptual analysis regarding factors which can help an organization attain sustainable competitive edge has been presented in detail in Chapter 2 of this book. Factors contributing to sustainable competitive edge have been clearly identified in that chapter, so that they can inform subsequent discussions in this book. As mentioned earlier, sustainable competitive edge refers to the ability of the firm to stay ahead and outlive its rivals. This is achieved through a strategy of continuous innovation as well as balancing the needs of stakeholders.

Chapter 2 clearly brought out that in order to be sustainable and stay ahead of the competition, firms must emphasize the following levers.

1. **Strategic focus:** Including clarity regarding the vision, goals, strategic positioning and co-evolution of the organization with environmental changes and, above all, ensuring execution through intense monitoring and feedback.

2. **Continuous innovation:** Including both sustaining and disruptive innovation.

3. **Implementation strategy:** Through focus on customer centricity, speed to market and agility; introduction of digitization and structural ambidexterity. It also involves enhancing people power and promoting a culture conducive to develop entrepreneurship, exploration as well as exploitation to facilitate continuous innovation.

4. **Ethical governance:** Keeping the threefold responsibility to people, planet and profit as the basis for sustenance and value creation for the stakeholders.

Boards and top managements of companies cannot ensure sustained competitiveness and longevity of the organizations they head, unless they adequately focus on and pay attention to the above strategic levers.

In this chapter, we present the empirical data (Appendix A) from the study conducted by the authors to assess the ground realities of what typical Indian boards do. Findings seek to answer questions as follows.

Which of the above levers of competitive edge are focused upon by the boards and to what extent? What type of roles are Indian boards playing in providing good governance as well as to build sustainable competitive edge of organizations? To what extent are Indian boards partnering with top managements of organizations to enhance firm-level performance?

Part 1 of this chapter, 'Building Sustainable Competitive Advantage: The Role of Boards' presents empirical data gathered from the following:

1. Senior-level corporate executives (operational heads) regarding factors contributing to sustainable competitive advantage.
2. Board members' views regarding the extent to which these issues (considered to be key by operational heads) are focused upon in boardroom discussions.

Part 2 brings out the details of the 'Thrust and Functioning of Indian Boards: Value Adding or Value Destroying?'

Part 1. Building Sustainable Competitive Advantage in Indian Organizations: The Role of Boards

The basic assumption in this part is that both managements of companies and their boards have a critical role to play in ensuring organizational sustainability and wealth creation for stakeholders. Therefore, understanding two key factors becomes relevant:

- The importance assigned to levers of sustainable competitive advantage by senior functionaries across companies
- The importance assigned to the same (above-mentioned) levers in boardroom discussions by board members

Perceptions of Senior-level Executives: Levers of Sustainable Competitive Advantage

- Priority assigned to the factors contributing to build sustainable competitive advantage of organizations
- Priority assigned to the factors derailing the sustainable competitive advantage of organizations

The perceptions of senior executives (Appendix C) have been taken in this work because these executives play an important role both in planning and implementation of the action agenda in various organizations. Hence, their views regarding where the focus of boards ought to be make a valuable contribution to the discussion on ways to building sustainable and competitive edge of organizations.

Perception of Board Directors: Levers of Sustainable Competitive Advantage

The same set of attributes (Appendix C) as above were presented to 70 board members to understand the time they spend discussing these factors in board meetings. This helped to assess the amount of attention which boards gave to these levers as compared to the importance attached by senior-level executives of companies.

Key Findings

Findings are presented as follows: (a) perceptions of senior-level executives—levers of sustainable competitive advantage; (b) priority given in boardroom discussions; (c) senior management perspective vis-à-vis boardroom discussion—ranks comparison and (d) factors derailing sustainable competitive advantage.

Senior-level Perspective: Levers of Sustainable Competitive Advantage

Senior management executives (170) from different companies (see Table 3.1) identified strategic leadership at the board level as the number 1 source of strategic advantage for organizations, followed by ethical governance at rank 2 and continued innovation at rank 3, speedy response to the market at rank 4 and so on. Thus, according to the senior management sample, these are the top four levers which can enable organizations gain sustainable competitive advantage and prepare for both the present and future challenges. The ranking indicates the relative importance assigned by the senior-level functionaries across public and private sector companies.

TABLE 3.1: Levers of Sustainable Competitive Edge: Senior Level

S. NO.	LEVERS	N = 170		
		FREQUENCY	%	RANK
1.	Strategic leadership at the board level	168	98.82	1
2.	Ethical governance	166	97.65	2
3.	Continued innovation	165	97.06	3
4.	Speedy response to market (time to reach market)	152	89.42	4

(continued)

(continued)

S. NO.	LEVERS	N = 170		
		FREQUENCY	%	RANK
5.	People with winning spirit	133	78.24	5
6.	Customer centricity	130	76.47	6
7.	Cost focus	115	67.65	7
8.	Quality focus	110	64.71	8

At this stage, readers will be curious to know whether the same level of importance is given by boards in their meetings to these levers.

Priority Given in Boardroom Discussions

Table 3.2 presents the mean scores assigned by the board members sample to each of the eight levers, indicating the extent to which these levers of sustainable competitive edge are discussed in board-level meetings. The top four levers discussed in the board meetings are as follows: cost management, quality, customer centricity and speed of response to market in that order. Comparison with Table 3.1 shows that these findings reveal just the opposite focus.

People with winning spirit (7), strategic leadership at the board level (7) and ethical governance (6) get the least priority in boardroom discussions, indicating that they are discussed only sometimes. Ironically, these are the key factors for preparing the organization for the future, building sustainable competitive edge, promoting renewal, taking

TABLE 3.2: Priority Given in Boardroom Discussions

S. NO.	LEVERS OF SUSTAINABLE COMPETITIVE ADVANTAGE	N = 70		
		MEAN	SD	RANK
1.	Cost focus	4.56	0.63	1
2.	Quality focus	3.89	0.94	2
3.	Customer centricity	3.23	0.90	3
4.	Speedy response to market (time to reach market)	3.00	0.90	4
5.	Continued innovation	2.27	0.87	5
6.	Ethical governance	2.17	0.85	6
7.	Strategic leadership at the board level	2.14	0.84	7
8.	People with winning spirit	2.14	0.84	7

Note: Mean scores on a 5-point scale—rarely, sometimes, many times, often and always.

organizations to the next orbit and building a lasting reputation both according to the strategies of great companies (Chapter 2) and the views of senior managements.

This certainly is a surprising finding: what is crucial for the future of the organization is given so little time in boardroom discussions. What could be the reasons for this? Does it reflect a certain mindset and a 'present' and 'immediate' focus among board members? Or is this a reflection of the level of business knowledge and awareness of all the board members?

Senior Management Perspective vis-à-vis Boardroom Discussion: Ranks Comparison

Table 3.3 compares the importance assigned by senior management (Table 3.1) versus priority assigned in boardroom discussions by board members (Table 3.2) to the levers of sustainable competitive advantage. Strategic leadership, ethical governance and continued innovation which senior management sample has rated to be of high importance—ranks 1, 2 and 3, respectively—are given low priority in boardroom discussions, the ranks being 7.5, 6 and 5, respectively. This indicates that those factors which are given high importance by the senior management for attaining sustainable competitive edge are given significantly low importance in boardroom discussions. In fact, boards are more focused on incremental innovation and exploitation of existing markets rather than exploring new opportunities and new markets which can help secure their future.

Comparison of the two rank sets, importance versus priority assigned, thus, brings out that important levers which can make an organization sustainable and competitive are hardly assigned any time for discussion in the board meetings. Although growing the business is the primary responsibility of the top management, setting direction, oversight and guidance, and monitoring of implementation need to be given importance in board discussions. Deliberating and brainstorming on the policies with reference to where the organization is headed, providing oversight and guidance are key board roles which are not being played to the needed extent according to findings of the present work.

Factors Derailing Sustainable Competitive Advantage

What hurts an organization's quest for sustainable competitive edge? This is useful information for those organizations

TABLE 3.3: Senior Management Perspective vis-à-vis Boardroom Discussion: Ranks Comparison

S. NO.	LEVERS OF SUSTAINABLE COMPETITIVE ADVANTAGE	IMPORTANCE OF LEVERS OF SUSTAINABLE COMPETITIVE ADVANTAGE SENIOR MANAGEMENT PERSPECTIVE	PRIORITY ASSIGNED IN BOARDROOM DISCUSSIONS
		RANK	RANK
1.	Strategic leadership at the board level	1	7.5
2.	Ethical governance	2	6
3.	Continued innovation	3	5
4.	Speedy response to market (time to reach market)	4	4
5.	People with winning spirit	5	7.5
6.	Customer centricity	6	3
7.	Cost focus	7	1
8.	Quality focus	8	2

Note: Spearman rank order coefficient [7] of correlation −0.74, significant at 0.05 level, indicates inverse relationship between the two sets of ranks.

which are trying to move on to the growth path and are ambitious to compete and win. Key internal management factors were examined, which if not effectively dealt with, can harm organizational sustainability and, above all, its capacity to compete successfully.

Table 3.4 presents views of the senior management group regarding factors which derail the sustainable competitive advantage of organizations. Findings indicate that the biggest derailer of sustainable competitive advantage is low strategic thinking with binocular vision (1). Strategic thinking with binocular vision gives an organization the ability to sense the signals at the periphery of their business context and scan the emerging future with a breadth of perspective, and it helps set and reset the future direction for the organization. Such capability helps the organization read the emergent environmental shifts and enables the top team to prepare for the same. Poor focus on R&D and innovation is at rank 2. Focus on innovation and innovative spirit will help the organization to make the needed improvements in products, processes and protocols and find innovative solutions to problems on a continuous basis. By not focusing on the future, the very survival of organizations is at risk, as companies keep themselves busy doing the same thing day in and day out, fighting fires and handling daily challenges. Such a present-focused approach will constrain the organization's capacity to adapt to the rapidly changing business environment. It will also allow other competitors to play catch up and out compete them.

The third derailer is inadequate understanding of government thinking and policies. Understanding of government thinking and policies if not keenly tracked, sensed, interpreted and appropriately handled, can jeopardize organizational strategy formulation and implementation. In fact, organizations need to develop alert antenna to keep abreast and even

TABLE 3.4: Factors Derailing Sustainable Competitive Advantage

S. NO.	DERAILERS OF SUSTAINABLE COMPETITIVE ADVANTAGE	N = 170		
		FREQUENCY	%	RANK
1.	Lack of strategic thinking with binocular vision	170	100.00	1
2.	Poor focus on innovation and R&D	167	98.23	2
3.	Inadequate understanding of government policies and thinking	164	96.47	3
4.	Poor ethical governance	162	95.29	4
5.	Inadequate understanding of market (poor market intelligence)	161	94.71	5
6.	Poor quality of leadership (CEO level)	156	91.76	6
7.	Poor culture of strategic monitoring and assigning accountability	152	89.41	7
8.	Poor delegation and empowerment	147	86.47	8

Note: Respondents group is the same as for Table 3.1.

try to anticipate the thoughts and actions of the policymakers. The fourth derailer of organizational sustainability is weak ethical governance (4). Dodgy behaviour on ethics, especially in dealing with various stakeholders, can hurt organizational reputation, undermine stakeholder trust as well as generate an unhealthy organizational culture. The impact of such behaviour is seen in the aftermath of numerous corporate scandals where people lose jobs and their entire savings. Unethical actions by companies create suspicion in the minds of all stakeholders, thus reducing goodwill, cooperation and support. Needless to say, the founders/CEOs and their companies lose all reputation and credibility.

The above-mentioned four factors—strategic thinking with binocular vision, focus on R&D and innovation, understanding of government policies and thinking and ethical governance—are the key determinants central to the future of the organization, its longevity and its capacity to stay ahead of the competition. Without such a future focus, organizations can lose direction. The rest of the derailers were ranked low from rank 5 to rank 8—inadequate understanding of the market, poor quality of CEO-level leadership, low strategic monitoring and assigning of accountability, and poor delegation and empowerment. These derailers (except for low strategic monitoring and assigning of accountability) reflect high inward orientation and perhaps, even a lack of organizational aspiration.

It may be highlighted that focus on Internal management alone is not enough, as it helps only in managing the present. Such inward orientation and lack of aspiration makes organizations more bureaucratic and status quoist, both of which are the enemies of growth and sustainability. Irrelevance and eventual death are certain for such organizations.

In order to prepare for the future, the essential requirement for ensuring organizational sustainability, companies must invest time and pay attention to four factors—strategic thinking, innovation, understanding the market signals and ethical governance—which constantly help them, both to manage their reputation and to prepare for the future. This is where the role of the board becomes prominent in the life of an organization, helping it set direction, guiding it, providing oversight and ensuring that it prepares to cope with the competition and prepare for the future, instead of being stuck on the endless treadmill of the present.

Key Findings: A Snapshot

The notable findings which emerged from Part 1 are as follows.

Findings indicate that Indian boards are more present focused rather than future focused. By dominantly focusing on the present, they are grossly failing in their responsibility to prepare the organization for the future. It is no wonder that many Indian companies are floundering or barely surviving and not growing according to their potential.

According to the sample of board members, strategy, innovation, ethical orientation and people power, the key levers of sustainable competitive advantage (according to the senior management group in this study as well as according to the wisdom from successful companies presented in Chapter 2), are hardly discussed by Indian boards.

This part of the chapter also provided insight into factors which derail competitive advantage—inward orientation hampers organizational effectiveness and growth.

Comparison of the factors to which boards pay attention in their meetings reveals that they are diametrically opposite to what they ought to be focusing on to develop sustainable competitive edge of the organizations they head.

Part 2. Thrust and Functioning of Indian Boards: Value Adding or Value Destroying?

This part brings out the details of the thrust and functioning of Indian boards—value adding or value destroying? Findings about what the board does, based on the sample board members are presented (Appendix D).

It must be mentioned that the present work does not examine the governance practices put in place by SEBI to ensure compliance, accountability and transparency. This part focuses on the thrust and focus of Indian boardrooms and the ways in which they contribute to building a sustainable and competitive organization. The basic assumption of this work is that good governance can be built on the foundation of good-quality board processes, board management and clarity of purpose and strategic direction. Thus, it is important that boards give thrust on these aspects, in addition to issues of compliance, transparency, accountability, stakeholder management, risks management and reputation protection. Data was gathered to identify the focus of board-level discussions on the above-cited aspects.

Findings of this part are presented around the following key themes: (a) what boards do, (b) thrust of boardroom discussions, (c) nature of Indian boards, (d) board agenda, (e) board behaviours and organizational collapse, (f) accountability of independent directors (independent directors) on the board and (g) needed board member competencies.

What Boards Do?

This section explores the ground reality of what boards are engaged in when they meet. Table 3.5 presents the findings regarding the focus of board-level discussions.

TABLE 3.5: What Boards Do: Focus Areas

S. NO.	AREAS OF FOCUS	N = 198		
		MEAN	SD	RANK
1.	Operational focus	3.48	0.80	1
2.	Reducing costs	3.42	0.61	2
3.	Customer focus	2.93	0.76	3
4.	Continuous innovation	2.86	1.13	4
5.	Evolving strategies for minimizing risk	2.82	0.82	5
6.	Concern for stakeholders	2.73	0.75	6
7.	Ethical focus	2.73	0.70	7
8.	Developing future leaders (succession)	2.73	0.75	8
9.	Oversight of policy and strategy-level issues	2.60	1.29	9

Note: Mean scores on a 5-point scale—rarely, sometimes, many times, often and always.

Table 3.5 indicates that boards give most (above average) thrust to operational matters. Some of the views shared by our sample group regarding this are quite illuminating, for example, CMD of a large public sector company said, 'chairman, MD, board are all busy with operational matters'. A total of 30 per cent sample of the present study said that boards monitor performance, IT and audit results to a high extent. Performance monitoring is the one thing they do on periodic basis. Boards repeat what top managements of companies ought to be doing rather than doing their own job of developing strategy, innovation, managing reputation, managing risk and so on.

Reducing costs has emerged at rank 2. The sample mentioned that cost reduction is focused upon a lot by boards, especially in the private sector where it is a major preoccupation. This was the unanimous voice across the sample of the present study.

On all other matters, whether pertaining to customer focus, continuous innovation, evolving strategies for minimizing risk, concern for stakeholders and ethical focus, board's focus is to a below average extent. Explaining why the other areas are not focused upon, a seasoned and senior board member said, the focus of the board on operational matters and cost reduction keeps everyone at the board level so engrossed in digits and numbers that they forget other important matters. Many times, the 'inward'-focused approach of the board results in their missing key developments taking place in the environment. It is no surprise, therefore, that few boards focus on discussing risk and how to mitigate risks. They are taken by surprise when the company is hit by various environmental factors.

Surprisingly, boardroom discussions don't adequately focus on key aspects relevant to building sustainable competitive edge of organizations. Operational matters and cost reduction, the top two thrust areas at the board level, pertain to issues relevant to managing the present business and get regular returns—wealth extraction. In fact, all future-focused matters important for wealth creation—continuous innovation, evolving strategies for minimizing risk, concern for stakeholders and ethical focus—are given below average attention.

Despite being at the helm of affairs of the company, the attention of the board is narrowly focused on immediate issues. In such a scenario, one wonders who is preparing the organization for the future.

Summary

Overall, the findings of this section clearly bring out that the focus of the company and the boards is on managing the present business (cost and operations focus) rather than preparing for the future. Future focus would mean building strategy, preparing people and organization for the future, identifying innovative approaches and solutions to build competitiveness. Building organizational reputation and giving attention to various stakeholders, both of which are important contributors to organizational sustainability, unfortunately, don't get much attention.

Thrust of Boardroom Discussions

This section refers to the issues which are given importance during board-level (and subcommittee) discussions.

Table 3.6 presents the thrust of boardroom discussions according to the sample. Examination of the mean values brings out that of the six key areas discussed in board meetings, audit committee reports get above average attention, followed by observations of statutory auditors.

Although findings of the risk management committee are discussed in the boardroom (rank 3), this is done to a below average extent. According to 15 per cent of the sample, with the experience of working on both public and private sector boards, in-depth discussion on the findings of the risk management committee take place much more in the private sector. In public sector, the focus on finding of risk management committee is less because they feel that there is a big brother (government) behind them. In the public sector, there may be a feeling that even if they take big risks and fail, the government is there to support.

TABLE 3.6: Thrust of Boardroom Discussions

S. NO.	ATTRIBUTES	N = 198		
		MEAN	SD	RANK
1.	In-depth discussion on audit committee report for continuously improving organizational performance	3.70	0.72	1
2.	In-depth discussion on observations of the statutory auditors	3.33	0.79	2
3.	In-depth discussion on findings of risk management committee to minimize risk	2.97	0.82	3
4.	In-depth discussion on HR issues and focus on building future leaders	2.73	0.72	4
5.	In-depth discussion on evolving strategy for growth and sustainable competitive edge	2.45	1.31	5

Note: Mean scores on a 5-point scale—rarely, sometimes, many times, often and always

There is no doubt that keen focus on findings of the audit committee reports and discussions on the observations of statutory auditors is very important for strengthening controls in organizations. Audits bring out issues such as financial bungling in some part the organization and 'bypassing' of established processes such as short cuts taken to manage time deadlines, collusion and ethical violations. These not only insidiously hurt organizational performance but also affect norms of workplace behaviour. If these are tolerated, they send bad signals down the line about top management's intent. The focus on audit is, therefore, much needed.

Discussion on risk and risk mitigation is also very important at the board level, as the company needs to be protected from various types of risks including economic risk, compliance risk, security and fraud risk, financial risk, reputation risk, operational risk and competition risk.

According to Table 3.6, HR issues and building future leaders are discussed sometimes. The scores make it amply clear that focus on building people power of the organizations is on the lower side. Majority of the sample (75%) highlighted that people- and HR-related issues are rarely discussed on the board. A strong view was expressed that there are some key people-level and culture-level matters on which the board has to take a clear position but does not do so to the needed extent—clarity regarding values at the workplace and plans to nurture leadership talent. These should be driven through systems and processes: HR, culture, organization, design, organizational structure, productivity, standard, contemplation standard, system of annual targets and key result areas. Key performance indicators and key result areas of the chairman and CEO need to be carefully crafted by the same board.

Featuring last on the list, evolving (business) strategies, one the most important levers for sustained competitive advantage, gets short shrift in boardroom discussions. Some of the observations and suggestions made by the sample are given below:

- Strategy is hardly discussed in board meetings. It is always the immediate and the urgent that grabs the attention of the board. Since strategy is so crucial to the future of the organization, boards need to re-examine their priorities on this matter.

- According to a former secretary of Government of India, who has been member on many boards,

> Boards look inwards when they should think and look outward; they need to change their focus... because the company may not remain the same with time. One needs to know the sustainability of the company, what will become of the company in 10yrs or 15yrs. Nobody asks such questions.

- Since the time horizon for chief executives in the public sector is not very long, CMDs and MDs focus less on building the future of the organization and seek to show maximum achievements during their tenure.
- Few boards do what they are supposed to do—prepare the company as per vision and mission document, get it implemented, review and monitor, and make changes as required.
- In well-managed private sector companies where the management is honest and in companies where they give employee stock ownership plans, they need to have the horizon of at least 5–10 years. In such companies, strategic focus is very much present.

The survey brought out that the thrust of boardroom discussions is on the following three factors: in-depth discussion on audit committee report, discussions on the observations of the statutory auditors and discussions on findings of risk management committee to minimize risk. Low importance is given to HR issues and building future leaders and evolving business strategy.

Nature of Indian Boards

There are times when a single adjective can succinctly capture many aspects of a phenomenon. With this in view, we asked the sample to select one word which according to them best described boards. Table 3.7 shows that two-thirds of the sample perceived boards to be ornamental, followed by country club. Only a miniscule percentage of the sample group described boards as committed.

Most of the sample (90%) said that boards were more ornamental or country club type and they further explained this as follows.

Members don't contribute much to the discussions. Boards are 'decorative', 'trophy' boards, 'good looking', members are 'distinguished people', 'they are well-known people', 'members have a good CV', 'they have worked in good organizations', 'they are people in the limelight', 'they make the board look good', 'board directors are high-profile people'.

Board directors on private sector boards 'are friends of the promoters, board members come for a chit chat, have a good lunch and leave'; 'it's an old boys club'; 'they are all chums and they just come and say hi, good you came, have snacks, have lunch and leave'. Many of them are friends ... when they meet it's like a 'get together at a country club'.

TABLE 3.7: Nature of Indian Boards

DESCRIPTION OF INDIAN BOARDS	N = 195	
	FREQUENCY	%
Ornamental	138	70.76
Country club	49	25.13
Committed boards	08	4.10

Another board member shared: 'I was an internal director on a leading private sector company board (in the steel sector). I found that they did bring high-profile people on board, but they were all friends and didn't know much about the business. They were supportive people and would not talk much about business but about the nation'.

A total of 65 per cent of the present sample said that the board tends to be highly supportive of the promoter. Few board members contribute to board functioning and look up to the Chairman/Promoter for direction.

Almost 40 per cent of the sample directors said that it is not uncommon to have family members on private sector boards. One of the interviewees shared about his board experience: 'the promoter had four family members—sons, daughter-in-law and wife—on the board'. Another board director said, 'promoters of small private companies keep people they know. But there are others who are on the board just for the sake of it, because the board needs a quorum to function'.

An HR veteran who has worked across public and private sector companies said, 'I was on the board of India's leading family-owned, promoter-driven conglomerate and I was amazed that there were at least 18–20 main members of the board. Now with such a large number, what serious discussions can happen? Members were ex-army, ex-police and other such people unrelated to business'.

The above data bring out the following points:

- Indian boards are viewed as more ornamental, followed by country club in terms of the behaviour of board members. The members are distinguished people with good background and credentials and make the board look good.
- Independent directors are generally not chosen based on their professional capacity and many of them may be clueless about what is transpiring on the board.

- Board members are loyal to the Promoter/Chairman rather than to the organization.

The above-mentioned points suggest that independent directors are appointed primarily to comply with SEBI regulations and not necessarily for any value addition that they can bring to the board. The selection of board members is done on whims and fancies and convenience of the Promoter/Chairman. Perhaps, there is no expectation that board members should contribute to board-level matters. In fact, independent directors are probably selected by the Promoter/Chairman for their loyalty and willingness to go along with decisions made by the latter. Given the above narration, it is, therefore, not surprising that Promoters/Chairmen can get away with lack of transparency and low accountability, as loyalty is given paramount weightage while selecting board members. Promoters/Chairmen of companies get their own way, propped up by their family and friends on the board.

Board Agenda

Heavy board agenda has typically been talked about by directors on boards and this has also been the experience of the authors who have been board members.

Board agenda refers to the number of items (issues) being brought to the board for approvals/sanctions and for information of the board. The high mean value (Table 3.8) indicates that our sample felt that the board agenda is very heavy. Evidently, the heavier the agenda, the lesser the time available for detailed discussions. This is more so when the frequency of board meetings is once every quarter. As a result, the quality of discussion is bound to suffer and important matters are passed by the board without thorough examination and discussion.

Our sample shared the following views.

TABLE 3.8: Extent of Heavy Board Agenda

N = 198	
MEAN	**SD**
4.30	0.52

Note: Mean scores on a 5-point scale—rarely, sometimes, many times, often and always.

Heavy Board Agenda

- Board agenda is very heavy, it is like a ritual.
- The board agenda is very heavy in both public and private sector.
- At times maybe preparing a heavy board agenda is deliberate.
- There are some companies where audit committee meeting, risk committee meeting and corporate social responsibility meeting all are scheduled on the same day and in the afternoon, they have the board. By the time the board starts, people are completely tired. People are completely disinterested, so things are just noted and passed.

Reasons for Heavy Board Agenda

The likely reasons for loading the agenda, according to almost all the sample (90%), are given below:

- Maybe the heavy board agenda is deliberate or maybe it reflects poor levels of delegation within the company, resulting in most decisions being in the hands of the Promoter/Chairman.
- It is quite possible that the top team maybe seeking safety in putting up everything to the board level. As a result, discussions that matter don't really take place owing to preoccupation with compliances and discussing matters

which the internal team ought to be handling. Even small matters are brought to the board; this takes up time and does not permit focus on bigger matters as per board role.

- Most of the sample (70%) said that the management always drives the agenda and decides what is put up to the board.
- Most of the board members in the sample (85%) found that the board's time is mostly spent on routine processes rather than governance. It could be because the mindset is of compliance rather than genuine discussion. In fact, boards are not interested in new ideas. They view board meetings more as a necessary evil to be complied with.

Outcomes of Heavy Board Agenda

According to 100 per cent of interviewed board members:

- When 100 items are packed in a single meeting, then discussions do not take place.
- There is too much to cover in too short a time. Because of short timelines, there is low possibility of in-depth discussions.
- Because agenda is circulated only 2–3 days in advance, there is less time for the board directors to prepare for the meeting by reading thoroughly.
- When this heavy agenda is combined with board members not getting enough time to read, board members are ill-prepared for any meaningful discussions.
- Board meetings are quarterly and there is never enough time for in-depth discussions.

It may be concluded from the above that the heavy board agenda also contributes to directors being unable to do justice to their roles on the board. A board is as good as the top team of the organization and, hence, strengthening the top team to function effectively is key to boards being able to do their job instead of getting dragged into issues which should be dealt internally by the management.

Board Behaviours and Organizational Collapse

Boards of companies play an important role both in the growth and in the fall of the companies they head. When they play their role diligently, it contributes to organizational sustainability and when they don't, the opposite happens.

Table 3.9 gives the views of our sample regarding behaviours of boards contributing to their collapse. Questionable integrity of board members is the most important factor endorsed by almost all the members in the sample (rank 1). Some of the views of the sample are now presented: most of the sample (70%) said that many Indian private sector boards

TABLE 3.9: Board-level Behaviours and Collapse of Leading Companies

S. NO.	ATTRIBUTES	N=198		
		MEAN	SD	RANK
1.	Questionable integrity	4.90	0.33	1
2.	Managing statutory auditors and rating agencies	4.68	0.53	2
3.	Lack of transparency	4.01	0.48	3
4.	Inadequate accountability	3.93	0.48	4
5.	Frequency of power used by influential board members to push decisions in the direction he/she wants	3.48	0.63	5

Note: Mean scores on a 5-point scale—rarely, sometimes, many times, often and always.

tend to be less professional in their management style since they are family managed.

Detailed views supporting this rank are given as follows.

In such family-run companies, it is the owner who runs the show. His/her say is what really matters. In typical Lala (family owned) companies, things are done at the whims and fancies of the chairman and the MD runs the show through a coterie. Important information and key issues are seldom brought to the board.

The inside directors and the independent directors look at the chairman for guidance. They follow his/her direction. They focus in the direction in which he/she focuses, thus giving him/her a blank cheque to do what he/she pleases.

According to 60 per cent of the interviewed sample, many board members are ignorant about their roles. They don't even know what is happening on the board. Board members come to the meetings, without even bothering to read the relevant papers, they make a few observations and then walk out of the meeting. When board members do not play their roles with due commitment and responsibility to the company, their integrity is questionable. Through their ignorance, or lack of time or collusion, they facilitate unhealthy practices which lead to the downfall of the very companies they head.

Most board members (75%) said, the approach of boards is more of compliance, 'ticking the box'. According to them, many companies are complying with requirements of SEBI and the Company Law, following the letter and not the spirit behind the laws.

One of the interviewees said, boards comply with norms set by SEBI. Nothing beyond the agenda (set by the Promoter/ Chairman) gets discussed in the meetings. For example, there is an instance of high-level corruption in the company, the management will rarely bring this to the boardroom, although it is important that the board should know.

Many interviewees (50%) opined that it is all a matter of intent of the Chairman/Promoter. If they have the right intent, then boards are well run. If the intent is not above board, then they can use the board as they want, get decisions passed which suit them and so on.

The above-cited information suggests that when board members are unprepared and ignorant and when directors don't ask questions even if they are knowledgeable, they are unwittingly colluding with the owner and the Promoter/Chairman can get anything done. In addition, when agendas are heavy, the promoter can get his/her way very easily. The above-cited factors become dangerous when the promoter has the wrong intent according to 50 per cent of the interviewees.

'Managing' statutory auditors and rating agencies is the next important factor which contributes to the collapse of companies. Our sample made the following observations regarding this factor.

Most of the sample (70%) were of the view that unfortunately audit firms and rating agencies can, at the behest of the company, manipulate company ratings. Some of the sample (15%) said that rating agencies have become a racket, a fake racket; they have become commercial. They are not projecting the true worth of the organization; there is no regulation of rating agencies, even CRISIL can be influenced. Otherwise the IL&FS story or DHL and Satyam would not have taken place.

Some others (55%) opined, rating agencies play an important part in the collapse of companies. In the IL&FS case, it was rating agencies who connived and did not play their role; they misled investors and the public.

Lack of transparency has been mentioned as the third important factor contributing to collapse of companies. A total of 50 per cent of the sample mentioned lack of transparency as the third-most important contributor to organizational collapse. A board member of one pf the India's rising star companies which committed one of the biggest frauds in recent times mentioned, 'many times we didn't even know what was happening in the company, we had to go by the agenda brought to the board'. Since the Promoter/Chairman sets the agenda for board meetings, he/she can very easily ensure that only certain sanitized information is brought for discussions rather than anything which can raise questions. In fact, many in the sample (55%) complained that they have seen boards where minor matters are focused on and important matters are either kept for discussion in the end or not brought at all.

Inadequate accountability of board members is ranked 4. Independent directors can come and can go as they wish, whether they contribute or not is not taken very seriously. In fact, there is no expectation of much contribution from them. The exodus of independent directors from boards of companies is a telling indicator of the refusal to accept responsibility.

The lowest ranked factor is **influential board members pushing their decisions.**

Summary

As Chapter 1 brought out, many of India's top companies have been declaring bankruptcy/ have been found to commit frauds, authorize fraudulent transactions, divert funds, etc. The findings of this section give some idea about the behaviour and attitude of board members contributing to dodgy actions by failed companies.

Questionable integrity of board members, managing statutory auditors and lack of transparency in decision-making are the key factors contributing to poor performance and even collapse of companies. Majority of the sample of board members clearly bring out that board members themselves behave in ways which contribute either directly or indirectly to fraudulent behaviours. They collude with the Promoter/ Chairman through either their ignorance or their deliberate silence in board meetings.

Accountability of Independent Directors (Independent Directors) on the Board

Of late, SEBI has made independent directors equally responsible for the performance of companies and they have been made liable when companies collapse [8]. The Companies Act, 2017, seeks to professionalize board functioning. When SEBI announced the new rule indicating the responsibility of independent directors in case of failures and bankruptcy, thousands of independent directors resigned [9] indicating that the position was no longer sought after and perhaps no longer glamorous [10] because it brings with it significant accountability for losses and poor decisions.

In this context, therefore, a question was asked to the sample to understand their views on the level of accountability which independent directors ought to take when things go wrong.

Table 3.10 presents responses to the question regarding the accountability of independent directors. Most of the sample

TABLE 3.10: Accountability of Independent Directors

S. NO.	ATTRIBUTES	N = 198	
		MEAN	SD
1.	Unethical board-level practices	4.95	0.26
2.	The poor performance/ collapse of companies	3.83	0.43

Note: Mean scores on a 5-point scale—rarely, sometimes, many times, often and always.

are of the view that independent directors are responsible to a high extent for unethical board-level practices as well as the poor performance and collapse of companies. This is further explained in the quotes given below:

- When friends are brought in on boards (as independent directors), there are mutual obligations and that's when problems start.
- The problem starts because family members are made board members—a common practice in promoter-driven companies.
- Most of the company boards where we see something going wrong, directly or indirectly, the founder is involved.
- On any board when family members are being nominated, they are inviting some disaster sooner or later.

Another dimension of unethical behaviour stems from the personal agendas of the independent directors on public sector boards. According to 10 per cent of the sample, many independent directors in the public sector have been known to push for personal favours to close pending cases. If they were not obliged, they created problems in the clearance of other proposals which the management was seeking to get passed by the board. Since they are government appointed for a fixed period, one can't do anything about their tenure. Similarly, in manufacturing companies and utilities, independent directors expect mutual benefits in the award of contracts according to 40 per cent of the sample.

Apart from active unethical behaviour by some independent directors, passive behaviours also contribute to the problem as indicated in the following statements:

- The tendency to just say yes to anything which is being brought to the board by the Promoter/MD is not good for the organization.

- Independent directors are silent on most issues during board discussions and that is the problem. Although board members are not involved in day-to-day matters, when it comes to integrity in functioning, there is a lack of questioning and silence and to that extent, they are guilty.
- The former CMD of a public sector utilities company said, nobody asks any questions to the MD. In my experience, independent board members never ask any questions.
- People don't really oppose views in the board meetings. Whenever there are people who are ready to debate, discuss, put their points across, the discussion gets richer, something which is left out can come out in that or if something is critical, it can come out.
- Even ex-bankers who become board members don't say much out of loyalty to the chairman who got them on the board in the first place. Generally, in public sector, I feel boards are just for the sake of it.
- Independent directors should be accountable because they are being paid money to ask questions and diligently see things, and if things go wrong, it means they have not played their part properly.
- It is the job of the independent directors to ask questions and collectively they are responsible for the company. Today, laws are very strict; every director is responsible. Earlier it was vague, but the Company Law has made it clear that all the directors are responsible. Therefore, every director needs to take responsibility for the company's growth.

Summary

Findings of the study on this question bring out the following key points:

- Independent directors are considered to be responsible to a high extent for unethical board-level practices of company boards as well as for the poor performance/collapse of companies. They cannot be absolved of responsibility.

- When family and friends are nominated to the board as independent directors, it is evident that they will follow the Chairman/Promoter. Therefore, their independence is itself in question.
- Although they are not involved in day-to-day matters and may not be directly benefitting, by not asking relevant questions in board meetings, they are colluding with the promoter and to that extent they are guilty.
- The views expressed by various board members in the sample indicate that it is through both omission and commission that independent directors are responsible for these phenomena.
- They can play a crucial and positive role if they choose to do so.

Needed Board Member Competencies

Some of the earlier tables have brought out that much of the problem of board-level functioning emanates from the type of board members, their capacity to contribute and their commitment to the owner rather than to the organization. This section examines the needed competencies of effective board members.

Table 3.11 presents the responses of the board members regarding needed board member competencies. Balance between domain expertise and understanding of the business has emerged as the most important board-level competency. Some of the views of the sample supporting the above competency are presented below:

- Each board member needs to be an expert in his/her own field, and he/she should be able to apply this to the challenges faced by the company.

TABLE 3.11: Needed Board Member Competencies

S. NO.	COMPETENCIES	N = 198		
		FREQUENCY	%	RANK
1.	Balance of domain expertise and business understanding	151	76.26	1
2.	Ethics, integrity and commitment	148	74.75	2
3.	Openness to ideas, willingness to explore	146	73.74	3
4.	Strategic mindset with growth focus	145	73.25	4
5.	Teamwork (influencing others, managing conflicts)	140	70.71	5

- If the board members are not competent, they will not be able to contribute. One can be a good board member if one is competent in that business, understands that business and has knowledge and experience in that business.
- The application of core knowledge needs to be done in the context of understanding of the specific business in which one is operating.
- Board members should have a wide knowledge base— understand finance, strategy and CG—and know how to apply this knowledge.
- Board members must understand leadership, strategy, entrepreneurship and finance. These are like the pre-qualifications to enter the boardroom.
- Any independent director will find it extremely difficult to handle the business of an industry without knowledge of

the sector. Handling complexity, detailing and decoding will be very critical.

According to the sample, the second-most important requirement is a mindset of ethics, integrity and commitment, where a person will make decisions with integrity and commitment, keeping the interests of organization and stakeholders in focus. The capacity to maintain confidentiality, making decisions in the interest of the organization and commitment to organizational well-being are the key requirements according to the interviewees. Some of the interviewees summed it up, thus:

- Integrity is a big part of governance; good behaviour and attitude are important because these are value adding for the board.
- Integrity of board members and their reputation in the market, how honest is so and so director and how honest is the board are crucial for the reputation of the board.
- The board's value depends upon the attitude, behaviour and honesty of the members. Leadership competencies also depend upon it; what style the board demonstrates, how things get done, all this ultimately sets the organization culture.

Openness to ideas along with willingness to explore them has emerged as the third-most important requirement. This competency becomes important especially when organizations are faced with disruptions and change and need to be responsive, adaptive and find innovative solutions. As explained by some of the interviewed board members:

- Directors on the board need to be open to ideas, willing to explore and accept that there could be differences and different point of views (vis-à-vis other board members).

- Flexibility for change, transformation and innovation are very important. People who are rigid will not be able to contribute much. Capability to handle change, transformation and flexibility will be very critical.
- The chairman also has to be open minded to listen to all the bad news. If he/she is not open minded and only wants to hear the good news, then the company will sink and the board members can't do their jobs.

Strategic mindset with growth focus has emerged as the fourth-most important competency. There is no doubt that unless a board member can visualize the likely future, he/she will not be able to contribute to decision-making for business sustainability. It is not enough to be strategic; the board member should be continuously concerned about ensuring business growth. As some of the board members lucidly explained:

- They need to be strategic thinkers who can map the broader business scenario. They need the capacity to think beyond, not just about the existing business but should think innovatively and see the big picture.
- They need a wide-angle perspective on the business which includes context sensitivity. This is not only connected to the business but also to economic, political and geopolitical contexts while taking the decisions.
- Capacity to read the current issues, events and context, especially signals at the periphery and connect the dots, will help to develop a hunch about the future. Strategic thinking by itself is inadequate unless combined with a growth mindset which will ensure that hunches are used to build strategies and perspectives for organizational growth.

The last and very important factor is teamwork, characterized not only by collaboration and cooperation but also by capability to influence others and manage conflicts, so that board carries on its business without getting diverted from its core focus of organizational governance and growth. The importance of working together is highlighted well in the following statement:

Along with teamwork, conflict handling is also important because unless there is conflict of ideas, rich outcomes do not emerge. Board members should have healthy debates where everyone is heard.

Other Suggestions on Board Competencies

Board composition and role of the chairman are the two key points which emerged from the open-ended questions in the interviews and are presented below.

Board composition: Most of the interviewees (80%) emphasized that the board should have diverse competencies. Some of the views are mentioned below.

- Experts need to be drawn from various domains—core business, finance company, IT, HR and so on—who can contribute to the discussions. Diversity is not necessarily because of gender, rather it occurs when there are different kinds of experience, specialization and thought processes.
- Composition of the board is critical. The board should have people of standing, people who are known for their depth of knowledge in a specific domain.
- There should be diversity (of talent and domain knowledge) on every board. The best boards are those where the board is diverse and has competent members and where there is an intent to use the talents available on the board.
- Diverse boards are very important as there is scope for great learning, and good ideas emerge from continuous debate and contribution of everyone.
- Effective board functioning is possible when there is a high-quality chairman (experienced person and a man of

integrity), who ensures transparent discussions and provides information and inputs.

- Board members should have a questioning spirit, and, above all, they should have some feel of the business so that they understand what is going on.

Role of the chairman: There is no doubt that the chairman has a key role to play in managing the board. Although the chairman is equal to other directors in terms of voting rights, the role played by the chairman is critical. Some of the views (40%) are presented below:

- Chairman must be knowledgeable and have the capability to manage board dynamics.
- By engaging board members regularly on what role is expected from them, the chairman can raise the level of the board.
- The chairman needs the capacity to keep the board members together and to manage dissension.
- The chairman should build a good board culture that deals with boardroom dynamics, power structures and develops unwritten practices to improve boardroom functioning and make it more effective.
- The chairman must have inter-company interfaces and ways to interact with other companies.
- The chairman should encourage pre-board chats to facilitate smooth board functioning.

Summary

The sample emphasized the following board-level competencies as essential for effective functioning of the board:

- Depth of domain knowledge (one's own area of expertise) as the necessary condition, along with application capacity (application to the present issue or problem at hand) and width of knowledge.

- Integrity and reputation of board members.
- Open-mindedness and exploring mindset to ensure that members have the capacity to examine different possibilities and opportunities without getting rigid and closed to new approaches to change.
- Strategic thinking combined with a growth mindset.
- The capability to work with other board members, reduce conflicts and increase collaborative spirit in the group.
- Capacity of the chairman to promote healthy debate, manage dissension, have productive discussions and keep the board together.

Overall Key Findings and Conclusions

Chapter 3 examined the ground realities of what typical Indian boards do. Which of the levers of competitive edge are focused upon by the boards and to what extent—strategy; continuous innovation; enablers of strategy of continuous innovation such as customer centricity, speed to the market, agility, people power and culture for entrepreneurship; and ethical governance keeping the triple Ps (focus on taking care of people, planet and profit)? Are Indian boards partnering with organizations to enhance firm-level performance? What type of roles are Indian boards playing in terms of both ensuring good governance and building sustainable competitive edge of organizations?

Major findings of the empirical study are presented below.

Part 1. Building Sustainable Competitive Advantage of Organizations: Key Findings

This part examined (a) the views of senior-level corporate executives regarding factors contributing to sustainable competitive advantage and (b) board members' views regarding the extent to which these issues are focused upon in board-room discussions.

Strategic leadership, ethical governance and continued innovation have been identified (by the senior-level executive sample) as the top three factors for ensuring organizational sustainability and competitive advantage. In contrast, it has been found that boardroom discussions give higher priority to cost, quality and customer and lower priority to the important factors identified by senior executives of organizations.

Based on the above finding, it is possible to conclude that boards of Indian companies are more present focused rather than future focused. It is no wonder that many companies are floundering or barely surviving and not growing according to their potential.

This part of the chapter presented data on factors important for effective business-level functioning and shone the light on the extent to which these priorities for business growth find a place in boardroom discussions. The first requirement for an organization is its stable existence and for this, effective management is one of the key requirements. If a company is poorly managed, no amount of compliance and good governance by the board is going to revive it. Hence, boards of organizations need to focus not only on governance but also provide oversight to the management of the organization to ensure its effective functioning and sustainable growth.

The authors feel strong dissonance regarding the low importance given to innovation, evolving strategy, HR issues and building people power in boardroom discussions. These three are important requirements for sustaining the business in the future. In today's disruptive environments, unless organizations think innovatively and build a culture of innovation and entrepreneurship, handling future challenges can be a daunting task. Positioning the right kind of people in the right place and unleashing people power and team spirit are essential for an organization to deliver with great focus. Without activating people power, organizational growth and sustainable competitive edge will be limited. Similarly, unless the organization is clear about where it is headed (goal) and has the right steps in place to reach there (strategy), it will keep floundering in the present morass and keep playing the catch-up game with the industry leaders.

Study of high-performing companies (Chapter 2) has brought out that organizations that last have a blue ocean strategy which keeps them ahead of the competition. They don't get mired in competing in a red ocean where there are too many competitors and too many wars with diminishing gains. Unfortunately, providing direction and strategic guidance to ensure the company's growth is virtually ignored by the board. Indian boards need to clearly re-examine the thrust of their boardroom discussions, so that there is a balanced approach to all important matters which they should pay attention to, encompassing both governance and performance.

Part II. Thrust and Functioning of Indian Boards: Value Adding or Value Destroying? Key Findings

What Boards Do?

The dominant focus of the company and the boards is on managing the present (cost and operations) rather than preparing for the future through building strategy, preparing people and organization for the future, identifying innovative approaches and solutions to build competitiveness. Building organizational reputation and giving attention to stakeholders, both of which lead to organizational sustainability, don't get much attention.

Thrust of Boardroom Discussions

The dominant thrust of boardroom discussions is on in-depth discussion on audit committee report for continuously improving organizational performance. This is followed by discussions on the observations of the statutory auditors. However, discussions on findings of risk management committee to minimize risk, HR issues and building future leaders as well as evolving business strategies are given lower importance and happen only sometimes. By not giving enough attention to developing future leaders and evolving a future-focused business strategy, boards are doing a disservice to the companies they head. It is a matter of serious concern that boards are not paying adequate attention to preparing the organization for the future.

Board Agenda

Board agenda is viewed to be very heavy by the sample for various reasons such as preoccupation with compliances and discussing matters which the internal team ought to be handling. Most of the focus of board meetings is on routine processes and compliances. It may be concluded from the above that the heavy board agenda also contributes to directors being unable to do justice to their roles on the board. A board is as good as the top team of the organization and, hence, strengthening the top team through empowerment and accountability is very important. Boards need to devote some time to assess the quality of internal management of the company and provide guidance on various matters which can strengthen the internal management—empowerment, monitoring, building suitable work culture to encourage innovation and good-quality decision-making. Once this is put in place, boards can strive to become more effective by focusing on matters which matter at the board level—governance and strategy.

Nature of Indian Boards

Indian boards are dominantly trophy boards. Members are generally not chosen based on their professional capacity and many of them may be clueless about what is transpiring on the board. Board members are loyal to the Promoter/Chairman rather than to the organization.

Wilful Negligence by Board Members and Poor Performance of Companies They Head

According to the findings, companies which perform poorly and/or collapsed probably did so owing to the questionable integrity of board members, the efforts made to 'manage' statutory auditors and lack of transparency of decision-making in that order. In other words, poor governance has been one of the biggest causes of poor performance of companies. Board members themselves behave in ways which contribute either directly or indirectly to fraudulent behaviours by the Promoters/Chairmen. They collude with the Promoter/Chairman through either their ignorance or their deliberate silence in board meetings. Another possibility is that the company has deliberately hidden information from the board. It is also quite possible that they support many board actions out of loyalty to the Promoter/Chairman.

Thus, it may not be surprising that there is a tendency among board members to condone and support decisions and actions of the chairman, instead of raising questions and getting involved in discussions. It is, therefore, not surprising that corporate scandals take place, either through ignorance or maybe through conscious collusion out of loyalty to the promoter.

Accountability of Independent Directors on the Board

Findings brought out that independent directors are viewed to be responsible to a high extent for unethical board-level practices of company boards as well as for the poor performance/collapse of companies. The key problems are owing to silence of independent directors in board meetings. Although they are not involved in day-to-day matters, by not asking questions, they are colluding with the promoter and to that extent they are guilty.

The above seems to bring out very strongly that although SEBI and other regulators can ensure compliance, the most important requirement is the intent of the Chairman/Promoter. If the intent is right, many things fall in place. Else, boards can be manipulated in any direction that the Promoter/Chairman chooses.

Board Members: Needed Competencies

Many competencies have been highlighted in the study. The key ones are as follows:

- Depth of domain knowledge (one's own area of expertise) as the necessary condition along with application capacity (application to the present issue or problem at hand) and breadth of knowledge across related domains of management.
- Integrity and reputation of board members.
- Strategic thinking combined with a growth mindset which needs both open mindedness and exploring mindset.
- The capability to work with other board members.

In Conclusion

At the end of this chapter, we go back to the basic question of whether boards are value adding or value destroying. Findings indicate that they are adding value only to a limited extent as they are not preparing the organization for the future. Everyone up the organizational hierarchy and at the board level is busy with operational matters and focused on reducing costs. The other core preoccupation of the board seems to be compliance and statutory matters. Who is looking out for the future of the organization and who is preparing the organization to sustain and be competitive are the big questions and sadly, the board, which is supposed to do this, is not living up to its role.

Strategy, innovation, ethical orientation, people power—the key levers of sustainable competitive advantage are hardly discussed by Indian boards. Future focus would mean building strategy, preparing people and organization for the future, and identifying innovative approaches and solutions to build competitiveness. Building organizational reputation and giving attention to various stakeholders, both of which are important contributors to organizational sustainability, unfortunately, don't get much attention.

The concern, however, is the low importance given to HR issues and building future leaders as well as evolving business strategies. By not giving enough attention to developing future leaders and evolving a future-focused business strategy, boards are doing a disservice to the companies they head.

There is a strong inward orientation and bureaucratic orientation which characterize Indian companies and both of them hamper organizational effectiveness and growth. The jugaad mentality of the typical Indian company does not take it too far. Indian companies and boards do focus on factors such as cost, quality and customer. The key question is whether it is a static process or it consists of incremental improvement or is it a dynamic process which is continually engaged in the dance of disruption and transformation in response to a dynamic environment and the demand for transformation. As Chapter 2 brought out, static and incremental improvements can no longer give a company much competitive advantage. Indian companies have to seriously focus on those factors which can take them far ahead and sustain them over the long haul. These are discussed in detail in Chapter 4.

References

1. Wikipedia.org. (n.d.). Mark Goyder. https://en.wikiquote.org/wiki/Mark_Goyder#:~:text=Governance%20and%20leadership%20are%20the,risk%20atrophy%2C%20bureaucracy%20and%20indifference

2. Perry, M. J. (2017). Fortune 500 Firms 1955 v. 2017: Only 60 Remain, Thanks to the Creative Destruction That Fuels Economic Prosperity. https://www.aei.org/carpe-diem/fortune-500-firms-1955-v-2017-only-12-remain-thanks-to-the-creative-destruction-that-fuels-economic-prosperity/

3. Charan, R. (2016). The Secrets of Great CEO Selection. Leadership Transitions. *Harvard Business Review.* https://hbr.org/2016/12/the-secrets-of-great-ceo-selection

4. Garratt, B. (1997). *The Fish Rots from the Head: The Crisis in Our Boardrooms: Developing the Crucial Skills of the Competent Director.* New York, NY: HarperCollins.

5. Useem, M. (2006). How Well-Run Boards Make Decisions. *Harvard Business Review*, Vol. 84, No. 11, pp. 130–138. https://pubmed.ncbi.nlm.nih.gov/17131569/

6. Ostrower, F., and Stone, M. M. (2006). Governance: Research Trends, Gaps, and Future Prospects. In *The Nonprofit Sector: A Research Handbook*, edited by W. W. Powell and R. Steinberg, pp. 612–628. New Haven, CT: Yale University Press.

7. Zar, J. H. (1984). *Biostatistical Analysis*, Table B19, 2nd ed. Englewood Cliffs, NJ: Prentice Hall.

8. ETCFO. (2020, 2 March). Independent Directors Prefer Resignation over MCA Tests. https://cfo.economictimes.indiatimes.com/news/independent-directors-prefer-resignation-over-mca-tests/74439146

9. Bhattacharya, R. (2019, 26 December). Resignations by Independent Directors Double in 2019 as Risks Grow. *The Economic Times*. https://economictimes.indiatimes.com/news/company/corporatetrends/resignations-byindependentdirectorsd oublein2019asrisksgrow/articleshow/72972968.cms?utm_ source=contentofinterest&utm_medium=text&utm_ campaign=cppst

10. Vijayraghavan, K., and Phillip, L. (2019, 20 November). Worried Independent Directors No Longer Keen to Hold Board Seats. *The Economic Times*. https://economictimes.indiatimes. com/news/company/corporate-trends/worried-independent-directors-no-longer-keen-to-hold-board-seats/articleshow/72135108.cms?utm_source=contentofinterest&utm_medium=text&utm_campaign=cppst

4

TOWARDS VALUE-ADDING BOARDS: RECOMMENDATIONS

The real strategic differentiation is to create true value, look forward, not backward....

—Pearl Zhu

Indian Boards: Key Concerns Regarding Business-related Thrust

Chapter 3 sought to empirically answer the fundamental question posed by this work regarding Indian boards: Are they **value adding** or **value destroying?** Findings of our research brought out that Indian boards are adding value to a limited extent, as they are more focused on the present and give inadequate attention to preparing the organization for the future. They focus more on compliance. On the business side, Indian companies and boards do focus on factors such as cost, quality and customer focus. However, strategy, innovation, ethical orientation and people power—the key levers for building future-focused and sustainable competitive advantage—are hardly discussed by Indian boards. In fact, there appears to be strong inward and bureaucratic orientations which characterize Indian companies, and both hamper organizational effectiveness and growth.

The key question, however, is whether the focus on the trio of factors, namely cost, quality and customer focus, is static (a one-time improve it and leave it approach); does it consist of incremental improvement (bits and pieces of improvement) or is it a dynamic process which is continually taking the company up the value chain in the never-ending dance of disruption and transformation. As Chapter 2 brought out, static improvements can no longer give a company much competitive advantage. Indian companies must seriously focus on those factors which can take them far ahead and sustain them over the long haul. A combination of incremental and dynamic improvement—at the level of customer, cost and quality—would be an important strategy.

In order to become value-adding boards that provide strategic leadership, board members need to have a reasonable understanding of the business context and the challenges faced by companies; they need mindset shifts, strategic thinking and actions, and prepare the organization to be in alignment with the above-stated actions (strategic thrust, organizational structure, technology, etc.). This chapter discusses these issues in greater detail.

A detailed analysis of the winning strategies utilized by great companies of the 21st century have been brought out in Chapter 2. The key thrust of this chapter is to lay emphasis on the types of shifts which companies need to make to become more competitive and sustainable. It goes without saying that managements of companies are the ones who need to have a close grasp on the nitty-gritty of building competitiveness on all fronts of the organization. Board members, however, need to have at least a reasonable understanding of issues and challenges faced by the organization, so that they can ask relevant and critical questions, draw the attention to relevant issues, monitor key factors, give the clearance for mobilization of resources for future-focused strategies and so on. Chapter 4 has been written in this spirit.

Issues and Challenges of Board-level Strategic Leadership

The Biggest Business Challenge Today

The current business environment can be likened to a war—a war where the enemy can come from anywhere and attack, a war where the organization cannot afford to be off guard and a war where the enemy has technologically sophisticated weapons to reach the customer and make other companies in the field irrelevant. The business war is a strange war, as it can be waged without attacking directly, a war where entire business can be wiped out without companies even becoming aware of what is happening until it is too late.

Strategies of such leading companies are based on the power of technology, AI, robotics and big data analysis which they use to maintain their lead. They stay much ahead of the competition propelled by their future-focused strategies, well-developed people power and the power of ideas and innovation. As one of the largest markets in the world, India has become a fertile ground for wars among companies who want to win a larger market share.

In order to stay relevant in such a context, Indian companies have no choice but to raise themselves to world-class levels and develop weapons that can help them take on the competition. The new opportunities being currently thrown up owing to geopolitical shifts must be quickly embraced. Companies must develop and use all the weapons that are available out there, learn from the competition and prepare themselves to stay relevant. This chapter discusses the weapons that can help Indian companies fight the war and stay relevant for a longer time period.

In such a daunting scenario, Indian boards have a key role to play so that they can enable organizations to build sustainable competitive edge. The key question is how can boards add value to the organizations that they head? This part aims to bring out the ways and means by which boards can provide strategic leadership to the companies they head.

Both the paradigms of doing business and the mindsets of Indian business leaders and board members need to shift from the old economy priorities and tactics to address the new contextual realities. As the famous saying goes, 'it's all in the mind'. Unless boards change the lens used to view their own collective role and responsibility and embrace their complete role (Appendix E), lasting change in how they address board-level challenges and actions is just not possible.

This chapter is presented in the following three parts.

Part 1. Back to the basics: The first step in the process of bringing such transformation is to bring shifts in the **mindsets**

and attitude of boards and top teams of companies, and, therefore, it entails boards going back to the basics.

The purpose of business and strategy priorities of the organization must be recast more in alignment with both current and emerging future business realities.

Part 2. Needed—a dynamic new business model based on continuous alignment with and anticipation of customer needs and aspirations: The three key weapons of business are the enduring trio of *customer centricity*, *cost and quality leadership* and *time to the market* albeit with one change, they must be dynamic and ever changing in line with customer-, context- and competitor-related changes. The dynamic component requires that companies make continuous innovation the centrepiece of their business model.

Part 3. The enablers of the dynamic business model: The key enablers are agile work system, ambidextrous organization design, appropriate work culture to support dynamic movement and change in anticipation of customer needs and aspirations, and ways to unleash people power.

Part 1. Back to the Basics: Recast Purpose and Strategy of the Organization

Recasting the strategic vision of the company depends on shifting of the board and top team to four kinds of mindsets and attitudes. These are as follows.

Mindset Shift 1. Wealth extraction to wealth creation
Mindset Shift 2. Enfold future into the present
Mindset Shift 3. Build a winning vision
Mindset Shift 4. Creative destruction

The purpose of wealth creation and growth through exploration of opportunities and optimization of the existing value proposition necessitates that Indian firms pursue the strategy of continuous innovation. This involves both sustaining innovation (important for organizational survival) and disruptive innovation (important for organizational growth). Both must form the basis of the strategic tactics of denting the opponent and defending (the organization) from attacks. In fact, innovation is not a stand-alone activity, rather it must be seamlessly embedded as the **centrepiece of the business strategy** of a company.

Mindset Shift 1. From Wealth Extraction to Wealth Creation

Indian companies need to uproot themselves from the strategies and tactics relevant in the old economy context. They need to move from the paradigm of wealth extraction which was at one time the dominant focus of businesses—riding on the power of business process re-engineering, downsizing, cost-cutting, six sigma, financial restructuring, etc. to squeeze the maximum out of their business. The importance and relevance of such efforts, no doubt, still exist and are at the core of incremental innovation. However today, incremental innovation is simply not adequate for firms to be sustainably competitive.

The mindset of the company must shift to wealth creation. Instead of simply staying ahead of their competitors, such wealth-creating companies will provide value and enjoy a lasting competitive edge through market-creating innovations. Innovations provide goods or services that delight a whole new group of customers beyond expectations and make them demand more and more. These customers then create a new market for the firm, thereby disrupting the existing market through innovation.

Market-creating innovations happen because companies explore opportunities and innovate solutions in their quest for wealth creation. Iconic products from Apple, Xerox and Starbucks came about because of such exploration of opportunities and innovating solutions, thereby putting these companies miles ahead of their competitors. Such companies attained high growth and profitability by creating value for customers in an uncontested market space (blue ocean), rather than competing in a red ocean, bloodied by numerous battles between competitors fighting for market share. According to Sun Tzu,[i] the legendary Chinese philosopher, the best **strategy in a war is to be victorious without shedding even a drop of blood.** What the Indian firm needs to do is to continuously look at creating value from the customers' point of view.

Mindset Shift 2. Prepare Today for Tomorrow: Enfold the Future into the Present

Every board needs to cultivate a Janus-faced approach and have an eye both on the realities of today and the opportunities and challenges of tomorrow. The company must have a vision for the near future, which should clearly articulate the purpose of its business. It should be action oriented and time bound as well as aspirational and measurable. The vision should be such that it can help the company to begin with the end in mind, craft an appropriate strategy and make strategic choices to compete and win.

Firms and their boards must be sensitive to the context, as it is the context that helps define the right action to cope with the challenges thrown up by the context. As Sun Tzu said, '…know the weather and know the ground, and your victory will then be complete'. The competitive business landscape has always been likened to a war. Firms must look around and look beyond to know what the context of business will be much in advance so that they can strategize and build their capabilities for it. They must visualize how the technology, product, consumer and competitors will evolve over time.

In a world where most of the decisions and solutions are data driven, the vision for tomorrow would definitely be assumption driven and based upon abductive reasoning and logical deduction. But the 'sound of the unborn child' can be heard only by those who are prescient, who have alert antenna and whose senses are trained for the unknown. It is, therefore, vital for the boards and top teams of the firm to continually monitor the unfolding reality and to periodically revisit and revise their vision. The whole idea is that the more well prepared the firm is, the greater is the likelihood that it will be able to seize the opportunity when it presents itself; the well-known quote 'chance favours the prepared mind' (Louis Pasteur) is appropriate in this context. Further, it will help the company identify looming threats and competitors. This will help them devise their strategic tactics as to whom to dent and from whom to defend. This is the strategy of enfolding the future into the present and about preparing today keeping tomorrow in mind.

Mindset Shift 3. Build a Winning Vision

Winning vison creates excitement. It captures the imagination of people, provides them with a sense of meaning and purpose to move collective energies in the needed direction. The more inspirational the content and the more it is actualized by the management, the more people accept the vision. In a world where all sources of competitive advantage soon disappear, it is people and the unlocking of their potential by vision and values that give the firm a competitive edge. In the emerging context, a vision can excite employees and others, when it has both a business and a social component, for example, doing good to society and to the environment, taking care of multiple stakeholders, extending reach to the needy in society and so on. The value priorities of millennials are such that they are no more excited by business goals alone. Organizations need to factor the social component into the vision statement.

Vision building cannot remain an HR activity. Instead it needs to be a collective effort led by the CEO or the entrepreneur. It should involve the opinion leaders, people with ideas, those occupying key positions in the organization and the stakeholders who are close to action. There should be structured dialogue with clients, suppliers, partners, junior employees in the frontline of research, marketing and sales. Deep diving with domain experts from within the industry and, more importantly, outside the industry is vital for seeing industry, product and technology in motion. History is witness to the fact that most disruptions within one industry had their roots in other industries. Fundamentally, a vision is useful only when it is owned by the organizational community and, hence, by involving them in vision creation, this requirement can be met.

Members must be tasked with questions such as what unique purpose is the key to our existence? Where are we going and where should we be going as a company? They should be asked to visualize what the future will be like and how and where do they see the company in that envisioned future. This would help the company understand the emerging landscape of business and identify the future opportunities and threats. This in turn will guide the firm in deciding the strategic initiatives, action steps and organizational mechanisms necessary for strategic execution and thus the realization of the vision.

The whole exercise of vision building should be held together by the senior leadership team so that the vision is sustainable. The company board also needs to be with the senior leadership team. Jack Dorsey, the founder of Twitter, has put it aptly, 'I don't want to build a company that is dependent upon any one person, including me … I want to build a company that survives the death of its founder and continues to carry on the same mindset'.

Mindset Shift 4. Creative Destruction: Life Begins from Death

'Life begins from death'. This is a profound Indian saying and aptly describes the relevance of creative destruction. Creative destruction is an important route for a company to stay innovative, youthful, lithe and ever renewing.

Creative destruction is the act of deliberately removing parts of the organization which are no longer adding value. It means that the company must give up their old habits and ways of doing business and substitute them with new and more appropriate approaches. In this activity, the top management must be guided by the vision and values of the company. It is in the backdrop of the vision as the North Star that a seemingly destructive step like Jack Welch's closure of businesses where the company was neither Number 1 or 2 or 3 starts making sense. A. G. Lafley began his second stint as P&G's CEO, with a strategic decision to weed the garden, selling off businesses in at least half a dozen of P&G's industry categories despite the fact that all of them were profitable. As he put it, 'Our strategy, in Peter Drucker's terms, was one of systematic abandonment. We wanted to free up the scarce resources, people, and cash to fund the innovations that were necessary to enter new businesses and transform important existing businesses.'

Creative destruction helps to push companies out of the comfort zone of the present and helps to push them beyond complacency. Top teams and board of companies must guard against cognitive closure. Being open minded is key to a company restlessly finding new ways to succeed. Such companies are more likely to explore and understand the changing needs of the customer as also to innovate new process and new solutions in keeping with the fast-changing business context.

In the contemporary world, the basic requirement for all firms seeking sustainable growth is to search for new opportunities, while optimizing the existing growth engine.

Exploration for the 'new' must happen hand in hand with exploitation of the 'existing opportunity'. This would require the firm to either innovate to improve its current offering and stay ahead of competition or innovate a new business model and disrupt the industry. It is crucial for firms to identify and seize new growth opportunities before the existing growth curve starts plateauing. Firms must remember the famous phrase of Marshall Goldsmith, 'What got us here, won't take us there'. Staying put and doing nothing can be suicidal. The success story of Intel proved that only the paranoid company survives. Firms must constantly analyze the competition, its determinants and drivers and find ways and means to stay ahead. Creative destruction does not just require a mindset change. It also demands that the functionaries right from the board to the other key stakeholders inside and outside the organization must be conscious of the fact that it is continuous innovation alone that can give them sustainable competitive edge, growth and success.

The Strategic Vision: Checklist for the Board and CEO

- Does my company have a dream?
- Has this dream been converted into a clearly articulated vision?
- What is the distinctive winning characteristic of the vision?
- Is the vision pitched at a higher level touching the larger issues and concerns of humanity?
- Does the vision have global reach and depth?
- Does the vision have an emotive content to inspire people?
- Are the strategy, structure and systems aligned with the vision?
- Is it a shared vision?
- Is the vision formulated through collective consensus or is it imposed?

- Are organizational members passionately committed to actualizing the vision?
- How often is the vision discussed, deliberated and talked about in the company?
- What percentage of revenue is derived from wealth creation mode as compared to the wealth extraction mode?
- What are the opportunities which could have been utilized but were missed or not capitalized by the company?
- How do we compare on product and service innovation vis-à-vis the top three companies in our industry segment?
- What is the percentage of revenue accrued from new products?
- Are the following examined from time to time?

    o What is our business?
    o Where is our business at this point of time?
    o What do we want to achieve in three to five years of time?
    o What do we want to achieve in 10 years of time?
    o What are our strengths and weaknesses?
    o What are the opportunities and threats vis-à-vis evolution of market, customer preferences, technological development, government policy change, business landscape and competitor's plans and moves?
    o Do we have the necessary resource and capability to withstand threat and seize opportunities?
    o Are we equipped to deal with the unforeseen?

Part 2. The Key Weapons

As mentioned earlier, the purpose of wealth creation through continuous innovation requires firms to have a business model that is centred around what customers value, how such value can be created, at what cost and at what price, and how it can be delivered. A business model is all about how enterprises need to work to capture value or to put it simply, make money. At the centre of this winning business model must be (a) customer centricity, (b) cost and quality leadership and (c) time to market. These are the key weapons which Indian firms need to develop in order to carve a sustainable competitive edge in the corporate Mahabharata. Winning the corporate war depends upon the extent to which Indian firms are able to mobilize and deploy these weapons, both faster and better than their rivals.

This part now presents the three weapons.

Weapon 1. Customer centricity
Weapon 2. Cost and quality leadership
Weapon 3. Time to market

Weapon 1. Customer Centricity

Customer centricity is about keeping customers (present and future) and their changing needs and wants central to the wealth-creating purpose of the company and meet these needs. Companies must, therefore, continuously innovate to outcompete their rivals. They can do so only when they anticipate and understand the needs of the customers. Involving the customer to co-create solutions, therefore, becomes the most fruitful strategy for any firm seeking sustainable competitive edge. In sum, to be customer centric, a firm must do the following:

1. Treat the customer as God and the centre of your universe
2. Understand the customer and his/her changing needs and wants
3. Involve customers in co-creating solutions for him/her
4. Innovate to provide and deliver value better than the rivals

1. **Treat customer as God and centre of the company's universe:** The raison d'être of every firm is the customer. As Mahatma Gandhi said, 'customer is God'. Firms survive only so long as the customer sees value in their goods and services. It is the customer who is the source of all opportunities, the biggest threat and the sole reason for the survival and success of firms. As one CEO of a leading international petroleum company said, 'The new order ... reminds us that companies, however big, are simply servants of society. We exist only because someone wants to buy what we provide' [1]. Companies must put customers at the centre and reorient their strategies around customers' requirement. The ability to provide value to the customer defines the competitiveness of the firm. In a free and competitive market, it is the customer who is the real sovereign. Those firms that recognized the sovereignty of the customer and sought to listen, learn, anticipate and satisfy the ever-evolving needs and wants have, more often than not, tasted success. Innovation is nothing but explorations striving to provide customers with better value in the creation and delivery of goods or services. It is high time that the mindset of Indian companies shifts from the trading mentality of making quick gains to a customer service mentality of building enduring relationships. If they do so, innovations will be inevitable and continuous innovation will become part of their DNA.

2. **Understand the customer:** Firms must have a dynamic and continuous interaction with the customer. This will enable them to know the mind of the customer and gather information regarding his/her needs, aspirations and above all frustrations. Firms must treat non-consumers as potential customers, target them and understand their specific needs and provide innovative solutions. They must try to identify the problem the customer is struggling to solve today and catch any signal that

the customer is emitting to show his/her dissatisfaction with the status quo. They should observe the current trends in customers' buying behaviour, strategic moves of the competitor and the evolution of technologies and be on the lookout for signals of change at the periphery. Various techniques can be used to get hold of information and data sources. It is a truism that customers don't buy goods or services, nor do they buy what the companies sell.

Wendell Weeks of Corning Glass said,

> your customer is unlikely to give you the disruptive idea because if they could, they wouldn't need you ... What they can do is identify their pain. Customers are really good at understanding it, but they don't always know how to solve their pain. You should listen to the problem and then ... figure out how to solve it [2].

Firms must be sensitive to the customer. They should have a robust mechanism to access and gather the 'voice of customers' with ease and speed and distortion free. This will not only provide feedback on the quality of their product or service, it will also them help them understand customers' experience and expectations.

In today's world of big data and digital technology, companies must use digital technologies to acquire information and data on customer needs. Capabilities in AI, ML and data science can help them gain insights into customer behaviour and choices. Today, most of this data gets generated in the mobile ecosystem and search engines like Google. Firms should have the capability to access such information, interpret it and respond to it. 'Chatbots' constitute an extremely useful tool to connect with the customer in real time and acquire information about his/her needs, product preferences and pain points.

However, despite the growth of technology-driven customer care initiatives, some things continue to be relevant, namely person-to-person contact and relationship marketing. There is everything to be gained by companies whose CEOs and top people meet customers to appreciate the 'moments of truth' in the words of Jan Carlson. CEOs and senior management of several companies in India and abroad use Twitter handles to connect directly with the people. Corporate czars such as Ratan Tata, Anand Mahindra and Nandan Nilekani and czarinas like Kiran Mazumdar Shaw are extremely active on social media with millions of followers. Such direct connect with customers contributes a lot to enhance corporate reputation and reinforce the brands. Companies can benefit when top managements maintain a significant and active social media presence.

3. **Co-create with customers:** In today's dynamic and complex context, it is desirable for firms, irrespective of whether they are a B2B or a B2C entity, to co-create value with their customers.

Co-creation requires a whole mindset change to get the voice of the customer in the board room, in the design cubicle, in the production room and in the marketing den. Co-creation depends upon the extent to which a firm has constant dialogue with its customers. Dialogue with customers must consist of direct exchange of information and opportunity for customers to share their views on value, value creation and value delivery process.

In the contemporary world, the community of customers is the new source of competence of a firm. The leadership now needs to view their enterprise as an extended portfolio of competences which exist both within and outside the firm. In fact, it is the acquisition of collective knowledge available with the suppliers, manufacturers, partners and consumers which will give a competitive edge to the modern-day firm. It will be only then that a company will be able to innovate solutions and deliver experiences beyond expectations. The centrality of customers and the configuring of the business model around them are the twin principles for both innovation-based growth and sustainable competitive edge.

4. **Innovate for enhancing customer value:** The experience of companies indicates that need-based marketing research cannot take companies very far. It will lull them into believing that incremental improvements in the existing product or service will be enough to satisfy existing customers. This is the easiest way of getting disrupted and blown out of the business. There are also several instances where customers have been found to like something better but would not prefer to pay extra for it. Firms thus should not 'overshoot', that is, create solutions that more than meets the customer's needs. Before innovating and adding any attribute, they should ask the fundamental questions: Will this be valued by the customer? Will the customer pay extra for it? After all, how many people would have agreed to pay for an extra blade in a Gillette Mach 3 cartridge and thus for an extra smooth shave. Beyond a point it would not matter to the customer. Firms should also draw lessons from the smartphone makers who sacrificed pixels and realistic photos so as to ensure easy and fast picture sharing and connectedness—the reason why people preferred smartphone over traditional camera.

In order to win, firms must disrupt what customers value. This is the strategy of the blue ocean. Disruptive innovation requires and must be preceded by disruptive thinking. Firms must constantly analyse what would be the impact on their offering and sales if they were to cut the product or service features by say 20 per cent and price by say around 80 per cent. This does not mean firms should introduce inferior products or services. Instead, the purpose is to excite the thinking as what a company can do in order to make that product simpler, convenient or affordable for the customers. Thinking disruptively can help a firm to seek new directions.

PCs, discount retailers, Uber ride sharing and Airbnb are illustrations of firms who disrupted by creating new markets and transforming the existing ones through simplicity, convenience, affordability and accessibility of their offerings.

Innovation in terms of customer value creation is neither about taking a shot in the dark nor an isolated and serendipitous activity conducted in the c-suite or in marketing break out rooms. Innovation in value creation is a humble, social, collective and systematic enterprise based on inputs from stakeholders. Firms need to solicit and follow product reviews, do crowd sourcing, organize hackathons, etc. They should use customer journey maps to identify new opportunities to serve the customer better. They should gather customer insights through online forums, customer meets, product launches and experiences of start-ups. They should network with the iconoclast, the common man, the front-line staff, the handpicked external experts, venture capitalists and specialist external agency–patent readers and technology trackers. Above all, firms must look around to know what is happening in the adjacent industry. They must realize that most of the disruptive innovation came from outside an industry's mainstream. Several historically great companies—Kodak, Digital Equipment Corporation, Sears and General Motors—stumbled only because they toed the expected line. These Goliaths listened to their most important customers and innovated to meet their changing needs. In due course, all of them ended up getting knocked out by seemingly innocent Davids' armed with one disruptive innovation which wiped out their existing businesses.

Customer Centricity: Checklist for the Board and CEO

- What is the job for which the customer is hiring my product or service?
- Why is that the non-consumers are not hiring my product or service? Do they have emerging unmet needs?

- What job is the customer struggling to get done? What are their dissatisfiers and needs?
- Do our products have more features or complexity than needed?
- Are the customers buying our product or service because they do not have any alternative?
- Who are the key people who will use the product or service and what are their jobs to be done?
- Who are the key people involved in the decision to purchase?
- Will the proposed idea ease the customer's pain? Can there be more cheap, convenient, accessible and better quality alternative to that idea?
- Could emerging technology simplify how end user's needs will be met?
- Will customers define quality differently tomorrow?
- What do customers, competitors, experts, technology-trend watchers across industries have to contribute about evolving needs, technology and change in customer tastes and preferences?

Weapon 2. Cost and Quality Leadership

In business, there are three perennial questions: Who are our target customers? What value we want to deliver? How we can create and deliver value? There are two supplementary but more significant questions with huge implications on strategizing: At what cost? And at what Price?[ii] One of the dangers of low-cost strategy is that it may turn out to be just denominator management. Firms pursuing competitive advantage only through denominator management will always be vulnerable to the next introduction of cost-reducing technology and process-optimization drives.

Only when 'denominator management' is used to complement 'numerator management' rooted in innovation-based growth that firms can create sustainable competitive edge. Numerator management is all about what customers value. S/he is bothered about price or simply stated, value for money. It is the value proposition that matters. It is not that costs are not important. They are important from the point of view of margin and what a company does with the margin. The key question is: Does the company use that margin to provide superior value, vis-à-vis the rivals, to the customers? The answer to this question will determine what is the low-cost leadership strategy being used for: wealth creation or wealth extraction, increase the size of the pie or grab a bigger share of the existing pie.

This section is about what a firm should do in order to create and deliver products or services efficiently and economically. They should do the following:

1. [Transit] from vertically integrated to virtually integrated value chain
2. Use IT to enable and integrate business
3. Globalize for cost-efficient value chain and profitable market access
4. Price right to make target customers purchase
5. Complement cost leadership with quality leadership
6. [Transit] From operational excellence to operational innovation

1. From vertically integrated to virtually integrated value chain: Organizations of the 20th century operated on the mode of self-sufficiency and organized themselves to take care of every requirement on their own. Several Indian companies whether in coal, steel or manufacturing sectors invested in infrastructure to build power plants, rail routes, roads, ports, etc. In large automobile and engineering companies, divisions were established which manufactured components and spares. Companies built business models with integrated upstream and downstream businesses. They became conglomerates. They went into unrelated areas where they had no competencies and much less core competencies. Soon the inefficiencies related to investment in unrelated businesses, unproductive assets and bloated administrative and financials costs to support the oversized manpower started eating into the bottom line of the companies. The early 21st century saw the heat of global competition in which companies started divesting and outsourcing some of the activities from their value chain. Many conglomerates were dismantled to become core-competency focused, lean and efficient entities.

There is no doubt that such vertical integration still offers a lot of advantages, provided the company can pass on the benefits of costs, assurance of quality and speed, reliability and flexibility of supply to the customers. Firms that are in the small and medium enterprise (SME) sector or whose businesses are afflicted with fragmented supply chain and logistics can greatly benefit by vertically integrated value chains. Even the firms in the technology, apparel and retail business can derive immense cost benefits through vertical integration with direct-to-customer route. This is more so in the context of the internet and mobile-based economy.[iii]

Firms can also derive cost-efficiency through horizontal integration. Unlike vertical integration which involved ownership and control of different stages in the value chain process, horizontal integration involves mergers of two or more companies located at the same stage in production supply chain. The most famous recent example of horizontal integration is the acquisition of Instagram by Facebook, Pixar by Disney, Corus by Tata Steel and Idea by Vodafone. Horizontal integration will allow the acquiring company to grow its market share, reduce competition, gain cost-efficiency through institutional knowledge, expertise and synergies, and acquire new customers. The post-pandemic normal will probably see more and more firms going for mergers and acquisitions (M&A) for this reason. The opportunity will be just right for some Indian companies that have strong fundamentals and aspire to grow through M&A to enter and consolidate themselves in businesses pregnant with huge possibilities.

There are risks involved in vertical integration. These risks are associated with the possibility of the company moving away from its core business, inefficiencies related to scale and inventory, obsolescence due to new technologies and loss of flexibility. Above all, the risk could be owing to the inability to adapt because of stickiness of assets and investments. Companies may thus suffer because of over-integration. Companies must do a cost–benefit analysis to compare the advantages of full vertical versus full horizontal integration and then decide on the action that generates better value.

There are alternatives to full vertical integration. Firms can go for partial integration like Zara or Apple did and choose to keep only two stages out of three (between sourcing-manufacturing/wholesale-sales/retail) of the value chain under their ownership and control. In the world driven by e-commerce and m-commerce, many Indian firms, especially in the SME sector, can choose to do backward integration (from sourcing to manufacturing) and partner with an e-commerce platform for sales and delivery. They can also choose quasi-integration by forming strategic alliances and joint ventures. Reliance's recent move to collaborate with Amazon to take on the Flipkart–Walmart behemoth in the retail business is emblematic of times to come as firms will look to consolidate across sectors. The growth of the internet has also made it possible for companies to build relationships based upon long-term contracts with external partners. This will ensure that the company neither loses control over its assets nor will it have to bear the heavy costs of acquisitions. Above all, with the help of IT, the company will be able to derive the same benefits as it would derive from vertical integration.

Over a period of time, firms should transit from vertically integrated business architecture to virtually integrated architecture. A virtually integrated company would involve the decomposition of the traditional company. The company will just own the brand and the customer like Airtel did. Everything else, right from the design, system development, product sourcing, logistics and even final assembly can be outsourced to supply chain partners with whom the company can have informal arrangements. Shipments of components as also service of customer order will be done through the internet or networked computer system. The partners will be linked by information and not by assets. The company will use the internet to integrate with the customer process and cloud-based supply chain management to network with multiple partners (the platform linking many with many). Virtual integration will thus help the company by ensuring the convergence of core competence and outsourcing. It will help them erect a winning partner-based ecosystem that will provide not only cost efficiency but also access to markets across the globe. In a digital economy, this will prove to be a perfect business model.

2. **Use IT to integrate and enable business:** Firms should apply advances in ICTs to integrate each and every part of their business. They should use app-based meeting platforms and videoconferencing for real-time communications and e-mail for lagged communication. They should use digital technologies to track the item quantities, trigger an order of additional stock when needed and thus manage inventory. Digital versions of documents can be stored on servers and storage devices and could be made instantly available to everyone in the company, regardless of their geographical location. Blockchains can be used to keep immutable record of transactions, optimize processes and enhance trust among partners. Firms must use data as part of their strategic planning process as well as the planned execution of that strategy. They should

use digital technologies to track sales data, expenses and productivity levels. Even in customer relationship management, the use of IT can help the firm capture every interaction with the customer. This will not only generate data for the company, improve its responsiveness to customer concerns and provide inputs and insights for innovating solutions but will also provide an exhilarating experience to the customers. By being digitally integrated, a company will eliminate the bureaucratic and governance costs incurred in monitoring, control and coordination for more efficient and effective functioning of the organization.

3. **Globalize—from make for India to made by India:** Indian companies tend to be highly internally focused, owing perhaps to the large size of the domestic market or owing to mindset issues. The mentality of making quick gains resulted in Indian corporates focusing more on the short term and did not spur their aspirations to become global MNCs. The proof lies in the fact that domestic companies did not create a globally distributed value chain right from manufacturing to sales. It is important that Indian firms globalize their value chain in order to create and sustain a low-cost positioning. This can help them enter the global market as a finished goods player who can charge a premium for the products, rather than remain just an intermediate goods exporter. Above all, the need to meet global standards in terms of price and quality and the pressures of global competition would also force them to become cost and quality conscious and competitive vis-à-vis global brands in the domestic market.

To create a global value chain, the company will need to partition and sub-contract activities in the value chain (product development, manufacturing, sales and customer service) and create an ecosystem in which these activities are performed by partner specialist companies. Since these specialist firms will be driven by their own priority to cut costs and enhance value (through process and technological innovations and economies of scale), Indian companies located at the core can harvest the benefits upstream.[iv]

Even becoming part of the global value chain can yield immense benefits to Indian companies. They can capture the benefits accruing from being part of the global value chain as has been proven in industries such as computer software, pharmaceuticals and autos. They can thus move up the value chain in manufacturing and service, especially in sectors that are science based or high technology based where India has a comparative advantage of highly capable and huge science and technology manpower. To move up the value chain, however, Indian companies will be required to do significant optimization and improvement-focused innovation to become more cost-efficient, provide higher value along with desired quality and product attributes at low cost.

Globalization will, thus, facilitate the Indian firms to capture market growth, pursue global-scale efficiency, profit from knowledge arbitrage and provide coordinated source of supply to global customers. Above all, Indian firms can use their multi-market presence to cross-subsidize and wage the battle in the home market. This has been the story of several winning firms such as Mercedes Benz, Ford, General Electric, P&G, Walmart, American Express and Sheraton to name a few.

4. **Price right to make target customers purchase:** Customers, especially Indian customers, tend to be extremely price sensitive. Hence, for any firm competing on costs, pricing their product or services right becomes extremely strategic. This is especially true for innovative products. Those firms introducing new or novel products are perennially conflicted about their pricing strategy. Should they start with the market-skimming price in which higher price is charged from the early adopters? Should they then lower the market-skimming

price to attract majority of customers?[v] Or should the innovator company start with market penetration price and turn their innovation into a commodity? Both the strategies come with their own downsides and risks. The problem with the market-skimming strategy is that competitors may price their product lower than the innovator and lure away the market. Similarly, the problem with the market-penetration strategy is that any subsequent increase in the price would erode the market in the absence of brand loyalty.

Firms selling innovative solutions should segment their market based upon where the customers stood in the technology adoption life cycle. They should then position themselves and target the segments of early adopter, early majority, late majority and laggards differently. This is particularly relevant if the technology of the product requires change in the behaviour by the user as in the case of discontinuous innovation. The failure of Segway and 3D printer, both of which were highly path-breaking products, happened only because they fell in between the fault lines of the technology adoption life cycle. In any case, firms which are market leaders and early movers must continually improve and optimize through process innovation or undertake myriad cost-cutting initiatives while they cross the chasm between customer segments. It is this strategy which has given success to several low-cost airline companies such as Ryanair, easyJet and Indigo as also other B2B capital equipment market firms. Thus, innovation is not just a matter of technology, it is also about marketing.

5. **Complement cost leadership with quality leadership:** Companies such as Toyota, Singapore Airlines and Apple to name a few have enjoyed dual competitive advantage: cost leadership and quality leadership. In fact, their quality initiatives led to the manufacture of qualitatively superior products at lower cost due to savings accrual from lesser number of

rejects, reworks and returns. This is one of the key reasons why firms must invest in quality improvement programmes.

Since quality is a matter of both cost and time, firms must create a fine balance between appraisal costs (investment in ensuring quality) and external failure costs arising from rejects, returns, rework and erosion of customer and brand loyalty. Another trade-off for the company is between quality and speed due to extra time needed for addition of performance attributes and enhancement and measurement of quality.

6. **From operational excellence to operational innovation:** There are, however, limits to the advantages derived from operational excellence despite its impact on quality and costs. This is because the benefits emanating from improvement in product quality and cost reduction are not sustainable. In the world of information diffusion and rapid obsolescence of products, cost structures can be easily duplicated by the competitors. This is more so when the existing mode of operations remains the same. The customer prefers to wait for the cheaper version from the competitor and thus postpones the expensive purchase from the original innovator firm.

To combat this tendency, firms seeking sustainable competitive edge must develop an entirely new way of work accomplishment. Companies like Walmart innovated in purchase and distribution of goods. Dell, Toyota and Shell are other examples of companies that were successful at operational innovation where time, cost and customer satisfaction all got enhanced.[vi]

In the world of disruptive change, sustainable competitive edge can, therefore, happen only when firms re-imagine their business process. This would mean firms re-examining how work is done, how jobs are designed, how departments coordinate, how performance is measured and rewarded and how the organization is designed. It is also about the implementation methodology. Operational innovation is a matter of iteration, evolution and spiral development. It is quite unlike the improvement implementation which is end goal envisioned, specified, fixed and unchanging.

Cost and Quality Leadership Checklist for the Board and CEO

- What are the cost drivers in the activity value chain of the product or services offered by the company? (Note: This would vary across industries, firms and activities.)
- Does the company perform competitive cost benchmarking of its activities in the value chain to identify its cost position vis-à-vis its rivals and industry?
- Does the company design appropriate interventions based upon its evaluation of the following cost drivers?

  o **Economies of scale:** Arising out of technical input/output relationship, indivisibilies, specialization and fixed cost.

  o **Economies of scope:** Arising out of a range of products and services to be produced, market to be served and customer to be managed.

  o **Learning curve:** Both at individual and activity levels and reflected in scheduling, labour productivity, asset utilization, product development and manufacturing process and material usage.

  o **Capacity utilization:** As a function of seasonal, cyclical demand as well as demand and supply fluctuations.

  o **Linkages:** Internally among various activities and externally with suppliers and channels.

  o **Interrelationships:** Transfer and sharing of various assets, managerial capabilities, know-how and learning from one division or business to another within the overall portfolio.

  o **Degree of integration:** From vertical to virtual, from backward and forward to whole enterprise architecture, from activities done in-house to activities contracted out and partnered in the world of open innovation and co-creation.

o **Timing:** Costs emanating from being a first mover, access to market, best location, best talent and best partner vis-à-vis the risk of failure and cost of market development.

o **Institutional:** Laws and legislations relating to labour, environment, resource use, transactions or in one word the tangible and intangible costs of doing business.

- What are the constraints the company faces in bringing about operational improvement and operational innovation?
- What are the processes among the following that can be re-imagined in the firm for bringing about operational innovation?

o What work needs to be produced?

o Who will do it?

o Where will it be done?

o When will it be performed?

o What are the circumstances in which it will or will not be performed?

o What will be the information required by those charged with work performance?

o What should be the magnitude and intensity with which work needs to be performed?

Weapon 3. Time to Market: Speed Is the Mantra to Win

Every morning both the lion and the gazelle have to run, each for different reasons. The lion chases the gazelle for food, while the gazelle runs to save its life. The lion knows that if it does not run fast enough, it will die of starvation; the gazelle also knows if it does not outrun the lion, it will be caught and devoured. Both of them have to run for their survival. In the corporate jungle today, it is not so much about the big eating up the small, it is more that the faster one eats up the slow. Many examples of companies such as Domino's, Amazon Prime, UPS and Uber prove the point about speed becoming the source of competitive advantage.[vii]

Among 135 odd pharmaceutical companies from all over the world racing against time and with each other to come up with life-saving vaccine to counter coronavirus, there are just 3 firms in Phase III, while the rest are still stuck in Phase I. It is also about flexibility and reconfiguring the entire innovation process. In the age of mobile-based economy and instant gratification, the notion of time as the basis of competitive advantage[viii] has become the key differentiator separating the winners from the losers.

Time to market is a key weapon in the competitive war. This will mean firms will have to meet customer needs and respond to the market changes faster than the competitor. This is the only way a firm can survive, grow and succeed sustainably. The phenomena of time to market depends upon how quickly a firm is able to pivot from sensing customer needs to developing solutions and from developing solutions to hitting the market. Firms that outpace their rivals in doing so will harvest profitability and growth. To ensure speedy and timely reach to the market, a firm will need to reconfigure its entire value chain architecture right from developing innovative solutions to the manufacturing and supply chain and finally to sales and service.

In accordance with the flow of the value chain, this section discusses what the firm needs to do at different stages of the value chain in order to compress time and space.

1. Use data and digital technology for sensing needs and opportunities
2. Use cross functional teams to speedily devise solutions

3. Speedily innovate products through collaborative models: lead user and open innovation
4. Use lean start-up methodology to hit the turf running
5. Use advanced manufacturing technologies to accelerate production
6. Digitize the entire supply chain to ensure fast, flexible and reliable delivery

1. Use data and digital technology for sensing needs and opportunities: Innovations begin from customer needs and expectations and require firms to speedily scan and sense the evolving needs and expectations of present as well as future customers. They should gather data from multiple sources—vendors, competitors, customers and the public. Ideas can also be gathered from other industries—BMW's iDrive idea came from the joystick used in gaming industry.

'Lead users' (customers who are advanced users of products and who try out solutions on their own) are invaluable to firms to understand the needs, problems, expectations and experiences of the customer and can be a great source of ideas for innovation. Interestingly, products ranging from PCs and 3D printers to hair colours to skateboards, mountain bikes, Gatorade drinks, surgical drapes of 3M, etc. have all been pioneered by 'lead users'. Although identification of lead users is a difficult and time-taking process, looking at the importance of the lead user and the threat from small and agile rivals, firms should make efforts to track them.

Traditionally, such customers were identified through a time-consuming and painstaking process involving mass screening of large number of customers, questionnaire-based survey, emails, social media interaction, personal interviews, etc. Today, technology[ix] helps firms to shrink the time taken by firms to identify and access the lead user from 6 months to just 14 days. The lead user mechanism tells us that firms should not solely depend upon marketing research to generate ideas for innovations. Instead, the lead user identification process should be made a useful part of the marketing research and corporate product development process.

Today, firms also have an entire toolkit of sophisticated digital technology (AI, ML and IoT) and data science to gather and optimally (even without human involvement) analyse data. We live in the world of web-based economy and mobile ecosystem. Every click, every swipe, every text on the search engine, the company website and the smartphone releases valuable data about people's habits, tastes and interests. Such data is invaluable for the company to design and develop solutions that are relevant, personalized and specific for its customers.

2. Use cross functional teams to devise speedy solution: Once data is gathered, the company should use the mechanism of customer-focused cross functional teams to speedily develop solutions. Cross functional teams should adopt agile development principles of working where teams are dedicated to developing and driving specific products to the market. This will enable team members to concentrate and work with focus for project completion rather than being distracted by myriad responsibilities. Teams will perform much better by using agile methods which involve sprints of 1–4 weeks in which specific questions are answered to narrow down options and at the end of which a prototype is developed and tested with the market until a minimally viable product is developed. The team should be encouraged to use effective group decision-making techniques such as brainstorming and design thinking to enable quick and optimal decisions. They should be empowered to take decisions. The firm should also create the necessary organizational architecture for the rapid implementation of their solutions.

3. Speedily innovate through collaborative models: In a volatile market, the firm with new and better offerings wins.

The innovation speed of a firm depends upon two factors: (a) the capability, strategy and organization of the product development team and (b) speedy transition from one phase to another like from product development to market. In view of the fact that Indian companies do not spend much on internal R&D, the technical capability of the new product development team may not be advanced in comparison to the global rivals. Indian firms, therefore, will be able to derive immense benefits if they collaborate with external partners. They should use the open innovation model and collaborate with others.

By partnering with other firms and institutions in the open innovation model, Indian firms will realize tremendous benefits. Partnerships will facilitate partitioning of tasks and thus division of labour, especially in those areas where the firm does not have technical competence. Working parallelly on different components would not only reduce project development time but will also save on the resources available for the fund-starved Indian R&D community. Working with others will speedily enhance the learning curve of the firm, reduce the possibilities of rework and potential mistakes. The company will gain immensely on matters of costs, risks and time related to innovation.

It is important for the firms to decide whom to partner with. Partnering with members of the scientific community in universities and research institutes and participating in the government-promoted ecosystems like Make in India or Startup India or SIDBI Mitra can help firms acquire the cutting-edge capability at the frontiers of knowledge. On the other hand, collaboration with market partners such as customers, value chain partners, SMEs or high-tech start-ups will yield even more benefits. It will allow the firms access to latest market knowledge, consumer trends and other external developments. It will enhance the firm's ability to utilize external knowledge and clarity of understanding of customer needs in the pursuit of innovation. However, the success of this model, as also technological diffusion, will depend upon the firm's internal technical capability and learning capacity.

The recent example of several research institutions, pharmaceutical companies and governments across the world collaborating to speedily develop the vaccine to fight COVID-19 is a lesson for all the firms. Such collaboration among these institutions united by a common purpose has made them shrink the normal time duration for drug discovery from 14 plus years to just over a year. What can be possible in situations of crisis can also be possible in the normal world. It is just about the mindset of firms—whether to collaborate and share the benefits or be the lone ranger and reap all the profits.

4. Use lean start-up methodology to hit the turf running: Companies should not lose time by trying to come out with one final and perfect product. They should take advantage of the build–measure–learn methodology to incubate their new product development process and to build a minimum viable product. They should then launch it, get customer feedback, learn quickly, improve accordingly and then relaunch. The bottom line is to innovate fast and adapt the solution incrementally. The use and success of lean start-up methodology depend heavily on the mindset of the company and its top management. The corporate DNA should favour experimentation, failing fast, regrouping, learning and developing products iteratively and incrementally. In today's world, elaborate planning and protracted execution are not only a waste of time and resources but also a loss of competitive edge.

5. Use advanced manufacturing technologies to accelerate production: This is the world of Industry 4.0. The operating paradigm of this world is 'acceleration' based upon the convergence of connectivity, advanced analytics, automation and advanced manufacturing technologies. In the last century, most Indian companies chose the easy route of technological collaboration with foreign companies to take advantage of the opportunities offered by globalization, liberalization and deregulation. However, owing to the lack of robust internal R&D and continuous improvement in manufacturing processes and technology, India missed out on the revolution in simple manufacturing. It lost its competitive edge not only to China but also to countries such as Korea, Taiwan, Vietnam and Qatar. The 2020 post-pandemic flattening of the world and the shortening of the supply chains have given India another chance. The policy shift towards self-sufficiency and self-reliance immanent in *atmanirbharta* has opened up a world of possibilities for Indian firms. It is important for Indian firms to adopt as quickly as possible the manufacturing practices and processes characterizing Industry 4.0.

In the 20th century world, it was enough for firms to have just-in-time production system and flexible factories. Demand used to be forecast based upon data of past orders and customer signals for the future. But in today's world of demand shocks and volatility, autonomous planning based upon AI and ML algorithms has proved to be most robust and useful for demand forecasting and planning mechanism. Planning right across the value chain can be further optimized by the usage of advanced analytics. Firms should use computer-aided design, computer-aided manufacturing, advanced robotics and AI-induced IoT to design and manufacture products with speed and efficiency. Developments in 3D printing technology have made it possible for firms to quickly manufacture spares, jigs and product components. Process automation and physical automation using advanced robotics can be used to supplement labour in order to ensure productivity, quality and speed. Automated factories can be deployed to shrink changeover time. Firms should employ advanced factory management technique. Advances in factory management such as automated data collection through sensors and machine's programmable logic controllers and its display on live dashboards can be used to enable real-time monitoring and supervision of operations. Firms need not rely on manual and human-centric process for quality check and quality control. Quality check can be boosted by machine vision algorithm for automatic quality check based upon predictive analytics. Above all, firms can use radio frequency identification and blockchains for the purpose of counting, tracking and tracing of stock keeping units. The demands on manufacturing in the context of COVID-19 and the unlocking of bottled-up demand have made it important that firms should be a nerve centre or a tower to coordinate and control the entire manufacturing process. This will ensure fast, uninterrupted and reliable reach to the market.

Advances in manufacturing technology like 3D printing can also help firms to become competitive domestically and globally. Firms can economize and become more cost-efficient by choosing to outsource production to external partners rather than developing solutions in-house. Now, firms also need not concentrate all manufacturing in one place. They can now distribute manufacturing to locations nearer to the market and ensure speedy supply of products or services to that market. It is this model which is being used by leading pharmaceutical companies to manufacture and deliver COVID-19 vaccines across the world. The global–local manufacturing model can be a feasible one for firms that seek to globalize to speedily access its global customers.

6. Digitize supply chain to reduce cycle time and order fulfilment time: Firms should take advantage of the developments in the world of supply chain with their programmes on 'plan, make, source and deliver'. They should use cognitive computing and AI tools to manage sourcing, selection of suppliers and monitoring of performance. Firms can utilize advances in automated warehouse and introduce blockchain to ensure cost savings (paperless transactions), data verification, asset tracking, smart contracts, accountability and compliance. Firms should also think of investing in or developing digitally integrated networks and in creating structured collaboration model. Data 'clean rooms' and digital marketplace can be used to create fast and flexible supply chain. Firms, particularly those in apparel business, using e-commerce platforms not only need to ensure personalized products and services but also speedy order fulfilment, and reliable and timely delivery. Above all, they should ensure quick returns and replacements.

Firms should know their customer, segment them, tailor individuated personalized offerings and engage them at each step of their customer journey. They should use advances in digital technology to recommend products, optimize campaigns, provide customer care and personalize advertising. With the emergence of the mobile-based economy, firms need to ensure faster loading of their websites and easy navigation to push sales. This is essential for all those firms that seek to sell products in areas with poor and unreliable net connectivity. This also means that the applications and websites have to get constantly updated and that too with zero downtime.

The search for improvement in time to the market is a ceaseless process. Firms must learn lessons from the Olympians. Great Olympians such as Usain Bolt, Carl Lewis, Phelps and Thorpe became great not because they won gold in the Olympics. It is because they won medals in several Olympics. This they did only because they'd start preparing for the next Olympics the moment the current race would end. In fact, the best among them prepared to relentlessly break their own records. Firms must raise the bar every time they compete to outjump their fast catching up rivals. Firms can learn lessons from the way champion high jumpers changed the jump methodology from the scissors to the western roll to the straddle to the Fosbury flop to stay ahead of the competitors. One does not know what the new jump strategy will be tomorrow and as also how distant tomorrow will be from today. Disruption is the need of the hour. The time-based competition has facilitated innovations in business models. It is time that Indian firms reconceptualize their business as an information business. This would be the first step in their becoming game changers, at least domestically.

Time to the Market Checklist for Top Teams and Boards

- Does the organization conceive its business as an information business?
- Does the firm seek to break from the past by re-imagining its business process?
- Does the firm recognize that the bases of competition have shifted from scale, position and speed to adaptiveness?
- Does the firm use search data, social media, product ratings and competitor scans to generate data on the changing needs of customers?
- Does the firm employ digital technologies to build flexible and adaptive cycle times—longer for basic product, shorter for differentiated and express for seasonal products?
- How does the firm create, measure, cultivate and sustain learning and its sharing?
- Does the firm have an infrastructure built to enable speed—big data, data science, digital technologies, enterprise-wide information system, integrated architecture with suppliers and channel partners and agile supply chain system?

Part 3. Enablers of the Dynamic Business Model: Growth through Innovation

Many brilliant business strategies have failed because the enabling organizational structure and culture were not adequately aligned. Organizational architecture plays a key role in strategy implementation. Leading companies carefully craft the organizational architecture and align the same with organizational strategy and action agenda for growth. Poor organization design and structure results in a bewildering morass of contradictions: confusion within roles, lack of coordination among functions, failure to share ideas, slow decision-making, lack of responsiveness to environmental changes and poor performance. Good strategy implementation requires organizations to streamline the operations, drive appropriate behaviours in people and ensure a seamless flow of communication and coordination. For instance, when Tata Group bought Jaguar and Land Rover from Ford Motors in 2008, Jaguar was going through a serious crisis. Tata could successfully execute its strategy and could turn the company around, only after Jaguar and Land Rover were restructured into a single legal entity. In March 2018, the joint entity made a record sale of more than 9,000 units in a month and emerged as a role model for its organizational design. The architecture of the organization enabling the strategy of growth through innovation should have the following characteristics:

1. Ambidextrous organizational form for exploitation and exploration
2. Agile organizational process for speed and flexibility
3. Entrepreneurial work culture and people power

Enabler 1. Ambidexterity: From Organizing for Exploitation to Organizing for Exploration

A typical Indian organization is characterized by a tall hierarchy, thick boundaries between functions/divisions, centralized decision-making, bureaucratic control, tightly defined roles, clear-cut responsibilities and standardized and rigid routines. Most of these organizations are run according to principles of management that took birth during the World War and the period of scarcity. The dominant paradigm was of organizations as machines and their strategic objectives were productivity, efficiency, predictability and stability. Tasks and people were grouped in terms of the functions. As companies grew, they differentiated their products and geographies. That is how the famous M-form, or the divisional structure, conceptualized in General Motors and popularized by Chandler in the management lexicon became appropriate. These were self-contained units in which people drawn from different functional areas were grouped to perform tasks arising from the unique nuances and specificities of product and its environment. In such organizations whenever integration of activities was required, that activity got centralized, such as strategy, R&D, HR, legal, advertising and promotions, and public relations. Some organizations changed to the matrix structure to cater to tasks that were interdependent (requiring people to rely on collaboration from others) and complex (in terms of need for range and depth of specialized skills). The mechanism entailed reporting to two bosses (functional and business). This created new turfs for battle, conflict, ego clashes and led to further problems related to accountability, resource sharing, information flow and speed of decision-making.

Whatever be the form, organization in India has silo-based functioning. Employee's mindset continues to be more focused on department/division goals and performance of narrowly defined functional/divisional roles.

The temptation is to consider the job to be done when their particular activity gets completed, without any concern either for the larger outcome or for the plight of customers. Turf battles are common with scant regard, commitment and pursuit of larger organizational goals. The dominant organizational DNA and mindset predispose people to lesser collaboration, information sharing, holistic mindset and contribution to the common purpose. Even project or product teams in Indian companies—characteristic of the matrix structure—end up becoming hierarchical, without holistic and customer-focused mindset. Such functioning was tolerable in a simple, stable and certain environment. In the complex, dynamic and uncertain business environment as of today, this form and functioning of the organization are a significant reason for the delay in decision-making, lack of responsiveness and adaptation to change, decline in performance and eventual death of the organization.

Organizations of today need to acquire, process and respond to a plethora of information. These relate to the business context, customers and their changing needs, and the opportunities and the threats vis-à-vis the rivals and disrupters sitting in any corner of the world—invisible yet connected through the internet. They then need to have the capability to innovate. Innovation requires transparent and intense vertical and horizontal information sharing and multi-disciplinary team-based functioning, fully empowered to take decisions. Above all, the organization then needs to ensure agile development of solutions and its speedy introduction into the market.

All this means that the companies must demolish the walls separating the departments and the divisions internally and that separating the company from the customer, allies and partners outside. One way they could do this is by creating teams—organized around processes (customer experience) or products (new product development) or projects (quality improvement). In such an organizational form, the supervisory tasks of monitoring, controlling and coordinating and thus integration of activities can be done by applying digital technologies. This will also lead to flattening of the hierarchy which in turn will facilitate empowerment and decentralization. However, empowering teams does not mean unleashing chaos. Companies will need to stipulate clear-cut delineation of responsibilities and accountability. The teams so formed will be responsible for exploring needs and opportunities and developing solutions. The responsibility of the leadership will be to provide shared vision, strategic guidance and resource support for exploration as also create metrics to measure performance and outcomes. Innovation requires implementation.

Execution is the key to strategy. While cocooning the exploration team is important to prevent tyranny of success manifested in the established current business to constrain and bias innovation, there still needs to be coupling (loose and not tight) with the established business for asset utilization, which can help in providing the innovation heft vis-à-vis the rivals in the market. Besides, internally, innovation and the change accompanying it unleash resistance from people who have vested interest in the status quo or from people whose competencies and comfort would be threatened. A strong, powerful coalition of leadership committed to growth and innovation is therefore essential for implementation. This is how organizations will be ambidextrous: both organic enough to explore, experiment and innovate and mechanistic enough to exploit, standardize and execute.

Teams, when given the right guidance, can help in making an organization boundaryless and networked with customers, allies and partners. Digitization can be used to facilitate sharing of resources, data, ideas, competencies with business teams internally and with external partner ecosystem. The developments in ICT today permit firms to create platforms for integrating all the teams, allies and partners together. There are examples of several companies such as Apple, Amazon, Alphabet, Facebook, Alibaba and Tencent who have reinvented their organization in this way and have been able to architect their success sustainably. Teams have also facilitated collaborations, open innovations and co-creation. We are in the world of augmented organization design where organizations can link up and leverage the competencies of partner firms to develop solutions or to enlarge their market share and clout or just to reinforce their existing competitive advantage.

However, such a transformation to ambidexterity will not be easy for established mature organizations with a legacy structure. One alternative for such organization is to add on structures for bringing in external perspective to drive innovation and guiding strategic investments in new categories and white space opportunities. Firms such as P&G, J&J, Nokia and Kimberly-Clarke have benefitted immensely by creating venture boards; Hewlett Packard has innovation councils. P&G's open innovation model has jettisoned the reliance on internal R&D for driving the company's innovation and growth. The model facilitates systematic tapping of ideas, resources and knowledge from external partners such as universities, academic research institutions, government or private labs and individual entrepreneurs. This mechanism to bring emerging technologies onto the radar screen or spur fresh insights combined with internal competencies to create novel technology has made P&G source approximately 50 per cent of its new innovations from outside the company.

Checklist for Organization Design

- Does the organization emphasize information, customer, innovation and agility?

- Do we have the right organizational structure to make innovation and growth happen?
- Do we have clearly laid out responsibility and account-ability for activities and outcomes?
- Do we encourage information sharing and transparency?
- What are the tools and platform through which information is shared across the organization, allies and partners?
- How are people, capabilities and activities integrated?
- How do we make people collaborate (ideas, information, resources and capabilities)?
- How are ideas and information sourced from allies and partners?

Enabler 2. Organizational Agility

Today, all firms are in the information business. This means that a firm which acquires, processes and responds to information speedily and flexibly has better chances of survival and success than those that are trapped in inertia, inflexibility and complacency. Although agile work and methods originated in the world of IT and other knowledge-based companies, these methods have proliferated even in traditional organizations like banks that seek to grow through innovation. Agile practices comprise both dynamic practices, needed for nimble and quick response to challenges and opportunities, and stable practices for reliable and efficient functioning. Dynamic practices such as sensing and seizing opportunities, rapid iteration and experimentation, technology-enabled systems and tools and continuous learning are necessary to drive innovation. Stable practices such as shared leadership, shared vision and purpose, strategic guidance, entrepreneurial drive, performance orienta-tion, information transparency and cohesive community inject discipline and ensure effective operation and systematic execution.

1. **Agile teams for agile outcomes:** Agile working is team based. Team and teamwork are all about shared mindset. The mindset to create wealth through value creation and innovation for the customers. This mindset will work like a North Star—illuminating, guiding and facilitating the mobilization and deployment of human energies for realizing the shared purpose.

Agility requires firms to set up a dual structure: a bureaucratic top-level structure with centralized management and standardized processes to provide stability and a network of agile teams to explore and seize opportunities. The stable top facilitates and creates conditions for teams to function. It provides actionable strategic guidance, standards and metrics of performance and outcomes and delineates clear responsibility and authority to the teams. At the beginning of the year, the company can decide its strategy in terms of objectives and key result (OKR) areas. Objectives are typically qualitative statements of what the company will want to achieve. The key result area is all about knowing whether it is being achieved or not. The company will thus create certain criteria and use metrics/milestones to measure its achievement from time to time. This is how Intel, Google, Twitter, Oracle, etc. set goals and monitor performance.

Teams are focused performance groups (tribes or lattice) with clearly stated goals. These teams are usually cross functional with members drawn from different functions, levels and business units, whose expertise and inputs need to be coordinated for outcomes like new product development. Apart from these teams, there can also be other standalone self-managed teams, which define their own way of working and are collectively responsible and accountable for end-to-end performance. Their performance is measured against key outcome indicators such as customer services, sales and marketing. Another team type is more stable, repetitive and long duration 'flow to the work pools' in which enterprise-wide tasks that are priorities have to be completed such as HR and legal affairs. An agile organization is like a mobile phone consisting of a stable hardware of centralized management and a dynamic operating system of agile teamwork.

2. **Agile working:** Central to all the teams is a commitment to the process of rapid learning and decision cycles. The ability to pivot requires that firms must move away from the traditional waterfall approach or stage gate approach for innovation to an experimental minimally viable product or deliverables in one or two sprints of one to four weeks. Between sprints, the team sits down to analyse the progress and the experience and other insights gathered. It reviews, modifies, plans and sets goals for the next cycle. Central to this agile way of working is a seamless and rapid sharing of information and learning across levels, departments, sub-units, businesses and the entire innovation ecosystem including other organizations and stakeholders. The focus on quick, efficient and continuous decision-making is at the core of lean start-up, iteration and experimentation. An innovation with 70 per cent features in place is preferred to the certainty of 100 per cent. Lean start-up is the new success mantra. Perfection can wait for subsequent iterations as amply demonstrated by Microsoft, Google and others who learnt from customer feedback.

3. **Venture capital-based planning and budgeting:** Firms will also need to bring about the changes in the way they plan, budget and allocate resources. The traditional model of planning and budgeting is based upon allocating limited resources to work that will generate the highest returns. In this, the senior leaders tightly control the purse strings, demand a rigorous business case, devise multi-stage approval processes and create a strict linkage between the allocated

budget and a highly specific and time-based (typically fiscal year end) output before they were to decide to fund a project. This may still be appropriate for certain parts of the business, but it has an adverse effect on agile teams and the returns they can generate.

Companies trying to support innovation through agile working should shift to allocating funds to the output, namely products, rather than to inputs and processes, namely projects. These products may vary from enhancing customer experience or business capability and technology platform or just website improvement. There may also be single or multiple agile teams whose job may be directed towards improving some part of the work process. Some teams may be focused on making it easier for customers to find the product, others may be concerned with the check-out experience and a third group oversees returns and exchanges. The product-centric approach will organize funds differently. It will be aligned to business outcomes like decreasing the time taken to check out on the website. The teams will thus become more autonomous in planning and scheduling their work. This funding model is well fitted with agile, which breaks large initiatives into small, manageable modules. It will also allow the senior management to reward teams that deliver good results with higher compensation or larger funding allocations. Ultimately, such arrangements help improve business outcomes. Companies across a variety of industries now organize their agile teams using products rather than projects. Retailer Walmart also focuses on products, attaching agile teams to business capabilities, such as human resources and digital marketing. One of the greatest benefits of this model is that instead of waiting until next year's funding cycle, it gives organizations the flexibility immediately to pull the plug on bad ideas so that they can execute on the good ideas generated mid-year. This model of mid-course corrections has also been employed by Google to fund its initiatives and the bubbles of good idea that may pop up from time to time.

Checklist for Organizational Agility

- Identify the aspect of value creation and value delivery which needs to be transformed. This can be customer centricity, employee engagement, productivity and supply chain.
- Determine why we need to be agile: Is it needed for the sake of competition or is it desired for ensuring competitive advantage?
- Does agility require an integrated end-to-end process transformation involving strategy, structure, systems, technology and people or can it be localized to just modularizing production or supply chain or talent management?
- Is the purpose and vision of the management communicated and shared by the organization down the line?
- Do the employees own and are they committed to the vision and purpose of management related to agility?
- To what extent is there an entrepreneurial culture consisting of individual and collective endeavours and organizational mechanisms for scanning, searching and sensing of opportunities?
- How is the firm organized to ensure agility?
- Do we have centralized governance and decision-making and standardized work process along with flexible, scalable network of teams operating with high number of standards, accountability, alignment, information transparency and collaboration?
- Which teams have primary and inherited OKR?
- Are there annual strategic meeting and quarterly cadence or business review meets to ensure coordination among the teams?

- Is there a culture of empowerment, trust in the capabilities, service mindset and above all the facilitating and democratic leadership style in the organization?
- Do we have teams to co-create ideas, products, services and solutions or values with external ecosystems consisting of customers, partners, networks, government, academia and even competitors?
- Is our scrum team led by product owner drawn from the business function and supported by the IT department?
- Does the firm pursue lean development involving continuous elimination of waste and Kanban to ensure continuous learning and improvement?
- How does the organization promote rapid iterative learning?
- How does the organization support development and deployment of minimal viable product or deliverable?
- Does the organization promote venture capital style funding for minimally viable start-up?
- Does the organization have a two-speed customer-facing agile system (e.g., customer experience) and a stable backbone of database and quality management at the back end (transaction integrity)?

Enabler 3. People Power and Culture

It is not organizations that fight wars. It is the people. Victory or defeat in any war—be it corporate or military—does not depend upon other material weapons. It depends on the people and their inspiration, imagination, willpower and determination to win. The role of AI, IoT and ML has increased exponentially in both value creation and value delivery. However, the role of people power in creating and sustaining the competitive edge of organizations reigns supreme. This is because it is not automation that enables a firm to innovate. It is the knowledge, technological skills and experience embodied in the human mind and their mysterious interplay in the creative imagination that enable a firm to innovate products, processes and attain a competitive edge.

People power is unleashed by the culture of the organization. The soul of the start-up refers to the entrepreneurial spirit which should pervade the company and drive its people to be flexible, adaptive and opportunity seeking. Established firms are usually characterized by large size, bureaucracy, hierarchy, inflexible processes and rigid control. This may lend strengths in terms of wisdom, social, intellectual and process capital, deep pockets and staying power. But during times of dynamic and disruptive change and need for innovation fueled growth, such organizations are flat footed, risk averse, conservative and sluggish. They become dinosaurs of a different era. The challenge for the giants is thus to re-invent themselves and mimic the form of the start-ups constantly seeking new business and the challenge of doing something new. The giants will dance or the bumble bees will fly only when the company is imbricated with the fervour, excitement and challenge associated with customer centricity, speed and innovation.

This enabler involves the following:

1. People power: Wage war for acquiring and retaining talent
2. People power: Develop the stock
3. Soul of the start-up: Harness the power of the collective
4. Soul of the start-up: Mobilize collective energy
5. Soul of the start-up: Inculcate opportunity-seeking mindset
6. Soul of the start-up: Promote unlearning and learning
7. Soul of the start-up: Instil the twin value of freedom and failure

1. People power—wage war to acquire and retain talent: Creating and sustaining competitive edge through innovation begins with attracting and retaining the right talent. This is a difficult proposition.[x] The 'war for talent' today is more intense in those industries and functions which require technologically sophisticated competencies. Job hopping is the new normal.[xi] A disengaged employee who is insincere with his/her job and stays on without any actual commitment towards the organization is a bigger disaster. Such employees proliferate in many Indian companies. Getting them to either shape up or ship out is the challenge. Shaping up requires efforts to be made by the organization.

One of the bigger problems for the Indian company is its inability to hire the best talent from campuses, not because it is inferior, but because it does not know how to market itself in the student community. No doubt the best graduates across the top engineering and management institutes are lured by global brands. However, there is still plenty of talent available out there that can be attracted by good Indian companies. Indian companies tend to shy away from branding themselves. In the world of competition, the need for branding is critical for getting the best talent on board.

Companies must establish, communicate and deliver a portfolio of functional, economic, social and psychological benefits attached with the employment to the prospective employee. A strong employer brand is all about a value proposition that is unique, distinctive, targeted and real. Google challenges and attracts the best talent because of its offer of complex jobs; Virgin Atlantic allures Gen Y with leadership in the sky. Superior Employer brand hinges on the quality of employment relationship and the extent to which the expectations of the employees are exceeded by the experiences of their employment in the firm. Participation and competing for being 'Great Place to Work' or the 'Most Admired Workplace' will make companies choose enhancement of employee engagement as one of the strategic objectives. This will at the minimum lead to the better alignment of the competencies of the employees with the job and its characteristics, competitively benchmarked rewards, career management and development interventions for upgradation and renewal of their capabilities. A company invested in talent will harvest exponential returns in performance and growth.

2. People power—develop the stock: In the dynamic environment marked by knowledge-based competition, firms seeking innovation-based growth must constantly accumulate knowledge resources for developing the right stock of intellectual capital for efficient and effective use. They also need to continuously renew it so that the exploitation of existing competencies and exploring and learning new ways for value creation can happen concurrently. This means that acquiring and retaining talent are not enough for creating superior people power. Firms should ensure dynamic alignment of knowledge resources with the strategic goals of the organization. This will make work meaningful and exciting for employees, and they will feel that their contribution is worthwhile. In a world characterized by frame-bursting efflorescence of new knowledge due to disruptive convergence of science and technology based disciplines and industries, there is an urgent need for the firms to constantly upgrade their intellectual stock. One way by which they can renew it is by sharing and diffusing the learning derived from constant integration of external and internal knowledge resources. In other words, the lessons learnt from programmes such as customer relationship management, total quality management, supply chain management and new product development must be disseminated throughout the rank and file of the organization. The company must seek to harness the four knowledge processes viz. accumulation, integration, utilization and reconfiguration. This is key to inculcation of competencies necessary for both exploration and exploitation related activities among its people. Firms must also encourage transmission and exchange of knowledge, experience and know-how both among employees and between employees and customers. This will lead to diffusion of shared competencies and new practices needed for adaptation and innovation. The absorptive capacity of the firm thus helps it augment its capability vis-à-vis its competitors. Indeed, developing new competencies faster and better than the global competitors is the surest way to effectively compete and win in time-based markets.

In sum, it is not just the best talent—the intellectual stock—which gives the firm its competitive edge. What is imperative in a dynamic environment is the scalability of the workforce. To do this, firms have to keep their human resources aligned with business needs and ensure their rapid transition from one level to another. This now is one of the basic firm-level competencies to attain a sustainable competitive edge.

3. **Soul of the start-up—harness the power of the collective:** It is culture that creates and unleashes the people power. The soul of the start-up is about the entrepreneurial spirit that should pervade the organization and drive it to explore and seize new opportunities, experiment, fail fast and learn rapidly. The power of the collective is the extent to which people internalize the shared vision and values of the organization and align their intentions and goals with the purpose and goals of the organization. Culture provides the conditions and the mindset which in turn enables and reinforces innovativeness in the organization.[xii] It is for this reason that firms renowned for their innovation-driven success advertise their culture. Apple invites talent to work for the sheer joy of producing technologically cutting-edge products; and 3M emphasizes itself as a science-based company; whereas, W. L. Gore talks about employee empowerment; Google about individuality and freedom; SAS about being a family; Toyota about engineering; IBM about empowerment and the right way. Amazon entices people with its slogan of being visionary and customer

centric and a workplace where people can enjoy and do great things and Tesla advocates moving fast, doing the impossible, innovating and we are all in it, together.

Organizational culture can powerfully enable firms to explore, ideate, experiment and innovate—both speedily and continuously. If culture is not shaped to align with organizational strategy, then culture itself can become the biggest stumbling block for the organization and its intent. There are many companies where strategy failed because of the lack of alignment between strategic intent and organizational culture. In a way, innovation is itself culture in which the amount of knowledge embedded in an innovation depends upon the amount of knowledge available and utilized in the organization. The organizational cultures shaped by K. V. Kamath when he transformed ICICI, by Kumar Mangalam Birla when he re-invigorated the Aditya Birla Group, by Sunil Mittal when he created Airtel and by Kiran Mazumdar in Biocon are by now legendary for the entrepreneurial spirit which they imbued in their people [3].

4. Soul of the start-up—mobilize collective energy: There are several examples of companies that have been successful without any formal vision statement. There are also an equal number of unsuccessful firms with truly grand vision statements. It is, therefore, necessary to distinguish between firms that have a vision and firms that are visionary. In order to develop sustainable competitive edge, firms need to be visionary. Being visionary requires the firm to align its core values, mission, strategy and practices. Companies such as Airtel, L&T and Biocon, and banks like ICICI have done this in textbook fashion [3].

5. Soul of the start-up—inculcate opportunity-seeking mindset: An innovative firm must have a culture which continuously scans the environment for opportunities and collaborators as also for threats and killer moves by competitors. Such companies look for signals for change at the periphery where they are most likely to be present, provided someone pays attention. Such opportunity sensing is embedded in the entrepreneurial nature of a company which restlessly seeks out newness and change. An entrepreneurial firm is one which is externally focused and seeks to grow through seizing of opportunities. Such an orientation requires retrieval of information for generating ideas, sensing needs and opportunities, tracking of technological developments and, thus, for devising innovative solutions. External orientation and openness to environment are a prerequisite for flexibility, adaptation and, thus, responsiveness to environmental dynamism. In the Indian context, the approach taken by ICICI to keep pace with customer expectations in the early 2000s is an unparalleled example [3].

6. **Soul of the start-up—promote unlearning and learning:** Entrepreneurial success depends upon the rapidity with which the company learns to unlearn and relearn in unending cycles. Learning enables an organization to anticipate and adapt to the dynamics of a changing environment. This depends upon the extent to which information as a resource is acquired by the organization and its internal processes are used for open sharing, processing and creative application. This capacity is especially crucial when the business environment is dynamic, complex and riven with ambiguity. Firms must, therefore, ensure that there is a seamless flow of information without any distortion, truncation or delay caused by the inevitable cracks between function, divisions and levels. They should encourage sharing and learning among and across business units and alliances. This will establish an adaptive learning culture that fosters and nurtures innovation. It is a critical facilitator of creativity and innovation because it supports enquiry, risk-taking and experimentation. Those companies that don't pay much attention to creating a learning

culture will experience rigidity, close-minded behaviour and ultimately get out of touch with external realities and become irrelevant. If organizational energies are not being guided towards learning, there is inertia and company culture gets caught in a downward spiral.

7. Soul of the start-up—instil the twin values of freedom and failure: The culture for innovativeness is woven around two core values: (a) employee freedom and (b) tolerance of failure.

It is important that firms committed to innovation create conditions for people to freely explore and ideate solutions. Innovative firms like 3M prescribe that their managers set aside 15 per cent of their time on ideating. That is how the idea of Post-it notes was born. Google sets aside 20 per cent time for people to ideate. That is how Gmail came about. HP also has personal think time. The idea of paid freedom, therefore, invites the person to discover his/her inner geek. At times, ideas that came from such 'think' time could not translate into innovative products, because of lack of subsequent experimentation and support. At other times, more innovative ideas came from outside. Providing freedom in the work culture is not only for promoting innovations, but it is also a great way to attract entrepreneurial and creative talent which flourish under conditions of liberty and abhor restrictions. In order to succeed, the company should also soften the boundaries between spaces where ideas germinate and where they take root. Delegation of power, empowerment and participative decision-making are essential to the culture of innovation and the basis for the success of cross-functional teams dedicated to finding/innovating solutions.

The other core cultural value to promote innovation is tolerance for failure. This single factor encourages people to explore, take risks, experiment and have the confidence to fail, knowing that they will not be penalized for doing so. Tolerance for risk signifies the willingness to deal with uncertainties and is, thus, related to the value of flexibility. Further, it is related to growth as it is only risk-taking which allows seizing opportunities that appear in the market. Apple, 3M and Google are all known for emphasizing such work culture as they seek to foster the flexibility and autonomy, enabling employees to work on creating new ideas. Supportive culture enhances employees' propensity to propose new ideas by providing a feeling of psychological safety. It is the processes and practices around these core values that invoke contextual ambidexterity. This contextual ambidexterity is the fundamental underpinning of exploitation and exploration. Cultural ambidexterity establishes, supports and reinforces organizational ambidexterity.

Checklist for People Power and Winning Culture

1. Does the company have a well-defined approach to attract and retain explorers and innovative thinkers?
2. Does the company have a strategy and plan of action in place for becoming a Great Place to Work?
3. Does the company have mechanisms and interventions for enhancing employee engagement?
4. Does the company allow its members to ideate, experiment, make mistakes and learn from failures?
5. Does the company have mechanisms for measuring, managing, recognizing and rewarding individual and team-based creativity and contribution in cost-saving or profit-enhancing innovations?
6. Does the company have mechanisms for recognizing and rewarding people for displaying innovation-related behaviour even if the innovation outcome may not have been achieved?
7. Does the company have institutionally arranged budget for training and development interventions to build competencies and expertise required for innovation?

8. Does the company change its action modes based upon latest knowledge?
9. Does the company conduct innovation and knowledge audits?
10. Does the company benchmark its processes and resources utilized for intellectual capital?
11. Does the company have systems and organizational processes to continuously learn from each other?
12. Is the organization like a university where knowledge is shared?
13. Does the organization have a corporate board with representation of scholars working at the cutting edge of the discipline?

Towards the Model of Winning the Corporate War

In human history, it is ironical that wars are waged by the army, but it is the nation that wins or loses. What will happen if the entire nation becomes an army? The contemporary corporate warfare can be decisively and sustainably won only if the entire organization is mobilized, energized and involved at all levels of war. The emergent model for winning in the corporate war is rooted in the power of the collective colossus. The emergent model is shown in Figure 4.1.

Winning Outcome through Fusillade of Continuous Innovation

The goal of the model is to triumph in the corporate battle-field. Firms will win only when they create sustainable competitive edge. To do that, they have to create wealth by untrammelled growth. This is possible only when the firm innovates continuously. Both improvement-oriented innovation and market-creating disruptive innovation are required for growth. Improvement-oriented innovation leads to

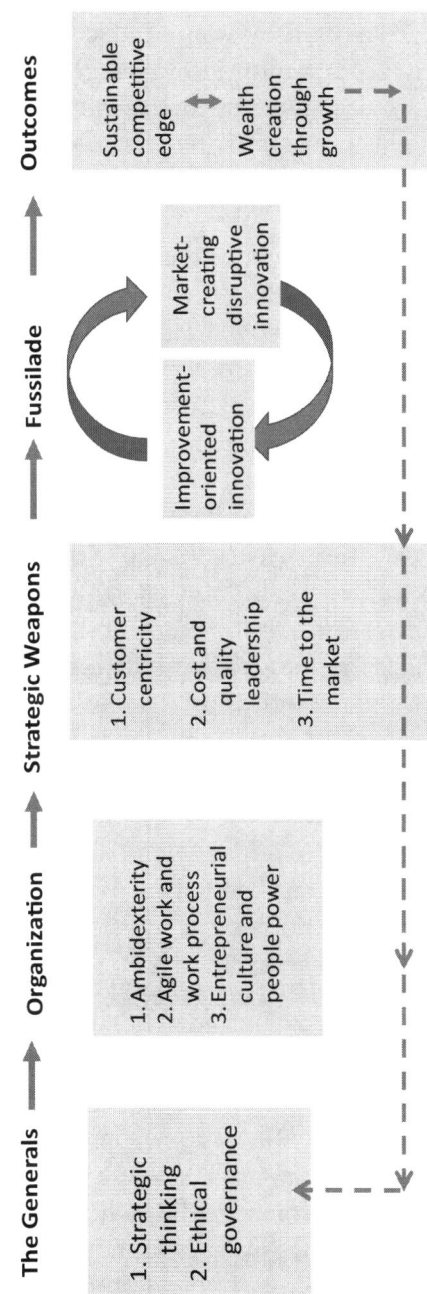

Figure 4.1 Towards an Emergent Model of Winning Corporate War

optimal exploitation of the existing product market to extract and appropriate more wealth. However, growth based upon only improvement-oriented innovation will be vulnerable due to its quick duplication by rivals, the rapidity of product obsolescence, the shift in the customer preferences, the evolution of the customer's needs, the advancements in technology and the disruptive innovation of the game changer. The competitive advantage enjoyed by the cost-optimizing firm at best will be temporary. It is only when the firm generates market-creating new or novel value to serve the unfulfilled and, at times, unknown future needs of customers, both existing and potential, as well as of current non-consumers that firm creates the basis for sustainable competitive edge. This innovation is a direct outcome of the blue ocean strategy of the firm which drives the orientation to explore, intuit and logically deduce future needs and opportunities. The optimization-based innovation can complement the disruptive innovation by enabling the company to buttress and reinforce its early mover advantage and, thus, remain ahead of its fast-catching competitors. However, no company can rest on its laurels. It is said that even if you are on the right track and you do nothing, you will be run over. Past success is no assurance of future success. A great Olympian never rests after winning the gold. S/he starts preparing for the next Olympics to be one step ahead of his/her rival.

The Business Model and Its Components: The Strategic Weapons

Both the innovation types flow out of the strategic weapons of the firm. In turn, the innovations sharpen, reinforce and enhance the strategic weapons. The whole architecture of the business model of a firm (the model by which it makes money) woven around value proposition is founded on the pillars of cost centricity, cost and quality leadership and time to the market. Value creation and delivery and innovations in them are all directed towards serving the current and future needs of the customers at a cost, price, quality, speed and flexibility exceeding their expectations. The entire process of sensing customer needs to developing solutions to its final delivery to the customer and providing after-sales customer care necessitates the following:

1. Gathering information about the customer, competitors, technology, market, etc., and its processing through the application of data science and digital technologies.
2. Creating a network of partner ecosystem right through the supply chain of plan, procure, make and deliver for cost-efficient, reliable and speedy creation and delivery of the product or services.
3. Applying advanced manufacturing techniques and factory management practices for manufacturing products at lowest cost, highest quality and blazing speed.
4. Digitization of the entire value chain and its integration by applying ICT to ensure cost, quality, speed and agility.
5. Globalization to derive efficiencies through global value chain and access to global market as also speed through distributed manufacturing and global–local delivery model.
6. Partnering with customers (including lead users), partners, allies and even competitors for co-creating and innovating solutions.

The Enablers

The use of the weapons depends upon the dynamic capability of the organization. These are different from the ordinary capabilities which just focus on the exploitation of current product, current market and current competencies. At best, this would lead to improvement-oriented innovations. Dynamic capabilities are exploration oriented. These are capabilities of scanning, searching and seizing opportunities and, thus, inspire market-creating disruptive innovations. Disruption can happen only when the firm is an early mover or fast learner in the market. This requires the organization to be agile, that is, capable of pivoting from sensing of needs to designing solutions to creating innovations and hitting the market with speed. To ensure that, there has to be robust people power, entrepreneurial mindset, strong support structure and enabling process and systems. The following are some of its key features:

1. Ambidextrous organizations with (a) a flat, lean, boundaryless—both internally and externally—structure, networked and augmented with customers, partners and allies to support exploration; (b) bureaucratic top-level structure with centralized management and standardized processes to provide stability and ensure strategic execution.

2. Empowered multi-disciplinary teams using agile methods and work process of rapid decision and learning cycle and following lean start-up methodology of experimentation and iteration to quickly produce minimally viable solution.

3. Use of venture capital type planning and funding to ensure empowerment, responsibility, accountability and alignment of agile teams with the strategic outcomes and goals of the organization.

4. Hiring and retaining best talent through superior employer branding and designing interventions for employee engagement and becoming Great Place to Work.

5. Heightening people power by creating culture of exploration, learning and knowledge management.

6. Installing a culture of innovation rooted in the shared purpose of wealth creation and entrepreneurial mindset and woven through the core values of freedom and failure.

The General

In a battlefield, warriors fight. But to win, the warriors have to be mobilized by the call of duty, the ennoblement of their spirit and the inspiration of a higher purpose. They have to be led. It is the occupation of the high ground that makes armies win in the battlefield. There can be no ground higher than the moral high ground. The larger purpose of the organization—creating wealth for the stakeholders, community and country—creates that high ground. This is what ethical governance is all about. The larger purpose can be realized only through the strategy of continuous innovation. This implicates that the cognitive bias and inertia rooted in past success and comfort can have no place. Creative destruction is the cornerstone of continuous innovation. The strategy of continuous innovation ensures win without even a combat. It makes the company invincible. However, the success of this strategy depends upon the extent to which the various strategic levers of competitive edge are worked upon. It is important for the board that it concentrates on all the levers, which actually work in tandem, and, thus, provide the competitive thrust to the organization and its sustainability.

To end, we once again quote Sun Tzu, 'If the sovereign heeds these stratagems of mine and acts upon them, he will surely win the war.... If the sovereign neither heeds nor acts upon them, he will certainly suffer defeat....'

Notes

i.   'To win one hundred victories in one hundred battles is not the acme of skill. To subdue the enemy without fighting is the supreme excellence.... The best policy in war is to attack the enemy's strategy.... The worst policy is to attack walled cities' (Sun Tzu).

ii. In Porter's generic strategies for competitive advantage, cost leadership is a strategic position which allows firms to capture higher value in terms of margin between costs and price. The bottom-line idea for firms pursuing lost-cost strategy is to combine low per unit profit with large sales to make enough profit aka the volumes strategy.

iii. There are several examples of companies such as Zara in fast fashion, Starbucks in quality of beans, Ferrero's purchase of Turkish company Oltin Gida for supply of hazelnuts and Louis Vuitton's retail of handbags that have benefited in their sales and global expansion plans because of vertical integration.

iv. It is by using this route that smartphone brands like Apple, garment labels such as H&M and Gap, and shoe majors such as Nike and Adidas leveraged the technologically integrated infrastructure of contract manufacturers to architect their competitive advantage.

v. Geoffrey Moore in his celebrated book *Crossing the Chasm* proposes that innovation-driven firms should, therefore, differentiate the market based upon where they stood in the technology adoption life cycle and target the segments of early adopter, early majority, late majority and laggards differently. This is more so when the technology of the product requires change in the behaviour by the user as in the case of discontinuous innovation.

vi. Similarly, Shell changed its order fulfilment process that resulted in reduced cycle time for converting orders into cash by 75 per cent and operating expenses by 45 per cent. This alone boosted customer satisfaction by 105 per cent.

Walmart became one of the largest companies in the world and the strongest brand by pioneering many innovations in purchase and distribution of goods. One of the best-known innovation was cross docking, in which goods trucked to distribution centre by suppliers get transferred from the trucks straight to the stores bypassing the storage warehouse. This combined with other innovations led to lower inventory and lower operating costs, both of which translated into lower price for Walmart.

vii. Some of the typical examples worth recollecting are: A Domino's pizza delivered in 30 minutes, otherwise free; orders delivered by Amazon Prime within specified time for which the company charges freemium price; a UPS delivery at the speed of business; Uber Eats rustled up in 10 minutes time.

viii. First introduced in the literature on strategy by George Stalk of BCG way back in 1988.

ix. Technology helps scrape specialized websites for user-generated concepts. This is then followed up with ML based semantic filters and memory models to isolate the most useful content and user. The solution can then be validated by company experts through their own analysis. The firm can then take up their ideas, concepts and prototype for adoption for further evaluation while developing solutions.

x. A McKinsey Global Institute study (2017) reported that a whopping 82 per cent of companies don't believe they recruit highly talented people.

xi. The average tenure of workers has reduced to almost half of what it was before. Much worse, as the 2015 survey by Gallup reported, more than 50 per cent of respondents were 'not engaged'; an additional 17.2 per cent were 'actively disengaged'. Another survey reported that 73 per cent of employees are 'thinking about another job' and that 43 per cent were more likely to consider a new one than they had been a year earlier. Voluntary turnover may have certain advantages in terms of facilitating the company to infuse fresh blood and new ideas inside as a replacement.

xii. Jim Collins states that path-breaking innovations such as Boeing Jets, 3M Post-it notes, HP Pocket Computer, Sony Walkman, etc. came about only because the companies created an organizational environment conducive for innovation. He called it 'social innovations'. For example, 3M's 'bootlegging', Ford's 'assembly line', W. L. Gore's 'lattice structure', P&G's 'profit-sharing' and Nordstrom's 'empowerment' were all social innovations that were instrumental in making them innovative.

References

1. Singh, P., and Bhandarker, A. (2002). *Winning the Corporate Olympiad: Renaissance Paradigm.* Noida: Vikas Publishing House.

2. Anthony, S. D. (2017). *The Little Black Book of Innovation: How It Works, How to Do It*. Brighton, MA: Harvard Business Review Press.
3. Singh, P., and Bhandarker, A. (2011). *In Search of Change Maestros*. New Delhi: SAGE Publications.

Further Reading

Adkins, A. (2016, 13 January). Employee Engagement in U.S. Stagnant in 2015. Gallup News. https://news.gallup.com/poll/188144/employee-engagement-stagnant-2015.aspx

Aghina, W., Ahlback, K., de Smet, A., Lackey, G., Lurie, M., Monica Murarka, and Handscomb, C. (2018, 22 January). Trademarks of Agile Organizations. McKinsey & Company. https://www.mckinsey.com/business-functions/organization/our-insights/the-five-trademarks-of-agile-organizations

Christensen, C. M. (2017). *The Innovator's Dilemma*. Brighton, MA: Harvard Business Review Press.

Christensen, C. M., Hall, T., Dillon, K., and Duncan, D. (2016). *Competing against Luck: The Story of Innovation and Customer Choice*. New York, NY: HarperCollins.

Day, G. S., and Schoemaker, P. S. H. (2016). Adapting to Fast-changing Markets and Technologies. *California Management Review*, Vol. 58, No. 4, pp. 59–77. https://doi.org/10.1525%2Fcmr.2016.58.4.59

Drucker, P. F. (1985). *Innovation and Entrepreneurship*. London: Routledge.

Edelman, D. C., and Singer, M. (2015). Competing on Customer Journeys. *Harvard Business Review*. https://hbr.org/2015/11/competing-on-customer-journeys

Felin, T., and Powell, T. C. (2016, August 1). Designing Organizations for Dynamic Capabilities. *California Management Review*, Vol. 58, No. 4, pp. 78–96. https://doi.org/10.1525%2Fcmr.2016.58.4.78

Goldsmith, M. (2008). *What Got You Here Won't Get You There*. London: Profile Books.

Johnson, M. W., and Suskewicz, J. (2020). *Lead from the Future: How to Turn Visionary Thinking into Breakthrough Growth*. Brighton, MA: Harvard Business Review Press.

Keller, S., and Meaney, M. (2017, 24 November). *Attracting and Retaining the Right Talent*. McKinsey & Company. https://www.mckinsey.com/business-functions/organization/our-insights/attracting-and-retaining-the-right-talent

Lesser, R., Reeves, M., and Goulet, K. (2013, 23 December). *BCG Classics Revisited: Time-based Competition*. BCG Publications. https://www.bcg.com/publications/2013/bcg-classics-revisited-time-based-competition

Mauborgne, R., and Kim, W. C. (2015). *Blue Ocean Strategy: How to Create Uncontested Market Space and Make the Competition Irrelevant*, 287. Brighton, MA: Harvard Business Review Press.

McKinsey Global Institute. (2019). *Digital India—Technology to Transform a Connected Nation*. https://www.mckinsey.com/~/media/mckinsey/business%20functions/mckinsey%20digital/our%20insights/digital%20india%20technology%20to%20transform%20a%20connected%20nation/digital-india-technology-to-transform-a-connected-nation-full-report.ashx

McKinsey & Company. (2020). *The Future of Business: Reimagining 2020 and Beyond*. https://www.mckinsey.com/~/media/McKinsey/Featured%20Insights/The%20Next%20Normal/The%20future%20of%20business/The-future-of-business-reimagining-2020-and-beyond

Moore, G. (2014). *Crossing the Chasm: Marketing and Selling Disruptive Products to Mainstream Customers*, 3rd ed. New York, NY: HarperCollins.

O'Reilly, C., and Tushman, M. (2013). Organizational Ambidexterity: Past, Present and Future. *SSRN Electronic Journal*, Vol. 27. https://www.hbs.edu/faculty/Publication%20Files/O'Reilly%20and%20Tushman%20AMP%20Ms%20051413_c66b0c53-5fcd-46d5-aa16-943eab6aa4a1.pdf

Porter, M. E. (1985). Competitive Strategy: The Core Concepts. In *Competitive Advantage*, pp. 11–15. New York, NY: The Free Press.

Porter, M. E., and Kramer, M. R. (2007). *Strategy & Society: The Link between Competitive Advantage and Corporate Social Responsibility*. Brighton, MA: Harvard Business Publishing. http://sustainability.psu.edu/fieldguide/wp-content/uploads/

2015/08/Strategy-and-Society-The-link-between-competitive-andvantage-and-corporate-social-responsibility.pdf

Trimble, C., and Govindrajan, V. (2005). *Ten Rules for Strategic Innovators: From Idea to Execution*. Brighton, MA: Harvard Business Review Press.

Tzu, S. (2018). *The Art of War*. New Delhi: General Press.

5

EFFECTIVE BOARDROOM GOVERNANCE: RECOMMENDATIONS

If a country does not have a reputation for strong corporate governance practices, capital will flow elsewhere. If investors are not confident with the level of disclosure, capital will flow elsewhere. If a country opts for lax accounting and reporting standards, capital will flow elsewhere.

—Arthur Levitt [1]

Ground Realities of Boardroom Governance in India

Key Findings and Conclusions

Findings from Chapter 3 Part II 'Ground Realities of Boardroom Governance in India' are not very heartening and reveal that, in general, Indian boards have a long way to go in ensuring effective governance. Independent directors are more ornamental rather than committed contributors to the organization. Findings suggest that the agenda of board members is not well aligned with building sustainable competitive edge of organizations.

Boards appear to be so immersed in the numbers that they are not mindful enough about managing various risks to the company and not concerned about building organizational strategy.

Independent Directors are appointed from different walks of life by the Promoter/Chairman, more to comply with the requirement of the regulator—SEBI. Our in-depth discussions with board members suggested that there is a level of casualness among both the Promoter/Chairman, who appoints independent directors, and the appointees themselves. The situation in the public sector is different; the government nominates independent directors, which include political appointees who may not have the necessary understanding of business.

There is a serious mismatch between the type of competencies needed to contribute effectively to boardroom governance and the reality of most Indian boards. Quality of board members, loyalty to Promoter/CEO, selection criteria with little focus on relevant domain knowledge and capabilities are some of the contributors to the competency mismatch and problems of many Indian boards. Boardroom processes are also inadequate as is the role played by the chairman, thus leading to poor-quality decisions and outcomes. Meetings seem to be conducted more as a formality than in a genuine spirit of brainstorming to find solutions for organizational well-being. Key issues of great importance to building organizational sustainability and competitiveness are not focused upon in boardroom discussions. In sum, the findings indicate that by and large, Indian boards are not playing their twin roles of providing both good governance and architecting strategy to shape the destiny of the organization.

The Challenge for Boards

There are many issues and challenges which constrain the capability of boards to be value adding to the organizations that they head. Unless board members have a reasonable understanding of the business and commitment to sustainable and competitive growth of organizations, they will not be able to play their roles effectively. There is no doubt that the intent of the Promoter/Chairman is critical to effective board functioning. However, if there is a strong board, then it can bring balance and enhance quality of boardroom discussions. Independent directors, in turn, will speak their minds, if they are appointed through a merit-based and transparent process based on clearly spelt out criteria. If they are nominated by the Promoter/Chairman for selection to the board, it is natural that they are beholden to them and would any day be loyal to them, rather than to the organization and its future. The regulators—RBI and SEBI—need to read the tea leaves here.

A board is as good as the top team of the organization and, hence, strengthening the top team through delegation, empowerment and clear delineation of accountability is very important. Boards need to devote some time to assess the quality of internal management of the company and provide guidance on various matters which can strengthen the internal management—empowerment, monitoring, building suitable work culture to encourage entrepreneurship and innovation and good-quality decision-making. While bringing such changes, the board has to ensure that the right person is in the right position to monitor the use of empowerment through assessing the decision quality. Once this is put in place, boards will get time to focus on matters which ought to matter at the board level—**strategy and governance.**

The Importance of Good Governance

Good governance is extremely critical to build the sustainable competitive advantage of companies. There are examples of companies which combine both economic and social goals and succeed in doing well. In fact, those companies that reached out to all stakeholders have been found to outperform other companies who focused directly on increasing shareholder wealth without concern for all stakeholders [2]. Good CG provides many advantages to the organization: it helps in reducing risk, attracting new investments and shareholders and more equity, besides promoting continued innovation and ensuring organizational longevity and sustainability.[i]

Boards have to actually 'head' the organizations they 'helm'; they have to bring the third eye perspective and have to be committed and give time to board work. It appears from the discussions that those who have little time, low commitment, less capability and knowledge of the business tend to be selected as independent directors. The other extreme criteria of selection utilized is to get people who are so busy heading their own companies, that they don't have the time to even attend quarterly meetings. One of the reasons for this is perhaps the intent of the Promoter/Chairman to retain total control of the business and to not have to answer any questions. The focus is on prestige rather than dedication to work for the board. This becomes a serious problem when the company is listed on the stock markets and the investments of minority shareholders are at stake. Owing to the regulator's requirement, boards do comply and conduct meetings; however, this is done more in letter than in spirit. The danger to investors losing their hard-earned money is very real in such companies. Boards, vested with the duty to ensure good governance, fairness and transparency, woefully fail at this core responsibility.

Recommendation to Increase Board Effectiveness

Good CG goes beyond rules and regulations and includes ethics and the values influencing the conduct of business. The core values which are adopted by the company, their statement of vision and mission, as well as their business principles and practices, need to be synchronized. Otherwise, it can just become a set of empty words with no credibility.

Needed: A Committed Board

Directors on the boards of companies need to be fully cognisant of their roles and responsibilities and must be committed to live up to these roles. Else, they should not take up such responsibilities. Clearly, this book is making the case for an involved and committed board which will have to meet more often than the traditional quarterly meetings. In the same spirit, sub-committees will also need to be more active and contribute more time and effort.

Companies don't operate in a vacuum, they have their own ecosystem and are dependent on myriad stakeholders for their sustainable growth. No doubt companies succeed and grow because they serve customers, who are themselves a part of larger society. Companies themselves gain from society and, thus, have a responsibility to treat society as one of the stakeholders. Given the general business environment as well as the socio-economic conditions facing human societies, companies need to think of all the stakeholders who contribute to their well-being either directly or indirectly.

Thus, the most relevant paradigm for boardroom governance is the stakeholder perspective. This approach keeps its focus not only on making profits but also keeps the interests of various stakeholders in mind. Undoubtedly, this is the need of the hour in today's tumultuous circumstances of job losses, mental illness and other forms of suffering [3]. Boards with such a mindset will tend to treat all stakeholders as partners.

This approach does not ignore the importance of competitive spirit—that's what has fuelled development through creativity in the modern world and has helped make the world a better place. Extreme competitiveness—growth at any cost—is by its very nature exploitative, inhuman and selfish; it is downright unethical and beyond a point, it is unsustainable. Companies need to be clued into the value priorities of the millennial consumers and employees who give greater importance to social values and buying ethically [4].

As De Bono [5] predicted, 'Companies that solely focus on competition will die....'

Board Mindset for Governance

The collective mindset of the board needs to move beyond regulation focus to ensure better quality of board members, better quality of board processes and better board-level leadership, if they have to do justice to their pre-eminent position on the top of organizations.

In our judgement, Gandhian trusteeship theory is also (with its strong moral fibre) is the most appropriate model for CG in India, since it seeks to build sustainable competitive edge as well as takes care of the interests of all the stakeholders. The trusteeship mindset is more relevant than ever today with the challenges of job losses and the widening chasm between the haves and the have-nots in the current context of disruptions. In the words of Gandhi,

> Supposing I have come by a fair amount of wealth—either by way of legacy, or by means of trade and industry—I must know that all that wealth does not belong to me.... The rest of my wealth belongs to the community and must be used for the welfare of the community [6].

The words of Gandhi ring truer than ever before: 'Wealthy businessmen will have to make their choice between class war and voluntarily converting themselves into trustees of their wealth' [7].

Board Mindset for Building Innovation Focus in the Company

Innovation is not a standalone activity and has to be built into the strategy of a company. Board members should give the thrust and push to promote innovation by asking questions. They can themselves also express ideas and/or promote ideas. This then should be taken forward by the internal team.

Creating any kind of culture or promoting any kind of ways of managing, or anything new that you want to have, requires a constant kind of focus. Hence, it is necessary that the board is able to effectively communicate the importance of this to the line of managers. Besides that communication should not be limited to the board meetings.

To ensure that the focus on innovation stays, board members must follow up by monitoring and by introducing innovation audits at least twice a year.

Building Board Credibility

Credibility of a company board is one of the key assets to build its reputation, increase trust in the market and attract greater capital investment. By its own credibility, the board enhances credibility to the company and vice versa. Credibility of board members depends on the selection criteria, past record of the board members and their achievements and reputations. If they have been appointed through a transparent process based on spelt out selection criteria, then they are viewed with respect and their acceptance is high.

Along with past credibility, the present performance is also closely monitored by the market. Board members live in 'glass houses' and are the cynosure of all eyes. Whom they meet, where they go, what they do, how they dress, their likes and dislikes, and use and abuse of company perks are matters keenly observed by all. In today's adrenaline-infused social media environment, board members are quickly judged/misjudged based on a single action/behaviour. Board members need to be mindful about how they project themselves, especially in the current scenario where the need is for compassion rather than flaunting of power and wealth.

They must instil trust and confidence among the stakeholders that the board will be the eyes and the ears of the company, that they will work for the growth of the organization and through their actions, build the reputation of the company.

Board members need to behave befitting people who occupy such high positions. The public relations department of a company on its part should be sensitive about board behaviours and work to protect the company's reputation. It has to provide the governance framework, ensure that it is implemented and that there is a sustainable growth of the organization. Governance is not only to ensure compliance but also to be transparent and open in the dealings, both ethically and from a business perspective.

Board-level Annual Agenda and Self-assessment

Every board needs to develop an annual agenda for itself. At the year end, boards must self-assess their performance against the agenda proclaimed in the beginning of the year. Transparent sharing of board intent and subsequent achievements will increase their credibility manifold.

Familiarization by Holding Board Meetings at Different Company Locations

Board members sit in ivory towers, and independent directors have no touch with the ground realities of the company. It can be argued that there is no need for them to be in touch with ground realities as they are not into operations. On the other hand, directors need to get some familiarization with the nature of the business, the infrastructure and so on. Conducting board meetings at different sites of the organization helps in the familiarization process. Board members can see for themselves different parts of the organization, interact with people down the line and serve to inspire people by their presence.

Talent Identification

Board members are invited as members of the committee set up for promotion of senior executives. They must move beyond marking mere ritualistic presence and becoming figureheads adding credibility to company decisions in such meetings. This can be possible when the company provides members ways by which they can meet talent one or two levels below. This can be done through different means—holding skip-level meetings in key parts of the organization (to the extent possible) is one such option which can help directors meet people, identify talent and bring them into the zone of consideration for promotions.

Empower the Next Level

The board must empower the next level, delegate power to handle routine matters, so that the board can focus on important matters rather than just responding to urgent matters. This will also declutter the board agenda. Close monitoring of the use of delegation will, however, be equally important to gauge whether they are able to use the empowerment to make better and faster decisions.

Attitude of Independent Directors

Independent directors need to be truly independent of the Promoter/Chairman so that they can bring a fresh perspective and approach to issues on the board and can stand up for themselves and raise questions to protect organizational interests. If the selection is itself at the discretion of the Promoter/Chairman, then by definition, they are not independent since they maybe beholden to those who select them for such positions.

Directors should view themselves as thinkers and entrepreneurs and not as managers. They are there to bring an outside-in perspective and to guide, not micromanage. The attitude of independent directors should be to contribute to the company to the best of their ability. They must regularly attend and prepare for the meetings, ask questions and constantly strive to contribute to the board. They need to closely study the minutes of the meeting, the action-taken reports and, above all, contribute to developing the agenda for the board meeting.

They should be proactive rather than passive. They should display constructive dissatisfaction, continuously seek to contribute better ideas and bring up better agenda items for board-level discussions. A positive and uncompromising attitude is required among independent directors, without sounding negative. This will lead to zero tolerance of wrongful behaviours and decisions which are harmful to the company.

Board Composition and Member Competencies

Good governance never depends upon laws,
but upon the personal qualities of those who govern...
The most important element ... therefore,
is the method of choosing leaders.
—Frank Herbert [8]

The essence of board composition is diversity of thought which can be assessed based on demographics such as member experience, education, exposure and gender. Ensuring higher diversity of talent on the board is the key. Boards should comprise a good mix of diverse talent and experience, which is related to different aspects of the business of the company. Bringing on board directors with complementary skills would be important for smooth and productive boardroom functioning.

Since board members can play such a critical role in the life of an organization, regulators (SEBI and RBI) need to spell out the needed board member competencies, the absence of which today is one of the biggest loopholes in the regulations. It is small wonder, therefore, that the names of family members as well as drivers and cooks feature as directors on the board, a complete subversion of the system of regulations being brought in to professionalize Indian boards. A second reason why this is done is that there is no monitoring or validation of data supplied by companies to SEBI. A basic principle of management is to monitor which needs to be taken seriously by the employees. If SEBI can at least do some surprise checks, it may help bring down such violations to a large extent. The accelerated migration to online systems can be used to its advantage by SEBI to validate data about directors by using Aadhar numbers or some such basic identifier.

SEBI should consider three necessary criteria for recruiting board members: *domain knowledge*—depth of domain knowledge (one's own area of expertise) along with application capacity (application to the present issue or problem at hand) and breadth of knowledge across related domains of management; *integrity and reputation* of board members and *strategic thinking combined with a growth mindset* (including open mindedness and exploring mindset). The capability to work with other board members needs to be one of the important and desirable conditions for board membership. Above all, integrity and commitment to the role are key to the selection of good-quality directors—in this social media age, everyone's reputation is freely available online. All it needs is for someone to verify and use it.

Appointment of board members in the listed companies should not be at the sole discretion of the promoters. Appointing the right kind of board members is essential and board composition should be carefully done. Every board should have people of standing, people who are known for their depth of knowledge in a specific domain.

Gender Diversity on the Board

While recruiting women as board members is desirable, it should not violate at least two of the above principles: (a) basic understanding of company business and (b) specialist understanding of a domain relevant to the business. Diversity of thought process is more relevant than gender per se, and the assumption that all those belonging to a particular gender have uniform thought process is fundamentally flawed.

Role of the Board Chairman

The chairman can play an important role in shaping the board character and priorities. The chairman needs to guide board members, enable their development and raise the average capability of the board. S/he needs to emphasize the vision, purpose and role of the board. Above all, the chairman has to be the conscience keeper of the board, ensuring that the twin goals of strategic leadership and governance are met.

Facilitation Skills of the Chairman

The chairman has a key role to play in carrying the board members and, hence, board management skills become very important. Skills to manage difference and dissension are very important too. A good board chairman needs to have the interpersonal skills to reach out to board members, explain to them and get their buy-in on important decisions so that things go smoothly in the board meeting.

Building Perspective on Key Issues among Board Members

There are all types of personalities on boards and different types speak out for different reasons: some to make their presence felt, while others to contribute. Personality issues can crop up and create needless misunderstandings and conflicts when complex and/or controversial matters are to be taken up for discussion. The chairman can convene a pre-board meeting and explain to the members the complete scenario and get their buy-in and smoothen the process of building understanding of issues.

Developing a Working Relationship

Board members need to have opportunities for developing a working relationship and understanding of each other so that they can function together in the organizational interest. The chairman can play an important role to bring board members together maybe over dinner or maybe a get-together.

Advantages of a Non-executive Chairman

The non-executive chairman has an important role to play in architecting the future of the organization and reminding the board about its responsibility to other stakeholders. Basically, the chairman can draw the attention of the board to all those matters which would otherwise get ignored because they lack urgency. The non-executive chairman can afford to be dispassionate as the role is such that there is some distance from day-to-day operations. On the other hand, when both the roles of chairman and MD are clubbed, the tendency is to be more concerned about the immediate requirements of operating as an MD (and dealing with the pressures of delivering results every quarter) than thinking about the future.

Chairman or Chairman and Managing Director?

In the Indian context, the combined CMD role is the most common feature of Indian companies. This is perhaps the key reason why Indian boards are not focused enough on the future since the bulk of the preoccupation of CMD is with managing the quarter-to-quarter challenge of delivering results. Separation of the roles of chairman and managing director is, however, fraught with complexity because there is a temptation for the chairman to intrude into the MD's role of running the business. One of the advantages of separation of the two roles, however, is that a non-executive chairman (with the right credentials and intent) can play a key role by bringing the board-level focus onto various non-routine, strategic and future-focused issues. This is unlike an executive chairman whose priority would be to get his/her own agenda passed by the board. The presence of a non-executive chairman of repute can ensure greater transparency of functioning and, therefore, increase the trust levels among the shareholders and stakeholders.

In practice, unfortunately, it is not easy to find a chairman who focuses on playing the broader future-focused role and resist the temptation to intrude into the MD's role. This makes the dynamics between the chairman and MD complex and hurts the organization. The alternative to this—combining the chairman and managing director roles—is, however, damaging to companies as reflected by one of the side effects found in our study data, boards hardly give importance to strategy and focus on the future in their discussions.

Before going for a blanket mandate to separate the two roles of chairman and managing 'director, as recommended by the Kotak Committee Report [9], greater effort needs to be put to identify people with relevant competencies, values and temperament to be non-executive chairman. Availability of such a pool is key.

Competencies of the Non-executive Chairman

The person capable of reflecting and thinking for the organization like a 'trustee' and ready to adhere to his/her role (rather than trying to run the organization) should be selected as a non-executive chairman. The person should be selected for domain expertise, values and temperament as well as board management skills to play such a key role.

Build an Open yet Committed Board Culture

It is not enough to recruit relevant talent to the board. A suitable culture has to be created, characterized by respectful yet open sharing of views. The chairman needs to encourage members to hold independent views, respect dissent and yet nudge them to come together for decision-making. The chairman needs to have command over group-influencing skills and tolerance for dissent.

A typical command and control type of leader who operates by imposition will get limited success as chairman, as s/he will not be able to carry the minds and hearts of the members. The deeply hierarchical society prevalent in India makes it critical that the chairman sets the tone of the meetings and, hence, encouraging dissent along with respectful conduct by board members is important. Clear signalling is required from the chairman that conflict of ideas is OK, provided members speak in the organizational interest rather than at cross purposes. Needless to say, the chairman has to play the role of a gatekeeper of conflict of ideas, ensuring that it is kept within bounds, just enough needs to be allowed, so that fresh ideas are triggered, yet not allowed to grow out of control, destroying relationships and the capability of members to work together in a congenial manner. The capacity of the chairman to promote healthy debate, manage dissension, have productive discussions and keep the board together is critical to productive board meetings.

Onboarding Directors

A formal process is required to onboard directors which includes familiarization, induction and training. Before the newly appointed board member attends the first meeting, there must be a schedule of familiarization about the company, especially for large and complex organizations. There should be an induction process for the board members. The orientation should comprise developing an understanding of the business context; strength and weakness of the company; site visits to familiarize with the organization; and clarification of role of the board in terms of compliance, governance, business and, above all, regarding the roles and responsibilities of independent directors. Incoming board members should undergo training by some competent body, where experienced directors are involved. Training should be provided to board members to develop awareness regarding the whole spectrum of board responsibility. Training is required not only on legal, financial, cyber security, risk, compliance-related aspects but also regarding boardroom functioning, board dynamics, roles, rights and responsibilities of board members and basics of business strategy.

Boardroom Functioning: Tactics

There are some seemingly trivial aspects of board-level functioning which, if practised, can add value to board meetings. These are now discussed below.

1. **Time spent on non-routine matters:** Every board must set aside 30 per cent time for discussion on non-routine matters so that important issues and concerns, though not on the agenda can be voiced. The chairman must play a big role in facilitating this.
2. **Quarterly mechanism of full-fledged performance review:** This refers to a mid-course looking back on how the company strategies are shaping up, whether they are giving the expected results or not. This mechanism can help to check whether the implementation of strategy is in the right direction and will help understand whether any mid-course correction is required to achieve business objectives.
3. **Board members' role in agenda setting:** As mentioned earlier, board functioning is strictly agenda based and driven by MD. Instead of being hampered by this, independent directors should also pull their weight and suggest specific agendas to be taken up for discussion.
4. **Time out discussions:** There should be 15-minute zero hour for open discussions in each board meeting. This will allow board members to raise issues which otherwise would not get a space for discussions.
5. **Good practices of boardroom functioning:** It must be emphasized that action-taken reports must be presented regularly to the board so that the board can track the implementation of decisions.
6. **Voicing dissent:** All decisions can rarely be consensus decisions. Board members should have the freedom to not only voice their dissent regarding board decisions but also needs to be recorded.

7. **Monitoring role:** However, oversight of policies is not good enough if the execution is not monitored, because there is difference between oversight and executive. The board needs to directly monitor key issues of relevance to ensure that stronger control systems are in place. Issues can range across all those matters which have been raised in meetings and need to be implemented.

Other Suggestions to Improve Board Functioning

Training institution: A high-quality training institution is needed where all directors can be trained to work effectively on boards. IICA should be strengthened and professionalized. Faculty with board-level experience from both public and private sector should be involved in teaching. Wherever necessary, subject matter experts should be involved.

Ministry of Corporate Affairs: It should develop a database of prospective directors with different kinds of expertise in domains such as IT, law, banking, insurance, business and HR.

Role of regulators like SEBI: Annual monitoring of members' participation in board meetings is essential. According to the Companies Act, in the case of absence, the rule is very clear, they automatically cease to be members of the board. This rule needs to be applied and can happen only when there is monitoring of attendance by board members (Appendix F).

Implementation of regulations: There is a need for an online mechanism to ensure implementation of the regulations. Periodic monitoring without much human intervention is important so that egos and vested interests don't get a chance to flare up.

Number of board memberships for a director: Currently, SEBI has pegged the maximum number of board memberships at 20. If higher involvement is needed, as advocated in this work, the number of memberships should not exceed six so that adequate time can be devoted by the directors to board work.

Governance in the Public Sector

OECD guidelines on governance of public sector companies should be followed. The government should stay at arm's length distance and act as custodian not owner (Appendix G). Public sector companies are mired in too many laws—company law, department guidelines and Department of Financial Services guidelines in the case of banks. The prevalent dual system of control over government companies has to end if public sector companies have to become more competitive. Ultimately, company law should prevail. Such clarity can immensely help public sector companies to become more effective in their functioning.

Monitor Implementation of Governance Regulations

Regulatory bodies have a key responsibility to ensure monitoring of the functioning of listed companies as per their guidelines, both on the hard and the soft parameters.

To Prevent Mismanagement of Large Loans Taken from Banks

Nominee directors (from banks) should be put on company boards, where the concerned bank has given a very large loan. For example, the bank should have the freedom to select and nominate a strong candidate who can oversee how the loan money is being utilized by the company and, thus, prevent diversion and siphoning of funds.

Checklist

Board members should raise the following issues:

- Strategies for the future
- Whether money which is raised for a particular purpose is used for the intended purpose or is it diverted
- Thoroughly examine company progress
- There should be discussion on managing competition
- Raise questions about stakeholder interests
- Ensure ethical practices down the line
- Examine the satisfaction levels of people

The board members should have an eye on the working of the chairman and the director.

Note

i. In a study of five Mexican companies, Lloret (2015) found that sustainable companies demonstrate successful long-term performance amid the restrictions imposed by economic, social and environmental systems, by developing a strategy that sustainably generates and captures value into the future. Sustainable practices are central to a company's business model and survival because a strategy of targeted, enduring actions affords competitive advantages.

References

1. Levitt, A. (1999, 7 October). *Corporate Governance in a Global Arena*. New York, NY: American Council on Germany.
2. Pfeffer, J. (2009). Shareholders First? Not So Fast. *Harvard Business Review*, Vol. 87, No. 7.
3. Deloitte, Global Center for Corporate Governance. (2020). Stepping in: The Board's Role in the COVID-19 Crisis. https://www2.deloitte.com/content/dam/Deloitte/global/Documents/About-Deloitte/COVID-19/COVID-19-The-boards-role-in-crisis.pdf
4. Singh, P., Bhandarker, A., and Rai, S. (2012). *Millennials Meaning of Workplace: Challenges for Building the Organizations of the Future*. New Delhi: SAGE Publications.

5. Search Quotes. (n.d.). https://www.searchquotes.com/quotation/ Companies_that_solely_focus_on_competition_will_ultimately_ die._Those_that_focus_on_value_creation_w/232639/
6. Gandhi, M. K. (1960, April). *Trusteeship*. Compiled by Ravindra Kelekar. Ahmedabad: Navajivan Mudranalaya.
7. Gandhi, M. K. (1946). Trusteeship. *Harijan*, pp. 63–64. https:// www.mkgandhi.org/trusteeship/chap02.htm
8. AZ Quotes. (n.d.). https://www.azquotes.com/quote/350134? ref=good-governance
9. SEBI. (2017, 5 October). *Report of the Committee on Corporate Governance*. https://www.sebi.gov.in/reports/reports/oct-2017/ report-of-the-committee-on-corporate-governance_36177.html

Further Reading

Lloret, A. (2016). Modelling Corporate Sustainability Strategy. *Journal of Business Research*, Vol. 69, No. 2, pp. 418–425. https://doi.org/10.1016/j.jbusres.2015.06.047

EPILOGUE

It is in our darkest moments that we
must focus to see the Light.

—Socrates

This book was conceptualized more than three years ago. The work began in right earnest two years back. Writing of the first draft of the initial chapters also commenced in pre-COVID-19 times. Six months down the line, we are living in a changed world where the new normal is still not visible to the human eye. The flattening of the COVID curve remains an elusive target, and there are no certainties as to when a vaccine will be in the market.

Widespread social and economic misery, deepened personal inequalities, crashed-out global growth rate, disarticulated supply chain and fractured production are the key features of this new world. Austerity is the new watchword. The government now has to ensure that the social side of state policy holds up—the ability to support expenditure on the social institutions of education, health (including public health), sanitation and public infrastructure such as roads, rails and transportation. This depends upon the speed with which the Indian industry—knocked out by the body blow of simultaneous demand and supply shock—is up and running. In terms of business, the pandemic has also underlined the continued importance of digitization, innovation, collaboration and acceleration. The tri-mantra of compassion, inspiration and resilience is needed to provide leadership in these trying times. They are in fact the new imperatives for a post-pandemic corporate India which needs to now more than ever show its human side.

There is an old saying, 'Capitalism without bankruptcy is like Catholicism without Hell [1].' Capitalist growth required that inefficiently managed and badly performing companies go bust. With its teeming million steeped in poverty, unemployment and social and economic backwardness, and spiralling public debt, India can ill-afford such destruction of assets. The slogans of 'Atmanirbharta' (self-reliance) and 'Make in India' given by Prime Minister Narendra Modi in the context of global meta-trends of deglobalization along with the threat from China's dominance in supply chain and trade-based diplomacy are a clarion call for developing self-sufficiency, high growth, inclusive development and shared prosperity. The recent fiscal stimulus to kickstart the economy is, therefore, not meant to infuse money into badly performing companies and to keep alive their inefficiencies. Instead, the economic and financial package along with the renewed emphasis on import substitution, innovation, skill building and policy reforms is to help the Indian corporates to capitalize on the historic opportunity of pandemic-induced 'flattened and borderless' world. The success of this endeavour hinges on the extent to which Indian corporates are willing to adapt and proact in response to the new realities. One positive outcome of the pandemic is that it has put organizations into the 'unfreeze' mode for change and speedy adaptation. It is time that the boards and the top managements play their role in reorienting their mindsets and attitudes to proactively grab the opportunities emerging in this business context.

Corporate India has some serious rethinking to do on the very purpose of business. Even the most fervent advocates of capitalism believe that capitalism is in crisis, and its economic model is broken. The free market has managed to generate a triple crisis for capitalism: it is financially unstable, environmentally unsustainable and politically unpopular. Capitalism has neither given growth nor enlarged the economic pie. Much worse, it has also not divided and redistributed the pie fairly. Ironically, as the living standard of most of the people globally has stalled and faltered, the wealth of the top 1 per cent businesses has soared. While the tech firms of Silicon Valley have contributed significantly to the American economy, the top 5 tech giants have also succeeded in destroying more than 100 companies (as Anand Giridharadas, author of the runaway bestseller *Winners Take All*, points out), to corner obscene amounts of wealth, destroying livelihoods and adding to the woes of the average human being.

The digital revolution has allowed technological entrepreneurs to build massive global companies without the big job-producing factories or large workforce of the industrial era. The result has been that more and more wealth is concentrated in fewer hands. Capitalism has succeeded in producing large wealth gaps that, in turn, is leading to even wider opportunity gap in societies.

The heart-wrenching sight of millions of starving and parched Indians trudging back thousands of miles on foot and cycles, precariously perched on trucks and lorries and dangerously hurtling down deserted highways is perhaps the largest peace-time migration in human history. The pandemic, just like the floods, simply brought to the surface some ugly truths of India's economy in May 2020. About 90 per cent of India's workforce is informal. They contribute around 50 per cent to the national economy, 71 per cent have no written job contract, no paid leave, no social security and more than a third get less than even minimum wages. The migration occurred due to the trust deficit experienced by migrant labour, and because capitalism has turned blind and lost its conscience. Capitalism is in dire need of a paradigmatic transformation.

It's moral claim to be superior to any other economic arrangement can be legitimate only when it is repositioned and redesigned on the Gandhian premises of trusteeship. Firms have to behave like trustees for society, managing and developing wealth in order to serve all stakeholders. It is only then that the moral fibre of the company will provide the strategic guidance for wealth creation, for the benefit of the stakeholders.

The competitive business landscape has always been likened to a war. With the erosion of the buffer of financial slack and the crippling of India's economic growth,[i] this war has become brutal, and the consequences of losing, grim. The pandemic blindingly revealed the significance of organizational resilience, agility, collaboration, innovation, learning to learn and adapt to win the war. The pandemic has shown the serious need for firms to have a shockproof and future-ready business model—using disruptive technologies to power the entire value chain. It also exposed the limits to the argument that development can only be driven by innovation for which competition is a necessary prerequisite. The pandemic has shown that when the shared future of humanity is in danger, people have the capacity to collaborate and drive innovation.

There is no doubt that technological superiority is needed to rule the world of business and to stay ahead of the competition. However, as Arianna Huffington[ii] said, 'Without prioritizing the human factor, digital transformation tools will never be enough'. This statement brings out the stark reality that in all the emphasis on technology, the human factor has been taken for granted. In fact, at a recent webinar, a consultant from one of the Big 4 consulting firms disparagingly talked about hot bodies, warm bodies and cold bodies —referring to human beings, humanoids and machines. The dehumanization which is evident in this thought process is chilling. Is this utter lack of human dignity the future awaiting us all, as we gradually get used to coexisting with robots and other mechanical entities who arguably can perform certain tasks better than us?

The pandemic has made us pause. Human beings are today mired in stress and anxiety owing to the uncertainties wreaked by COVID-19. It has reminded us that behind all the business models, strategies, innovation and technology is the power of human creativity and imagination. Unless people get a soothing touch and sense of security, they will not be able to unleash their imagination and creativity, nor will they be motivated and inspired to go beyond the minimum requirements. Human beings are being taught the key lesson of the need for resilience and humility and of the fervent need to reconnect with our human side and that of communities and societies. There is an urgent need in today's context for compassionate leadership and the capability to inspire people towards greater positivity and optimism, even as we are surrounded by so much doom and gloom. The wise words of Socrates 'Be Kind, for everyone you meet is fighting a Hard battle' have never been truer and sum up the ultimate expression of humanity.

Eventually, it is about how we see the post COVID-19 normal: Do we see the post-pandemic world as a problem or an opportunity? Great leaders have always seen opportunities in problems. Non-leaders see problems in opportunities. If India is to become more self-reliant, then Indian firms must rethink their strategy and business architecture to compete globally. The pandemic has also shown, without doubt, that the strategy of growth through continuous innovation and the right business model (comprising customer centricity, value proposition and time to market) can be equally effective both in times of warfare with competitors and for fighting invisible enemies. It is said that the best weapons in corporate warfare are always those that can be used for both: attacking to triumph and defending to become invincible. It is this twin capability that gives sustainable competitive edge to firms.

It is time that top managements and the boards of Indian companies develop their strategy around the following 10 Ps of leadership to architect sustainable competitive edge for their firms. These 10 Ps provide sustainable competitive edge to companies since they are holistic in their coverage and enduring in their utility. Disruptions may come and go but focus on these 10 Ps can provide guidance to companies in building, assessing, evaluating and recalibrating their strategies. They help leaders (boards and top teams) to pin their focus on what matters to build organizational resilience—the key requirement in today's times.

The 10 Ps for Building Sustainable Competitive Edge

1. **Purpose:** Wealth creation through growth based upon continuous innovation.
2. **Place:** Understand the emerging context of business and the locational complexity which can help look for blue ocean opportunity and strategy building.
3. **Players:** Identify your global competitors, local competitors and global–local competitors now as well as in the emergent future. Develop business strategy for denting and defending or even disrupting through innovative solutions.
4. **People:** Keep customers and their needs (both current and future) the central premise for value creation and delivery. To ensure that, develop entrepreneurial culture and heighten people power.
5. **Period:** Achieve time to market through digitization, agile teamwork, agile work process, digitally enabled and IT-integrated supply chain, distributed manufacturing and global–local delivery mechanism.
6. **Partners:** Create a partner ecosystem (both domestic and global) with supply chain partners, value chain network, allies as well as customers to co-create solutions and innovations.

7. **Process:** Ensure cost and quality leadership through global and digitally enabled and integrated value chain, application of advanced manufacturing (Industry 4.0) and modern factory management system, and operational innovations for process optimization and efficiency.

8. **Planning of execution:** Ensure execution through (a) organizing—boundaryless, networked and augmented designs; ambidextrous involving organicity for exploration and ideation and mechanistic for exploitation and idea implementation and (b) performance management through venture capital based planning and funding, strategic guidance, cascading OKR, metrics and its balanced score card.

9. **Planet:** Do business with least harm to the community, ecology, energy, climate and pollution to ensure sustainability.

10. **Perceptions and cognitions:** Display Janus-faced strategic vision—at once looking behind and looking ahead, managing for the present and preparing for the future and using both binoculars and the microscope.

Finally, boards and top leaders should show wisdom, compassion and courage—the three qualities which define character according to Confucius. Posterity will judge them on this measure of moral compass and its display, especially during these disruptive times.

Notes

i.   GDP of India contracted by 23.9 per cent (the worst in the history of independent India) in this April–June quarter as against growth of 3.1 per cent in the January–March quarter. This was across all sectors with most being in the construction sector (50%), followed by transport, trade and hospitality services (47%) and manufacturing (39%). Consumption demand, the driver of growth, fell by 27 per cent and investment demand (measured by gross fixed capital formation contracted by 47%). Incidentally, in the FY 2019–2020, according to the International Monetary Fund, the actual GDP growth in India (1.9%) and China (1.2%) as against the USA (–5.9%), the UK (–6.5%), Germany (–7%) and Russia (–5.5%) show the slump in global economy Mohanty, P. (2019, July 15). Labour Reforms: No One Knows the Size of India's Informal Workforce, Not Even the Government. *Business Today.* https://www.businesstoday. in/sectors/jobs/labour-law-reforms-no-one-knows-actual-size-india-informal-workforce-not-even-govt/story/364361.html

ii. https://economictimes.indiatimes.com/news/company/corporate-trends/without-prioritising-human-factor-digital-transformation-tools-will-never-be-enough-arianna-huffington/articleshow/78207673.cms#:~:text=Without%20prioritising%20human%20factor%2C%20digital,Arianna%20Huffington%20%2D%20The%20Economic%20Times

Reference

1. Borman, Frank. (1996). https://www.forbes.com/quotes/3057/

APPENDICES

Appendix A

Research Method

Sample and Data Collection

Stage 1. Purposive sampling technique was utilized. Board members were contacted by the three authors, and questionnaires were administered. Some of them were contacted during senior-level training programmes, others during board meetings, yet others through known people on boards of various companies. People who had in the past attended training programmes with the authors and had then, over a period of time, been elevated to the board level in various organizations were also contacted. Because of the utilization of this approach along with administration of the survey questionnaires by the authors (either face to face or telephonically), the response rate on the questionnaire was 100 per cent. We received 200 filled questionnaires of which we had to discard two since they were incomplete.

The study consists of two kinds of sample groups from whom data was gathered using three different questionnaires:

1. One hundred and seventy senior-level corporate executives (operational heads of organizations across companies— 120 from public sector and 50 from private sector) responded to questions regarding the relative importance of the enablers of sustainable competitive advantage of the

organization as well as derailers of sustainable competitive advantage (Appendix D).

2. Seventy board members (both internal directors and independent directors—40 from the public sector and 30 from the private sector) responded to questions on the extent to which the factors contributing to sustainable competitive advantage (Appendix V) are focused upon in boardroom discussions.

3. One hundred and ninety-eight board members (both internal directors and independent directors—140 from public sector companies and 58 from private sector companies) answered a survey questionnaire (Appendix F) regarding what boards do, thrust and focus of boardroom discussions, nature of Indian boards, board agenda, board behaviours and organizational collapse, accountability of independent directors on the board and needed board member competencies.

Stage 2. Initial findings were not very insightful in the absence of qualitative data. On average, most of the sample group could not spare more than 20–30 minutes in Stage 1 of the interviews and, hence, there was hardly any scope to get an in-depth understanding from the board members. Therefore, a second round of data gathering was done to get an in-depth understanding of board members' views. With great difficulty, we could conduct in-depth interviews with 19 veteran board members across public and private sector boards. Each interview lasted at least for an hour.

Data Treatment and Data Analysis

Data analysis has been conducted in three parts.

Survey Data

Data was cleaned, coded and entered in SPSS software. Since no difference was found in the responses across both public and private sectors, the data was clubbed for conducting overall analysis and to ensure ease of presentation.

Data was analysed using simple techniques such as mean, standard deviation, frequency and percentages.

Interview Data

In this book, interview data has been largely used to substantiate the findings of the questionnaire data and to add richness of content and depth to the core findings of the survey data. Open-ended questions were posed (see the next section) to get an in-depth understanding of the dynamics of board functioning. The interviews were content analysed to identify most frequently occurring responses. Simple coding was done followed by keywords analysis to identify commonalities across the interviews. These keywords were then categorized at Level 1 followed by Level 2 (a higher conceptual level of analysis). These were then converted into themes and used to support the key findings which emerged from the survey data.

Open-ended Interview Themes

- Role of the board for sustaining company's competitive edge
- Competencies of an effective board member
- Characteristics of an effective board
- Focus of the board in boardroom discussion
- Role of boards in promoting innovation and strategic thinking in an organization
- Roles and responsibilities of the independent directors
- Your views on the separation of the chairman and MD roles

Appendix B

Levers of Sustainable Competitive Edge

LEVERS	DEFINITION
Strategic leadership	Strategic leadership is the leader's ability to anticipate, envision and empower people to create the needed organizational change.
Ethical governance	This refers to rules, practices and processes built on the foundation of a set of core organizational values to enable organizations meet their goals as well as serve the larger public interest through fairness, transparency and accountability.
Continued innovation	This is an ongoing process of continuous improvement (both incremental and radical) in activities, processes and services through out-of-the-box and even radical solutions.
People with winning spirit	People with winning spirit have the mindset to be proactive, surpass limits, work with team synergy and give their best, whenever required, for organizational well-being.
Speedy response to market (time to reach market)	Quick response to customer needs in terms of understanding requirements, developing solutions and taking them to the market ahead of the rivals.

(continued)

LEVERS	DEFINITION
Customer centricity	Customer centricity refers to keeping the customer needs and their fulfilment at the core of value creation and the business model of the firm.
Cost focus	Focus on cost and its minimization is to create wider margin between cost (of the suppliers) and price (amount customer is willing to pay) so that profits increase.
Quality focus	Quality focus refers to adherence to the standards of quality of product or service and commitment to its continuous improvement as competitively benchmarked with the rivals and the industry.

Appendix C

Levers of Sustainable Competitive Edge: Enablers and Derailers

The following questionnaire was given to 170 senior-level executives (public sector = 140; private sector = 30) as well as to 70 board members (public sector = 40; private sector = 30). The senior executives were asked to highlight the relative importance of the levers (enablers and derailers). On the other hand, the board members were asked to indicate the importance given to the enablers in boardroom discussions.

Levers of Sustainable Competitive Edge: Enablers

A list of eight levers of competitive advantage is given as follows. All of them are important levers; however, we are interested in to know how you view their relative importance. Based on your experience, kindly rank them in order of importance (1 being the most important and 8 being the least important) in the space provided.

S. NO.	LEVERS	RANK
1.	Strategic leadership at the board level	
2.	Ethical governance	
3.	Continued innovation	
4.	Speedy response to market (time to reach market)	
5.	People with winning spirit	
6.	Customer centricity	
7.	Cost focus	
8.	Quality focus	

Levers of Sustainable Competitive Edge: Derailers

A list of factors known to erode competitive edge of the organization is given as follows. Based on your experience and understanding of organizations, please rank the items from 1 to 8, 1 being the most important derailer (relatively speaking) and 8 being the least important derailer of organizational competitive capability.

DERAILERS	RANK
Lack of strategic thinking with binocular vision	
Poor focus on R&D and innovation	
Inadequate understanding of government policies and thinking	
Poor ethical governance	
Inadequate understanding of market (poor market intelligence)	
Poor quality of leadership (CEO level)	
Poor culture of strategic monitoring and assigning accountability	
Poor delegation and empowerment	

Appendix D

Survey Questionnaire

198 board members (public sector = 140, private sector = 58)
Indicate the extent to which boards are focused on the following. Kindly tick mark in the relevant box for each attribute mentioned.

AREAS OF FOCUS	RARELY	SOMETIMES	MANY TIMES	OFTEN	ALWAYS
1. Operational focus					
2. Reducing costs					
3. Customer focus					
4. Continuous innovation					
5. Evolving strategies for minimizing risk					
6. Concern for stakeholders					
7. Ethical focus					
8. Developing future leaders (succession)					
9. Oversight of policy- and strategy-level issues					

You have worked on the boards of companies in both public and private sectors. Based on your experience, kindly rate (by ticking in the relevant box alongside each statement) extent of board-level focus and thrust on the following issues.

S. NO.	ATTRIBUTES	RARELY	SOMETIMES	MANY TIMES	OFTEN	ALWAYS
1.	In-depth discussion on audit committee report for continuously improving organizational performance					
2.	In-depth discussion on observations of the statutory auditors					
3.	In-depth discussion on findings of risk-management committee to minimize risk					
4.	In-depth discussion on HR issues and focus on building future leaders					
5.	In-depth discussion on evolving strategy for growth and sustainable competitive edge					

How would you describe the typical Indian board? Tick two.

1. Ornamental, 2. Country club, 3. Committed

Rate the extent to which the following attributes contributed to the poor performance/collapse of leading companies and banks such as IL&FS, Kingfisher Airlines, Bhushan Steel, Air India, RComm and many others. Indicate with a tick mark in the relevant box for each attribute mentioned.

S. NO.	ATTRIBUTES	RARELY	SOMETIMES	MANY TIMES	OFTEN	ALWAYS
1.	Questionable integrity					
2.	Managing statutory auditors and rating agencies					
3.	Lack of transparency					
4.	Inadequate accountability					
5.	Frequency of power used by influential board members to push decisions in the direction he/she wants					

Rate the extent of accountability which should be attributed to independent directors for the following.

S. NO.	ATTRIBUTES	RARELY	SOMETIMES	MANY TIMES	OFTEN	ALWAYS
1.	Unethical board-level practices					
2.	The poor performance/ collapse of companies					

Based on your experience, kindly rate (by ticking in the relevant box alongside each statement) the following.

COMPETENCIES	RARELY	SOMETIMES	MANY TIMES	OFTEN	ALWAYS
Balance of domain expertise and business understanding					
Ethics, integrity and commitment					
Openness to ideas, willingness to explore					
Strategic mindset with growth focus					
Teamwork (influencing others, managing conflicts)					

Appendix E

Roles and Responsibilities of Directors

General Duties of Directors under the Companies Act, 2013

- To act in accordance with the articles of the company, in other words, to act within powers.
- To act in good faith in order to promote the objects of the company for the benefit of its members as a whole.
- To act in the best interest of the company, its employees, shareholders, community and for the protection of environment.
- To exercise due and reasonable care, skill and diligence and independent judgement.
- To avoid direct or indirect conflict of interests.
- To avoid undue gain or advantage either to himself/herself or relatives, partners or associates
- To not assign his/her office to any other person

SEBI (LODR) Regulations: Reg 4(2)(f)

The key functions of the board of directors are as follows.

1. Reviewing and guiding corporate strategy—major plans of action, risk policy, annual budgets and business plans—setting performance objectives, monitoring implementation and corporate performance, and overseeing major capital expenditures, acquisitions and divestments.
2. Monitoring the effectiveness of the listed entity's governance practices and making changes as needed.
3. Selecting, compensating, monitoring and, when necessary, replacing key managerial personnel and overseeing succession planning.

4. Aligning key managerial personnel and remuneration of board of directors with the longer-term interests of the listed entity and its shareholders.

5. Ensuring a transparent nomination process to the board of directors with the diversity of thought, experience, knowledge, perspective and gender in the board of directors.

6. Monitoring and managing potential conflict of interests of management, members of the board of directors and shareholders, including misuse of corporate assets and abuse in related party transactions.

7. Ensuring the integrity of the listed entity's accounting and financial reporting systems (including the independent audit and that appropriate systems of control are in place, in particular, systems for risk management, financial and operational control and compliance with the law and relevant standards).

8. Overseeing the process of disclosure and communications.

9. Monitoring and reviewing board of director's evaluation framework.[i]

Note

i. For more details, see https://www.mca.gov.in/Ministry/pdf/CompaniesAct2013.pdf; https://www.sebi.gov.in/sebi_data/attachdocs/1441284401427.pdf

Appendix F

The Companies Act and SEBI Regulations

The Companies Act and SEI regulations ease the process of doing business and improve CG by making companies more accountable.

There are variations in some of the provisions, while there are some areas where there are no stated guidelines.

	THE COMPANIES ACT, 2013	SEBI
Gender diversity on the board	Second Provision to Section 149 Provided further that such class or classes of companies as may be prescribed shall have at least one woman director. Companies (Appointment and Qualification of Directors) Rules, 2014 Rule 3. Woman director on the board. The following class of companies shall appoint at least one woman director: 1. Every listed company	Regulation 17(1)(a) Board of directors shall have an optimum combination of executive and non-executive directors with at least one woman director and not less than 50 per cent of the board of directors shall comprise non-executive directors.
Minimum number of board meetings	Section 173(1) Every company shall hold the first meeting of the board of directors within 30 days of the date of its incorporation and thereafter hold a minimum number of 4 meetings of its board of	Regulation 17(2) The board of directors shall meet at least 4 times a year, with a maximum time gap of 120 days between any 2 meetings.

(continued)

	THE COMPANIES ACT, 2013	SEBI
	directors every year in such a manner that not more than 120 days shall intervene between two consecutive meetings of the board. Provided that the central government may, by notification, direct that the provisions of this subsection shall not apply in relation to any class or description of companies or shall apply subject to such exceptions, modifications or conditions as may be specified in the notification.	
Updation of knowledge of the board members	Schedule IV(III)(1) The independent directors shall undertake appropriate induction and regularly update and refresh their skills, knowledge and familiarity with the company.	Regulation (4)(2)(f)(iii)(4) The board of directors shall encourage continuing directors training to ensure that the members of board of directors are kept up to date. Regulation 17(3) The board of directors shall periodically review compliance reports pertaining to all laws applicable to the listed entity, prepared by the listed entity as well as steps taken by the listed entity to rectify instances of non-compliances. Regulation 25(7)

(continued)

Appendix F

(continued)

	THE COMPANIES ACT, 2013	SEBI
		The listed entity shall familiarize the independent directors through various programmes about the listed entity, including the following: 1. Nature of the industry in which the listed entity operates 2. Business model of the listed entity 3. Roles, rights, responsibilities of independent directors 4. Any other relevant information
Induction and training of independent directors	Schedule IV(III)(1) The independent directors shall undertake appropriate induction and regularly update and refresh their skills, knowledge and familiarity with the company.	Regulation (4)(2)(f)(iii)(4) The board of directors shall encourage continuing directors training to ensure that the members of board of directors are kept up to date. Regulation 25(7) The listed entity shall familiarize the independent directors through various programmes about the listed entity, including the following: 1. Nature of the industry in which the listed entity operates 2. Business model of the listed entity

Role of Boards

(continued)

THE COMPANIES ACT, 2013	SEBI
	3. Roles, rights, responsibilities of independent directors 4. Any other relevant information

	THE COMPANIES ACT, 2013	SEBI
Disclosure of expertise/skills of directors	Section 152(5) A person appointed as a director shall not act as a director unless he/she gives his/her consent to hold the office as director and such consent has been filed with the Registrar within 30 days of his/her appointment in such manner as may be prescribed. Provided that in the case of appointment of an independent director in the general meeting, an explanatory statement for such appointment, annexed to the notice for the general meeting, shall include a statement that in the opinion of the board, he/she fulfils the conditions specified in this Act for such an appointment. Rule 5 of Companies (Appointment and Qualification of Directors) Rules, 2014 Qualifications of independent director: An independent director shall possess appropriate skills,	Regulation 36(3): Documents and information to shareholders. (3) In case of the appointment of a new director or re-appointment of a director, the shareholders must be provided with the following information: 1. A brief resume of the director 2. Nature of his/her expertise in specific functional areas 3. Disclosure of relationships between directors 4. Names of listed entities in which the person also holds the directorship and the membership of committees of the board 5. Shareholding of non-executive directors

(continued)

	THE COMPANIES ACT, 2013	SEBI
	experience and knowledge in one or more fields of finance, law, management, sales, marketing, administration, research, CG, technical operations or other disciplines related to the company's business.	
Separation of the roles of non-executive chairperson and managing director/CEO	Provision to Section 203 Provided that an individual shall not be appointed or reappointed as the chairperson of the company, in pursuance of the articles of the company, as well as the managing director or chief executive officer of the company at the same time after the date of commencement of this Act unless: 1. The articles of such a company provide otherwise 2. The company does not carry multiple businesses Provided further that nothing contained in the first provision shall apply to such class of companies engaged in multiple businesses and which have appointed one or more chief executive officers for each such business as may be notified by the central government.	Schedule II: Corporate governance Part E: Discretionary requirements D. Separate posts of chairperson and chief executive officer The listed entity may appoint separate persons to the post of chairperson and managing director or chief executive officer.

Role of Boards

Appendix G

G20/OECD Principles of Corporate Governance

The six principles of CG are as follows:[i]

1. Ensuring the basis for an effective CG framework
2. The rights and equitable treatment of shareholders and key ownership functions
3. Institutional investors, stock markets and other intermediaries
4. The role of stakeholders in CG
5. Disclosure and transparency
6. The responsibilities of the board

Note

i. For more details, see https://www.oecd.org/daf/ca/Corporate-Governance-Principles-ENG.pdf

ABOUT THE AUTHORS

Pritam Singh was a distinguished scholar, thinker, academic leader and role model. He was the Midas Touch director who transformed IIM Lucknow, India; MDI Gurgaon, India and IMI Delhi, India. He was well known as an inspiring and wise guru to CMDs of companies, top directors of organizations and academic leaders heading the prestigious IIMs. He had served on more than 20 boards of leading Indian companies. He had authored 10 academically reputed books (3 of which are award winning) and published 60 research papers. He had served on many important government committees. Dr Singh was the chairman of the Defense Acquisition and Procurement Committee (2016) and member of the prestigious Prime Minister's Committee on Institutions of Excellence (2017–2020). He was the recipient of more than a dozen prestigious national and international awards. He was the first Padma Shri awardee in management education for his work in transforming management institutions.

Asha Bhandarker, Distinguished Professor of organizational behaviour at IMI Delhi, India, is well known for her contributions to research, teaching, training and consulting in the field of organizational behaviour. She has published over 40 research papers as well as articles in peer-reviewed journals, both nationally and internationally. She has published eight books with reputed publishers like SAGE. Dr Bhandarker has received many awards for her work, including the Senior Fulbright fellowship, Best Paper Award, Best Case Award and Best Teacher Award. She is Director on the Board of Punjab National Bank and IMT Ghaziabad, India. As a trainer and consultant, she has worked with numerous organizations in the public and private sectors. She has been a visiting professor at the School of Public Policy, George Mason University, Fairfax, USA, and at the Darden school of Business, University of Virginia, Charlottesville, USA, and visiting fellow at the London Business School, London, England.

Subir Verma is a Fellow (PhD) from IIM Ahmedabad, India, MA (gold medallist) and MPhil in Political Science from University of Delhi, Delhi, India. He has more than 30 years of research, teaching, training and consulting experience at reputed institutions. He has been Dean, Academics, at IIM Ranchi, India and Dean, Corporate Relations and Placements, at IMI Delhi, India. Dr Verma has headed postgraduate programmes, placements and international accreditations at MDI Gurgaon, India; IMI Delhi, India; and FORE School of Management, Delhi, India. He is an active trainer on leadership, team building, mentorship, change management and negotiation skills. He has conducted several programmes for reputed firms such as ONGC, SAIL, CIL, IOCL, Indian Postal Service, RBI, SBI, PNB, BOB, Dena Bank, Intel, HP, PepsiCo, Nestlé, Coca-Cola and Maruti. He has been a consultant with the World Bank, Jharkhand government, Nestlé, GETIT and Siemens Power, among others. He has edited/co-edited five books and has presented his research papers in prestigious international conferences such as AOM (Academy of Management), APROS (Asia-Pacific Researchers in Organization Studies), EGOS (European Group for Organizational Studies), IHRM (International Human Resource Management) and ISA (International Sociological Association).

Through her book, Sai takes women on a journey that challenges the unconscious, the beliefs and the not-so-obvious in life and at the workplace. With self-reflective tools aplenty, she compels the readers to introspect, reflect and truly transform into who we can be. This book is a must-have gem for future women leaders.

Hema Ravichandar
Strategic HR Advisor and Former Global Head HR,
Infosys Technologies Limited

Break the glass ceiling

For special offers on this and other books from SAGE, write to marketing@sagepub.in

Explore our range at
www.sagepub.in

PAPERBACK
9789353287160